THE SIGNS

PROPHESY FOR 2000 A.D. AND BEYOND

THE SIGNS

PROPHESY FOR 2000 A.D. AND BEYOND

CANYON ADAMS

EPIPHANY PRESS®
UNITED STATES

Epiphany Press
United States
Send all Correspondence to Epiphany Press at
unionsundown@journey.com
or to Canyon Adams at
bigbuzzcut@aol.com

Cover Design: Dawn Dockins, Country Prep Imaging™
Text Design: Epiphany Press

ISBN: 1-893172-24-4

Library of Congress Catalog Card Number: 98-74582

Epiphany Press is a division of Union Sundown, Inc.
The opinions published herein do not necessarily
reflect or represent the opinion of Union Sundown, Inc.
nor any of its members, officers, divisions, investors, or
affiliates.

Printed and Manufactured in the United States of America

10 9 8 7 6 5 4 3 2

To Cherie, For Everything...Thanks!

Contents

Chapter 1

The Sign of Jonah

As I sit down to write this book, I realize what a monumental task there is that stands before me.

For starters, I am hyper-aware of the fact that I will need to move forward against the ever present opposition of religious myth, the universally accepted religious belief system which, although backdropped by a handful of generally understood biblical principles, stems primarily out of doctrines and practices contrived by mankind itself. In the face of such doctrines and practices, most of which have been woven into the fabric of our culture and reinforced internationally generation after generation for centuries, I am but a small, isolated voice in the wilderness. A pindrop. And insignificant whisper. A man with a computer, a publishing contract, and a few decades of biblical readings and research under my belt and tucked away in the attic of my mind. In that sense, I remind myself of a line written by Bob Dylan in 1965:

"I need a steamshovel mama to keep away the dead. I need a dump truck baby to unload my head..." I have a great deal of biblical research and concept that I would like to write about and bring to the forefront of *universal* religious conscience; yet, I am very cognizant of the fact that much of what I have to say cuts sharply against the grain of what has become globally accepted "Christian" belief. And who am I to speak up controversially amid that which the rest of the world--the majority of practicing "Christians"-- so fervently adheres to and believes?

Or more importantly, how do I possibly accomplish the task of writing about such things as God's 7000 year plan, or Jesus' establishment of a government on earth that will last 1000 years; or how do I speak out against such unfounded and un-biblical beliefs as the "rapture theory" or the obser-vance of Easter and Christmas, without coming across to the reading public as some pompous, over-the-edge zealot; or some misinformed, myth-spreading candyman myself? Or worse yet, as some self-righteous preacher harping about with one of those "repent-or-be-damned" diatribes? How do I present this material, and on what resource can we all rely to prove such material to be true? To be truer than church doctrine? To be truer than tradition and truer than weekly sermons and universal rituals? The answer, I am convinced, is to simply use the Bible. Period! To rely solely on the words of the Bible and to prudently start with its truth, stay with its truth, and end with its truth. Period!

A great disservice is accomplished when one searches out-side the Bible to answer questions or to formulate under-standings and beliefs of any religious nature. Thousands upon thousands of deaths--both physical and spiritual--have been accredited to man-made doctrines and religious assimi-lations. Beliefs and rituals, which are not necessarily bibli-cally based, have been passed along from generation to gen-eration through literature and art and declarations and man-ifestos. We fall prey to ultimate confusion and misunderstanding when we adhere to such systems of belief and practice without employing the indisputable reference of the Bible as our sole source of truth and fact. As a writer, a label which I will loosely attach to myself for the purpose of this book, I would perpetuate a great dishonor if I were to move away from the Bible and, instead, rely on man-made doctrines and dissertations to fuel my discussion of the end time prophesies. *Especially of the end time prophesies!* There are thousands of man-created materials on the subject out there; but, unlike the Bible, they are not written by God; they are written and inspired instead by the author of confusion. I, therefore, have committed to relying solely on the Bible to reinforce anything I write, discuss, or bring forth herein. And likewise, I implore each reader of this book to depend solely on his or her Bible as well. Do not believe me. Do not believe any man or any reference. Do not, at face value, believe any church or preacher or doctrine. Turn, instead, to the Bible and read what has been written and inspired by God. Therein will all the facts become plain. Therein will the truth be known and understood.

I have included several Bible passages in this book; they have been derived from various translations (King James, Plain English, etc.), and they have been included to bring the reader's attention to the concepts and premises upon which the subject matter of this book has been based. But, in an attempt to encourage each reader to turn to the Bible and read its books and verses in their entirety, I have consciously omitted the usual numbers of chapters and verses which are so very typical of Bible translations. In other words, when I have quoted, for example, a passage from the Gospel of Luke, Chapter 21, Verse 26, in most cases I have made a conscious and purposeful effort not to write out "Luke 21:26." Instead, I have merely preceded the passage with the word "Luke" and then wrote out the actual verse in bold print. By approaching quotations in this manner, I believe I will avoid the isolation and limitation of focus so often accomplished by chapter and verse citation; and I will, at the same time, I hope, encourage readers to delve further into each passage and read it from their Bibles in context with other verses in that particular Book or Gospel.

In theory, this approach to citation works as follows: a reader searching, for example, in the Book of Revelation to find a quoted verse from Revelation 13:10, knowing only that the quote came from somewhere in the Book of Revelation, will also, in their search, read small excerpts from Chapter 4, Chapter 12, Chapter 15, etc. And once the actual verse is located, more than just 13:10 will be read. A reader is more likely to go beyond the original quotation and read, say, verses 13:1 through 13:18; thus, placing the quoted verse into its proper context. It may, on the surface, appear to be more work; but I believe it is an excellent method to help each reader move beyond the words of the writer and to rely completely on what the Bible itself has to say on the subject.

And that is, truly and in the final analysis, the only correct way to proceed. The Bible stands on its own in timeless and unshakable truth; and most importantly, it interprets itself. *The Bible interprets itself*! And although the churches, in general, have taken bits and pieces of it and have constructed huge followings and great infrastructures around their selected tidbits, turning man-created interpretations into longstanding and unchallenged doctrines, the Bible is free standing and self-contained. It was written to be a complete resource within its own pages. Questions arising in one part of the Bible are answered in another, consistently and without fail. Concepts which are vague in some areas of the Bible are crystallized in other areas, because scripture is true; it was written to be true, and it remains true. Only when the mythological thinking of man begins to creep in does truth become jumbled. Only then does whipped-up distortions begin to fog the facts.

The result of such has been a complete human movement

away from our true identities in scripture and in history, and a complete misunderstanding as to our true purposes in the overall plan of God. As a culture, many of us have become spiritually and religiously ignorant. Many have become blinded to the clear messages of the Bible. For example, many citizens of the United States of America do not even remotely know where we, as a 21st century mega-culture, the richest, most productive, and most blessed country in the history of man, are mentioned in the Bible, *which we most certainly are*; therefore, we have no clue as to when the Bible is speaking directly to us as a country, or when it is referring to somebody else in another time period or another geographical location.

The truth has always been before the eyes of mankind; yet, a great deal of religious confusion and ignorance has existed throughout the ages. And, alas, I blame the churches for the bulk of this confusion. The Bible has been at their disposal for centuries! Millions and millions of people have turned to the churches for understanding; yet, in too many cases, the people have received only great *mis*understanding. Half truths and incomplete perceptions have too often been passed along and accepted as doctrine. Facts have too often been confused by beliefs. Biblical truth which, again, stands alone is generally overshadowed by the towering mythologies of man. The result has been mankind worshipping blindly and often in vain a God who they do not even know nor understand.

I reflect on the experience of Jesus for a moment. In the Gospel of Luke, the story is told of Jesus preaching in the synagogue in the presence of many misinformed worshippers:

Luke: **He went into the synagogue on the Sabbath day and stood up to read. And there was delivered unto Him the book of the prophet Isaiah. And when He had opened the book, He found the place where it was writ-**

ten, *"The Spirit of the Lord is upon me, because he hath anointed me to preach the gospel to the poor; he hath sent me to heal the broken-hearted, to preach deliverance to the captives and recovering of sight to the blind, to set at liberty them that are bruised, to preach the acceptable year of the Lord."* **And He closed the book and gave it again to the minister and sat down. And the eyes of all them that were in the synagogue were fastened on Him. And He began to say unto them, *"This day is this scripture fulfilled in your ears."* ...And all they in the synagogue, when they heard these things, were filled with wrath, And they rose up, and thrust Him out of the city, and led Him unto the brow of the hill that they might cast Him down headlong.**

Think, for a moment, of the magnitude of that passage. Jesus Himself was standing in this particular town's place of worship. He was telling the people in the synagogue straight out, *"I have come to fulfill this prophesy."* And instead of accepting His message, the people grew enraged and took Jesus out of the city to throw Him off the edge of a cliff and kill Him. Simply because the words and facts He was presenting to them from scripture--*the truth*--was in opposition to what the people themselves had already concluded and believed in their hearts as truth. The event was a classic case of The Word versus the myth; and the myth, due to the fact that it was believed by a greater number of people at the time, won out in popular opinion. The believers of the myth attempted to kill the messenger of the truth.

Yet now, in retrospect, we know differently. We now know that during Jesus' time, the religious beliefs of man were foolish, especially as they were in confrontation with the teachings and the truth of Jesus. But let's not judge that generation so harshly; hindsight is always 20/20. We may believe that, if we had been alive during the days of Jesus, we ourselves would certainly have known better and would have listened to Jesus and would not have joined the crowds of people who opposed Him and tried to kill Him. But people of that particular day thought the exact same thing about their own ancestors. Those church-going people thought that, if they had been alive during the time of the prophets, they would not have taken part in the execution of those prophets. But Jesus pointed out to them the folly in their thinking in Matthew 23:30:

Matthew: **"And you say, 'if we had been alive in the days of our fathers, we would not have been partakers with them in the blood of the prophets.' Therefore, you be witnesses unto yourselves, that you are the children of them which killed the prophets. Therefore, behold, I send unto you prophets, and wise men, and scribes: and some of them you shall kill and crucify; and some of them shall you scourge in your synagogues, and persecute them from city to city: O Jerusalem, Jerusalem, you that kill the prophets and stone them which are sent unto you."**

Now, please understand that I am in no way placing myself in the category of prophets. And please don't think for a moment that I am by any means taking the stance of the self-righteous. I am not. I am merely pointing out the fact that new and different information, which may be in opposition to longstanding beliefs, whether it be brought by a prophet or merely pointed out by a "writer," has traditionally been met with great resistance. The prophets were resisted. Jesus was resisted. Paul and his followers were resisted. And writers throughout the ages who have brought forth information in opposition to popular belief systems have also been resisted.

But I challenge each reader of this book to let down his or her potential resistance for the time being, and to proceed throughout these pages with an open heart and an analytical mind. And I, for my part, will present only the facts as they exist in the Bible. I will bring to light the relevant informa-

tion from scripture's own interpretation of itself, and I will
likewise commit to discount the interpretations and misin-
terpretations of man. I may present an occasional hypotheti-
cal concept or theory; but as we walk together through this
examination of God's plan and the various prophesies as
they relate to our time, we can safely and consistently rely
solely on the only resource of truth and understanding offered to us from the beginning of time: the Bible.

And so, as we begin, I would like to take two specific directions in this particular chapter. One, I would like to further
set the philosophical tones to which the contents of this book
will be based, which, I believe, will add to the general
strength and bond of our conversation. And two, I would
like to discuss the Sign of Jonah, a sort of categorical
springboard I have used in my personal pursuit of biblical
truths to question and challenge some of the longstanding
and traditional religious beliefs of our culture.

This book was actually inspired by the increasing amount of
hub-bub I have been hearing on TV and in the papers and
out on the street regarding the year 2000 and the supposed
approach of the end of the world. There have been increasing concerns about wars and rumors of wars in various parts
of the world, great anxiety expressed by many over the Y2K
crisis; and a considerable upsurge of TV personalities--
celebrities and evangelists alike--coming to the forefront
with predictions from psychics and prophets, and verses
from sources ranging anywhere from isolated biblical prophesies to over-zealous translations of the poetry of Nostradamus. And while I understand that noise is, after all,
just noise, I find myself growing increasingly irritated by all
these so-called "experts."

Within the realm of "Christianity," a term which I use, you
will note, with extreme caution and great reservation, a certain degree of "church truth," as I will call it, is universal
and ever-present. That is to say that certain core beliefs

consistent to the practice of "Christianity" are present and universal to the belief system; although, in some instances, those beliefs vary from denomination to denomination by the ways in which they are approached . An example of that would be in the observation of the weekly Sabbath. All areas of "Christianity" acknowledge the fact that God set aside a day intended for rest and worship. Some churches believe this day to be Sunday. Others believe it is Saturday. Others believe that it simply doesn't matter which day is set aside, just as long as *some* time is reserved for attending church. Some church members worship on whichever day they decide is correct by going to church for an hour. Others worship all day long and completely refrain from work and commerce, observing the "day of rest" in a very literal sense. All adhere to the same general belief, yet practice it in very different ways.

Another example can be pointed out in the churches' observation and understanding of Jesus himself. Universally speaking, "Christianity" acknowledges that Jesus lived, died, and was resurrected for the salvation of mankind. Some churches focus solely on that particular role of Jesus, seeing Him as a presence who arrived on the scene roughly 2000 years ago to take away the sins of the world. Others acknowledge the fact that Jesus actually *created* the world, was the manifested presence of God in the Old Testament, appearing before the likes of Abraham and Moses; and that He was born into the world as "the second Adam," defeating Satan for the salvation of mankind in a way that Adam was meant to do but could not.

Each view is similar, yet very different. And the same holds true for the ways in which Bible prophesies are handled and interpreted. On a universal level, "Christianity" acknowledges the presence of prophesies throughout the Bible; yet, each denomination approaches these prophesies from completely different points of view. Some denominations focus solely on the Book of Revelation. Some rely on Jesus' projections discussed in the four Gospels. Others recognize that two-thirds of the Bible is prophesy, and they therefore extract predictions from throughout its pages. And, likewise, the interpretations of these prophesies, whichever ones are recognized and acknowledged, vary greatly from denomination to denomination.

My intention in the writing of this book is not to take sides with various issues and interpretations and pit them against the beliefs and interpretations of the other side. That would be the equivalent of putting on boxing gloves and jumping into the middle of a street brawl with the intention of stopping the fight; it would be a mere exercise in counter-productivity and futility. Instead, my intention is to discuss biblical prophesies as they relate to God's 7000 year plan for mankind, which began roughly 6000 years ago, and which will be culminating in the relatively near future in a period of great despair for the world followed by a 1000 year period of unprecedented peace and prosperity on earth. My scope will touch on all 7000 years of the plan, but will focus on prophesies as they relate to the latter portion of the plan, primarily the various time periods in the 5000th and 6000th years of the plan, as well as the 33 to 100 years or so directly in front of us. And in conducting this discussion, I will rely directly on biblical references as they outline the actual prophesies themselves and then serve to interpret those prophecies within the context of itself through other biblical references. In other words, I will discuss biblical prophecies as they are presented and interpreted IN THE BIBLE, within its own language and organization. I won't go out to the church doctrines and man-made belief systems in an attempt to bring forth any degree of understanding; such an exercise would only serve to present, as it always does, confusion and *mis*understanding. I won't take the side of any particular church doctrine; although, I will most likely speak out strongly against the ridiculous "rapture" theory and the universal "*kathlikos*" church. But, in general, the only side I will take will be the side of the Bible, which, as I have already mentioned, was written to stand on its own and interpret itself *within* itself.

To read the Bible as a stand-alone reference is not as easy of a task as it at first appears. So much additional information has been woven into the ways in which we have traditionally approached and understood its teachings. And as I proceed, I am intensely aware of the greater task at hand: the task of *un*teaching and *un*conditioning very deeply entrenched and, I am sure, well defended sets of beliefs and cognitions surrounding religious doctrine and biblical interpretation that each reader will possess. It is a touchy undertaking at best! Each person has grown up to adhere to a certain doctrine concerning religious philosophy, spiritual orientation, and biblical understanding. For most people, those philosophies and understandings have been church initiated and have stemmed from the teachings of a particular religious affiliation or denomination. Through the course of time, these beliefs have been interwoven into the fabric of our society in general. And in most cases, those teachings have begun at a very young age, continually, through interactions in Sunday schools and catechisms, from books lying around the house or in office lobbies and libraries, from movies and images on TV, and from several other sources such as music or mere word of mouth. A whole barrage of input regarding religious doctrines and beliefs have been at our society's disposal--at OUR disposal--all of our lives; and through the internalization of this information, we have each formed our own system of beliefs.

Likewise, so much as been written about biblical prophesy. So much information and misinformation has been disseminated throughout the ages, through the churches and through the result of man's own fears and creative compulsions, that the truth continues to teeter on the edges of confusion and absurdity. Religious beliefs and convictions have been strongly established in our societies as a whole and in our hearts as individuals. Our church leaders continue to swing back and forth in agreement and disagreement with each other on issue upon issue; and in their wake, scores of zealots have reared their heads in the public forum to lend their own interpretations to the mix. But much of the man-generated information we have learned should, accordingly, be viewed with a raised eyebrow and more than just a wince of question and skepticism. Man has taken the information made rich and plentiful in the Bible and, throughout the ages, has channeled it into beliefs and interpretations and rituals filled with theocentricism. The result has been a multitude of religious affiliations (e.g. Catholic, Christian, Lutheran, Methodist, etc. etc. etc.). Unfortunately, however, in many cases, these beliefs and interpretations and doctrines and affiliations have had very little, beyond a foggy resemblance, in common with the information made abundant in the Bible.

A good example of where this same (albeit unrelated) type of learning phenomena--and subsequent need for unteaching--can be viewed in another area of society, unassociated with religion, is found in the way in which the subject of English grammar is taught and learned in the American school systems. A high school English teacher asks, "*What is a verb?*" The students answer, "*An action word.*" WRONG! (As an ex-English teacher, this is one of my personal pet peeves!) The same incorrect definition--"*an action word*"--learned by these kids in 2nd grade remains with them in 9th, 10th, all the way through high school. In the earlier grades, for the sake of simplicity at a given moment, the common misnomer "*action word*" is attached to the definition of a verb; and the limited cognitive development of the 2nd grader is simply unable to determine that words such as *is, are, will,* and *should,* to name a few, simply do not adhere to the definition, although they are generally used as verbs. Likewise, words such as *quickly, suddenly, slowly, abruptly,* etc. for just a few examples, show a whole lot of action but are generally used as adverbs, not verbs. So, the 2nd grader learns--and internalizes--an incorrect definition of a verb that stays with him well into high school. And thousands of high school English teachers across the country realize that _un_teaching the lessons of the past, for the purpose of clearer understandings in the present, is a very fundamental classroom task year after year.

Such is the case in the writing and teaching of biblical fundamentals. A certain degree of _un_teaching and rethinking has to take place in order for the reader to fully accept the material from a newer, fresher, and less biased perspective. It is never an easy movement away from old, established beliefs into newer, unfamiliar perspectives. It is generally a leap of faith, so to speak, a scary walk out onto the tightrope of the unknown. However, in doing so, greater and more in-depth understandings can be accomplished. By challenging familiar information, knowledge increases and new worlds become completely opened up.

Specific to the contents of this book, a reader who is willing to place familiar beliefs aside and fully examine the Bible with an open and analytical mind, and who is willing to let the Bible interpret itself within the context of itself, shedding, if only momentarily, the definitions and interpretations historically created and followed by man, will certainly walk away from this book--and from the Bible--with a greater understanding of God, of Jesus, of man, of man's purpose and destiny, and of the dozens and dozens of prophesies that relate directly to our world now and in the years just ahead in the 21st century. A reader who is willing to approach the material in this book with a careful and open mind, and who is willing to use the Bible and prove the material by biblical teachings alone, will learn, among other things, that the earth will not end in our lifetimes. That Jesus will return to earth relatively early in the 2000 A.D. millenium and rule mankind with absolute authority *on earth* for 1000 years. That Jesus, upon His return, will again be met with opposition; and that much of this opposition will be generated directly from the world's churches and from those inhabitants of the earth who may, even in this current day and age, refer to themselves as "Christians." That Jesus will overthrow this man-made belief system of churches and "Christians" and will reestablish His own system of government, placing His truth in the hearts of all His followers, recruiting human beings who understand His truth to be priests and teachers in the carrying out of His objectives in this earth-based government.

We will discuss the fact that the "Israel" referred to in the Bible is not merely a country in the Middle East, but consists today of the United States and Great Britain as well. That "the beast" mentioned in Revelation 13 (666) is not a man nor an antichrist, but a country (an empire and a kingdom.) That although Jesus will return to the earth in great splendor and spectacle, He will not be recognized or accepted by the majority of people because the world has been misled into recognizing a false picture of Him. For example, the picture most people associate with Jesus is that of the Good Shepherd from Pagan art, the mild mannered and meekly structured man with long hair and a beard. This image has been blazoned into the conscience of the entire planet. Show a picture of the soft-framed gentle man in a robe, with His long hair and beard, to any person in the world and ask that person "who is this?" And the answer would most readily be "Jesus." It is the picture we have grown to recognize as Jesus. However, the Bible paints a much different picture For example, did Jesus have long hair?

1 Corinthians: **Why, nature itself teaches you that long hair on a man is a disgrace**...

Is Jesus meager in physique? Is He small structured and docile? Consider His act of tossing the money-changers out of the temple:

John: ...**Jesus went up to Jerusalem, and found in the**

temple those that sold oxen and sheep and doves, and the changers of money sitting...He drove them *all* out of the temple, and the sheep, and the oxen; and poured out the changers' money, and overthrew the tables; And said to them that sold doves, "Take these things hence; make not my Father's house a house of merchandise!"

Notice the word "all." There were many of the merchants and money-changers and only one Jesus; yet, He drove them *all* out. He was yelling and pushing over tables, and throwing the changer's possessions on the ground. He was basically shutting down their businesses and driving them out into the streets; yet, not one person challenged Him. Instead, He was not attacked but obeyed. This is not the way a mob generally handles a mild mannered "Good Shepherd" throwing a tantrum, is it? Common sense tells us that if Jesus was the gentle little man with a beard single-handedly tossing the merchants out into the street, and the opportunity to earn money was being lost in the process, two or three of the bigger guys on hand would have ganged up on Him and probably knocked Jesus for a loop. Instead, they were driven out into the street.

Consider also that Jesus was a carpenter, not necessarily a finishing carpenter but possibly a man who built whole houses. A man who worked outdoors with hammers and nails and heavy lumber. And that when He recruited such type of men as fishermen and tax collectors, He was basically rounding up some pretty physically capable people, all of which followed Him without much resistance. And when He went into the churches and challenged their doctrines, people generally ganged up and tried to attack Him, not one-on-one, but in numbers. These things do not indicate that Jesus was the 97-pound-weakling from Nazareth, the dainty little figure from a Pagan painting. He was very physically capable. In addition, Jesus owned a house, paid taxes, drank occasional alcohol, and had a whole gamut of human emotions. These facts are mentioned throughout the four Gospels; yet, most of the world does not fully recognize such aspects of Jesus. And when He returns to earth, all of these misconceptions will contribute to the fact that He will be challenged and confronted by a well-deceived population.

And during the discussion of such facts, my hope is that readers will invoke a challenge within themselves to read the Bible and question some of the things which each reader has traditionally envisioned and believed. And as we walk together through biblical prophesies to analyze and challenge what has traditionally been taught and defined through the inventions of man, we will put many pieces of prophesy together, from the Bible itself, to better understand just what these prophesies have been saying to us all along; and how they pertain to the times we have lived in and which are directly ahead of us in the near future.

In some instances, the prophesies will be clear and immediately defined. In other places, various biblical texts will have to be pieced together and viewed as a whole to clearly understand their meanings. For example, let's take a quick look at "the mark of the beast," that infamous number 666 from Revelation 13, which will be covered in greater depth in chapters 6,7, and 8. The biblical text directly referring to this mark is in the Book of Revelation.

Revelation: "...**and he causeth all, both small and great, rich and poor, free and bond, to receive a mark in their right hand, or in their foreheads: that no man might buy or sell, save he that had the mark, or the name of the beast, or the number of his name. Here is wisdom. Let him that hath understanding count the number of the beast: for it is the number of a man; and his number is six hundred sixty and six.**

Man has been creating definitions for this mark for nearly 2000 years. Some say it will be a mark from a branding iron that will be burned on the hands and heads of citizens all over the world (imagine *that* happening in suburban America). Some believe it will be three numbers-666-that will be tattooed on our wrists and foreheads in order for us to buy and sell. Some have speculated that it will be some form of global social security number, or a micro-chip that is going to be placed in our heads and hands as some form of purchasing mechanism compatible with cash registers throughout the global economy. These are all, of course, crazy interpretations of man which have nothing to do with the facts offered up strongly and clearly in the Bible. But because this passage is generally read only in its isolated context and is not compared to verses elsewhere in the Bible, its meaning remains misconstrued. And because of the time of the writing of the Book of Revelation, and the use of future tense by John as he was recording the events which were being revealed to him at the time, many readers of the book, including readers of our time, continue to pro- ject this *"mark of the beast"* as something that will happen in the future; something perhaps technical and scientific, which is what readers in the technical age of the latter half of the 20th century invented as a possible rationale regard- ing the mark.

But when we discount man's imagination and compare this passage from the Book of Revelation with various other pas- sages of the Bible, we can easily conclude that, although the mark of the beast was seen as something that would be be- stowed upon mankind in *John's* future, it is very well some- thing that has already been placed upon mankind in *our* past. And many may wonder just how such a mark, on our hands and heads, could possibly have happened already in our past, since, as the passage reads, it would be placed *on the hands and heads* of "**all, both small and great, rich and poor, free and bond.**" As a society, we know that there are not marks on our hands and heads, so we continue to speculate that it will be something that happens in the future. However, as we look at other verses in the Bible, we can easily see that the sign of the Lord is also on our hands and heads.

Further examination of additional biblical passages reveal that the marks on our hands and heads are symbols. In other verses we learn that they are symbolic of thinking and worshipping (with our heads) and working (with our hands). Whereas God commands us to think and work and worship according to His laws, the book of Revelation points out that *"all men, great and small, rich and poor,"* will be, instead, thinking and working according to the laws of the beast. I have written an entire book on this particular subject entitled, **666: The Beast Revealed**. In it, I discuss the beast and the mark in greater detail. And, as mentioned, we will discuss it in further detail in later chapters of this book. But at this point in the chapter, please let me just say that the mark of the beast has been upon us for centuries already! Upon our fathers and mothers and their fathers and mothers and their fathers and mothers, dating back hundreds and hundreds of years!

We have been working and thinking in accordance to the laws of the beast. But to understand the mark, one must first understand the beast. Later, we will follow biblical passages to understand both the beast and the mark; but for now, without jumping ahead, and without just throwing too much information out before establishing the foundations by which it can be understood, let me just say that the answer to the beast AND the mark which we all have lies in our calendar. Look at the calendar. Stare at it for a long time. Go through it week by week and month by month. Understand it. Therein lies the answer to the beast and its mark.

But before we get too far ahead and too well off track, let's get back to what this chapter was originally about, which was *"the sign of Jonah."*

When I was twelve years old and still a Catholic, possessing only very limited knowledge of biblical teachings, one of the most confusing things to me regarding the church and the Bible was the church's "Good Friday," and the Bible's "sign of Jonah." At the time, they both seemed to be talking about the same thing to me; yet, each one was contradictory to the other in a very fundamental way. The church was teaching that Good Friday represented the day upon which Jesus was crucified and buried in the tomb. He supposedly remained in the tomb until Sunday morning--Easter morning--at sunrise and then He was resurrected. *The Sign of Jonah*, on the other hand, which Jesus gave as a sign to the wicked generation of His time, as recorded in the Gospels of Matthew and Luke, stated something strangely similar yet completely different:

Matthew: **For as Jonah was three days and three nights in the belly of the great fish, so shall the Son of Man be three days and three nights in the belly of the earth."**

At twelve years old, I remember reading that passage and thinking, "Wait a second. There are not three days and three nights between Good Friday and Easter." And I counted the days. Friday....day one. Friday night....night one. Saturday....day two. Saturday night....night two. Sunday morning? This falls short! There were simply not three days and three nights! And for me, even at age twelve, something smelled rotten in Denmark regarding this conflict. I found myself faced with probably my first true blue religious dilemma. Should I believe the Bible? Or should I believe the church? Truly, as I think back now, I probably would not have made up my mind so quickly if it weren't for the fact that Jesus Himself spoke those words. I am, today, a firm believer that children have a natural in-stinct towards Jesus; but back then, I just knew that I trusted Him over anything or anybody else. And since He was speaking of the three days and three nights, I concluded rather quickly that the Bible was correct and that the church was somehow wrong in its calculation of this Good Friday /

Easter thing.

I began researching the sign of Jonah and examining other church denominations which followed Good Friday. To my amazement, almost all churches of which I was aware at that time--Lutheran, Baptist, Methodists, to name a few-- observed Good Friday and Easter. I continued to seek an answer that would help me clarify such a flagrant discrep- ancy between the Bible and the church; and within a few years, I began to gain better understanding of both the pas- sage and the gaping difference between church and doctrine. My understanding has helped me develop a sort of gage, or pretest, when viewing churches, their leaders, and their parishioners. I have used it as a sort of litmus test to all churches everywhere, testing them for their validity and un- derstanding; and for their knowledge of the Bible. And I chose to begin this book with "The Sign of Jonah" because I want to challenge each reader to take a look at it and draw his or her own conclusion regarding the sign and the current practices of the churches. By exmining this one point, the goal of *un*-teaching that which has been previously learned might be accomplished. And also, this chapter may set a foundation from which to approach the rest of this book and its collection of passages and perspectives. By understand- ing the Sign of Jonah, it is possible that the whole Bible can be approached with an open, inquisitive, questioning mind.

Jesus clearly stated that *"...as Jonah was three days and three nights in the belly of the great fish, so shall the Son of Man be three days and three nights in the belly of the earth."* Jesus was crucified and buried in the afternoon. Once in the tomb, he spent THREE DAYS AND THREE NIGHTS in *"the belly of the earth."* Easter, according to the practicing churches of our day, is supposed to represent the day on which Jesus was resurrected. Most churches practice that He rose from the dead at sunrise on Sunday morning. And they likewise practice that He was, therefore, crucified in the afternoon of what is known as Good Friday.

But, as I discovered at age twelve, regardless of how you cut it, there is simply not "three days and three nights" between Friday afternoon and Sunday morning. It's more like two days if we cut it just right; two *nights* max. And I am aware that this might, on the surface, sound like an extremely trivial detail. But, first of all, Jesus stated that The Sign of Jonah was the world's only real sign concerning Him:.

Luke: **...Jesus answered the crowd and said to them, "An evil and adulterous generation seeks after a sign; and there shall be no sign given to it but the sign of the prophet Jonah: For as Jonah was three days and three nights in the belly of the great fish, so shall the Son of man be three days and three nights in the belly of the earth.**

Think about this. Is it a trivial matter for Jesus to say one thing and for the church to screw it up so terribly? And secondly, as we will examine shortly, and as a matter of fact, Jesus was *not* resurrected on a Sunday morning; He rose from the dead on a Saturday evening shortly after sundown. Which takes His crucifixion, death, and burial, according to the sign of Jonah, all the way back to Wednesday afternoon.

Why is this important? For many reasons. First, it points out for us just how carelessly invented and randomly scattered our so-called holy days, such as Good Friday, really are. Two, it helps us see how so very often church doctrine is accepted without challenge or questions as to sources of proof. Thirdly, and by no means conclusively or least importantly, our ability to understand these basic errors helps us raise an eyebrow on our current calendar system, which was created by *"the beast, dreadful and terrible"* and which has served to distort our entire connection to God's plan for two thousand years.

21

Understanding such seemingly trivial events--such as
church observation of a loosely invented and flagrantly miscalculated holy day--is extremely important in putting all
the pieces of the greater biblical puzzle together, and also in
seeing the ways in which churches just lead and how parishioners sometimes just follow.

During Jesus' time, clocks and watches were not available,
and days did not begin and end at midnight. Instead, days
began and ended at a time that was observable by all: at
sundown. A single day started at sundown, which means
the first part of the day was actually night time. Thursday,
for example, would begin at night, at sundown, and run
through the night, into morning, all afternoon; and it would
end at sundown of the following day, at which time the next
day, Friday, would begin. Sunday would actually begin on
Saturday night at sundown. It would run all through Saturday night, into Sunday morning, all Sunday afternoon, and
it would end on sundown of Sunday night, at which time
Monday would begin. Days went from sundown to sundown. The first day of the week, then, started at sundown
on Saturday night. The last day of the week, the Sabbath,
began on Friday at sundown and ended on Saturday night at
sundown.

When calculating Jesus death, burial, and resurrection, it is
important to keep the sundown to sundown day-schedule in
mind.

The books of Matthew, Mark, and Luke clearly state how,
after Jesus was buried, Mary Magdalene headed towards
Jesus' tomb *"when the Sabbath was over, at sunrise,"* only
to discover that Jesus had already been resurrected. John
points out that she headed toward the tomb while it was still
dark. Here are those detailed accounts from the King James
Version of the Bible:

Matthew: **In the end of the Sabbath, as it began to dawn**

toward the first day of the week, came Mary Magdalene and the other Mary to see the tomb.

Mark: **And when the Sabbath was past, Mary Magdalene, and Mary the mother of James, and Salome, had bought sweet spices, that they might come and anoint him. And very early in the morning the first day of the week, they came unto the sepulchre at the rising of the sun.** (Note: Remember this part about the rising sun; we will refer to it later.) **And they said among themselves, Who shall roll us away the stone from the door of the tomb? And when they looked, they saw that the stone was rolled away: for it was very great. And entering into the tomb, they saw a young man sitting on the right side, clothed in a long white garment; and they were affrighted. And he saith unto them, Be not affrighted: Ye seek Jesus of Nazareth, which was crucified: he is risen;** _**he is not here**_**:**

Luke: **Now upon the first day of the week, very early in the morning, they came unto the tomb, bringing the spices which they had prepared, and certain others with them....and found not the body of the Lord Jesus.**

John: **The first day of the week cometh Mary Magdalene early,** _**when it was yet dark,**_ **unto the tomb, and seeth the stone taken away from the tomb.**

All accounts are true. Mary rested on the seventh day of the week, the Sabbath (sundown Friday to sundown Saturday) and headed for Jesus' tomb sometime _before_ sunrise in the morning, _"while it was yet dark."_ Jesus was already out of the tomb. He was resurrected just shortly after sunDOWN the night before. All of the above passages directly disprove what most churches believe, which is that Jesus was resurrected at sunrise on Sunday morning. Jesus was resurrected on Saturday night, just after sundown.

Later, we'll see how those infamous "sunrise services" observed by most churches in their celebration of Easter have little to do with Jesus or His resurrection and are, instead, merely spin-offs of Pagan sun-worshipping practices disguised as a celebration of Jesus' resurrection at sunrise. But the 4 gospels explicitly point out that Jesus was resurrected well before sunrise.

The Gospels also point out that Jesus died around 3 pm.:

Matthew: **Now from the sixth hour there was darkness over all the land unto the ninth hour. And about the ninth hour Jesus cried with a loud voice, saying, My God, my God, why hast thou forsaken me? ... Jesus, when he had cried again with a loud voice, yielded up the ghost.**

Mark: **And at the ninth hour Jesus cried with a loud voice...and gave up the ghost.**

When one reads the previous passages, and when one understands that the Sabbath lasted from sundown on Friday night until sundown on Saturday night, that the 9th hour (of sunlight) was roughly 3 o'clock in the afternoon, and that Jesus clearly stated He would be *"three days and three nights in the belly of the earth,"* one merely needs to calculate THREE DAYS AND THREE NIGHTS between the two time periods to come to the obvious conclusion: Jesus was crucified on a Wednesday afternoon.

And some may still simply say, "So what!" So what? In the world today, there are millions and millions of people going to church and praying for the death of Jesus on Good Friday afternoons. And the same number of people face the sunrise on Easter morning to worship Jesus' resurrection. Neither practices are correct; yet, both are rarely questioned in terms of their validity. They are just observed. They are observed because the whole culture and the whole church does it; the priests and ministers do it. It is traditional. Worshipping people throughout the world believe in it. And we, as people with hearts truly yearning for the truth, too often overlook another statement of Jesus made in the Gospel of Mark:

Mark: **"Howbeit in vain do they worship me, teaching for doctrines the commandments of men. For laying aside the commandments of God, you hold the tradition of men."**

Jesus told us about the Sign of Jonah; yet, churches continued throughout the ages to teach and believe that Jesus was crucified on Friday afternoon and resurrected on Sunday morning. Generation upon generation has been led into believing it. Many people simply do not open the Bible. Few people attempt to validate their practices.

In my teenage years, I asked myself this one question; and I ask it right now of each reader of this book: if something as universally practiced as the sunrise service on Easter and the observation of Good Friday can be so easily proved incorrect, does it not stand to reason that many other man-and-church interpretations of biblical events could possibly be analyzed and challenged as well? As a kid, according to what I knew at the time, I used the Sign of Jonah to test whether or not the churches were practicing correctly. If they were observing Good Friday and engaging in sunrise services on Easter morning, I concluded that they were incorrect; that they were following, as Jesus stated, *"the traditions of men"* as opposed to the *"commandments of God."* I concluded that the churches were, for the most part, teaching incorrect doctrine and that their parishioners were incorrectly learning this doctrine as fundamental truths.

And thus, we come back to the point I made at the beginning of this chapter: the monumental task of unteaching what has been accepted as truth, and to opening the door and presenting opportunities to view things with a more receptive mind, is at hand. I contend that once a reader is

25

willing to approach the Bible with a careful, inquisitive, and open mind, an entire universe of understanding can then be accomplished.

Some may want to inquire of the church, maybe even sit down with a minister and review the contents of this book. I encourage that, but I must also say, "Remember the Sign of Jonah!" If your church, or any church, observes Good Friday and sunrise services on Easter morning (or Easter in general for that matter!), I would like to kindly suggest that the evidence is before you that the church already has *something* amiss. It is already doing something incorrectly and out of accordance with what the Bible teaches. And we will explore the reasons behind this depressing fact in later chapters. For now, I would like to personally recommend, as I have done myself, that readers side-step the teachings of the church for a moment and examines biblical scriptures on their own.

And one other very important thing that I must repeat: as you continue through the chapters of this book, please do not simply take my word for anything. I have included biblical scriptures to help put 2-and-2 together and determine facts as they stand by themselves, free from man's confusion. But please take it upon yourself to open your Bible frequently and examine the scriptures over and over again, drawing conclusions in your own heart: free from church doctrine. Free from the analysis of Canyon Adams. Free from the hype and fear-inducement of the public that generally accompanies discussion of prophesies.

And as you will see, God has a clear-cut plan for mankind which is, in all reality, quite contrary to what is being taught in our places of worship. And God's plan is not terrible and frightening. Yes, there will be some dark time. Yes, there will be trials and tribulations. Yes, there will be diseases and disasters and wars and sicknesses, and calamities the likes of which have never been known to mankind. But the end is not global disaster. It's not death and hell for all the inhabitants of the earth. In the end, God will restore all things and provide for mankind a time of peace and prosperity on Earth that will last 1000 years.

The news is good! The road ahead may be hellacious, but the news is good. In our hearts, we can have hope and faith. In our minds, we can have knowledge. And in our whole beings, we can have God.

With an open heart and mind, please let us proceed:

Canyon Adams

Chapter 2

The United States, Great Britain, and Europe in Bible Prophesy

---

In order to understand biblical prophesy, one must first understand biblical *identity*. To formulate a clear picture of how and why world events have unfolded in the past, and how they will certainly unfold in the future, it is imperative to know the identity of those people and countries and cultures to which the Bible primarily speaks. Once these national identities have been established and are clear, Bible prophesy becomes much easier to follow and comprehend. Simply put, if we know who we are and where we've been, we have a much better chance of seeing where we are going. To this end, then, we will follow biblical passages to determine the identity of those people in the Bible who have become "God's chosen people"; that is, the people in the Bible who are known and referred to as "the children of Israel," and who progressed through the ages to become lost, to become found, and to ultimately become what is now known as Europe, Great Britain, and the United States.

It seems a very strange and unique phenomenon to me that, in spite of the fact that Europe has been central to the historical evolution of the entire planet, and that the United States of America is the richest, most productive, and most exhalted nation in the history of the world, their biblical identities remain a mystery to millions and millions of people, now and throughout history. Millions of church-going citizens within the boundaries of both the United States and Europe have no idea as to where they are mentioned in the Bible, or even that they *are* mentioned in the Bible; and this serves to compound the problem of understanding prophesy. If we cannot recognize our individual and national identities in the Bible, it is difficult to understand the prophecies which pertain to us and how they will ultimately effect our lives and our countries. But the fact is this: much of the Bible's prophecies are written for modern times, and they directly involve the United States and Europe. In many instances, the Bible is speaking directly to these two countries.

Consider for a moment the relatively brief and dynamic history of the United States. Whereas other countries in the world have histories dating back thousands of years, the history of the U.S. as an independent country goes back just a little over 200 years. Civilization is roughly 6000 years old. In the scope of 6 milleniums, a 200 year time span is an extremely short period of time; yet, during that time period, the United States has risen to a world power the magnitude of which has never before been known to mankind. As a nation, the United States is a wealthy, powerful, healthy, and educated superpower. A super-*presence*. We are a free people, free to make choices and pursue happiness. Our industrial and agricultural strengths are unsurpassed. Our military might has stood up time and time again against the forces of oppression throughout our history and in all parts of the world. In the history of human civilization, there has never been another country like the United States; nor has there ever been another world center such as Europe, nor another omnipresent and far reaching united kingdom such as Great Britain.

And so, it is extremely perplexing that anybody might think the Bible would not mention such great, unique, and significant countries. Equally as perplexing is the fact that the many churches and religious leaders of the world today appear not to be knowledgeable of the matter either; and they, therefore, minister in general terms and allow their parishioners to remain in the dark as to who they are in biblical context. Many believe that the Bible is an accounting of the history of ancient Israel and is, at least in terms of its Old Testament, significant only to the history of that particular time period and country. But the truth is that the Bible could just as easily be titled *"The Complete and Supernatural Histories of Europe, Great Britain, the Middle East, and The United States."* And the subtitle could be *"And a Detailed Account of the FUTURES of These Countries."* Most of what is written in the Bible is prophesy; and in modern times, the Bible is speaking primarily to the people of these countries, showing them their detailed histories, consulting them during their present-day trials and tribulations, and revealing to them the way in which their futures will unfold.

The Bible is primarily a book speaking directly to the people who have become modern day Europe, Great Britain, the Middle East, and the United States.

To understand this fact, one must first understand a few principles concerning the way in which the Bible works. First and foremost, as I have mentioned, the Bible stands on its own and interprets itself. There is no need to reach out to the creative rhetoric of man. The Bible itself will take care of all explanations and interpretations Secondly, the Bible was not written nor intended to be read in a linear manner; that is, it does not read from beginning to end like most other books. Instead, it was intended to be read by piecing bits of information together *"...a little bit here, a little bit there..."* in order to construct a complete picture.

31

In Isaiah 28, God points this particular principle out:

Isaiah 28: **"Whom shall he teach knowledge? and whom shall he make to understand doctrine?.... For precept must be upon precept, precept upon precept; line upon line, line upon line; *a little bit here, a little bit there.*** (Some interpretations say *"here a little, and there a little,"* meaning the same thing.)

The Bible is meant to be read line upon line, a piece here and a piece there, *"...here a little, and there a little..."* In practice, this can be experienced by trying to read the Book of Revelation by itself. As an isolated book, it is difficult to understand and, consequently, lends itself to the bizarre interpretations of man. But when it is read in conjunction with the Book of Daniel, and knowledge is put together with other knowledge, *"precept upon precept.....here a little and there a little...."* things begin to become clear and understandable. A newer and clearer picture begins to unfold. And such is the case throughout the Bible.

Another very important principle that must be understood when reading the Bible is that many events happen in TWOS, or in "dual" or "tandem" with one another, especially where prophesy is concerned. Things that happen one time in the Bible are more or less preludes to other similar things that happen--or will happen--on a greater scale at a later time. This is known as the Bible's "Dual Events Principle." Events that happen once will happen on a greater scale later on. For example, Jesus came once, and He will come again in greater and more glorious fashion. Adam came and created sin through which all men must die. Jesus came as "the second Adam" through which all men may live.

1 Corinthians: **"For as in Adam all die, even so in Christ**

shall all be made alive.... The *first* Adam was made a living soul; the *second* Adam was made a quickening spirit."

This particular principle, the Dual Events Principle, is extremely important to remember and apply in reading and understanding the Bible, especially as it applies to prophesy. The principle is vital, and it exists throughout the scriptures. As we examine the identities of both Europe and the United States in the Bible, this principle will become clearer as we look at, for example, events from our recent and well known American history and compare them to events in the Old Testament. Clear parallels can be observed as we do this.

Likewise, we will need to apply the principles of *"a little bit here, a little bit there,"* taking texts as they exist throughout the Bible and reading them together as a collection, as opposed to citing them as isolated verses existing on their own. As we read the Bible in this manner, the old myth of how *"...the Bible contradicts itself.....,"* which I have heard for years and continue to hear, will be proven false. The Bible does not contradict itself. It is, in fact, an very tightly written collection of writings, all of which have been written by different authors in different time periods, but which, of course, were actually written and inspired by one author: God.

With the above principles of *"a little bit here, a little bit there,"* and *Dual Events* in mind, we can begin to explore the identities of the United States, Europe, and Great Britain in the Bible.

The histories of these countries began with the calling out of Abraham by God in Genesis 12. As we follow the Bible's account of the lineage of Abraham through his son, his grandsons, and his great grandsons, we will see the histories of the people who would eventually grow to become the national composite of these geographical areas—Great Britain, Europe, the United States, and the Middle East. Beginning in the Book of Genesis, God looked upon Abram and decided that he would be the individual upon which God would create a chosen people. God called out Abram, eventually to be named Abra<u>ham</u>, which stands for "father of many," and told him to go to a land which God would show him and there he would be made into a great nation:

Genesis 12 **"The Lord had said to Abram, 'Leave your country, your people and your father's household and go to the land I will show you. I will make you into a great nation and I will bless you; I will make your name great, and you will be a blessing. I will bless those who bless you, and whoever curses you I will curse; and all peoples on earth will be blessed through you."**

Important in the above verse are three facts: (1) God was calling out Abram from the rest of the world. (2) God was promising to make Abram a great nation. And (3) God also promised that "...*all the peoples of the earth will be blessed through you.*" This single passage, complete with these three facts, marks the beginning of the histories of the United States, Great Britain, and Europe.

The name Abram, without the "h,"simply meant "exalted father," but in chapter 17, God changed his name to Abraham, meaning again, "father of many." And His promises to Abraham continued:

Genesis: **Neither shall your name any more be called Abram, but your name shall be Abraham; for a father of many nations have I made of you. And I will make you exceedingly fruitful, and I will make *nations* of you, and kings shall come out of you. And I will establish my covenant between me and you and your seed and thy**

seed after you in their generations for an everlasting covenant, to be a God unto you, and to your seed after you.

Abraham, upon being called out, was established by God as the father of many nations. It was a promise, a covenant, between God and Abraham that would be *everlasting* and would be passed on to his children and his children's children, down through his "seed," or through his continuing genetic line. And God points out to Abraham that this genetic line would be extensive:

Genesis: **I will make your offspring like the dust of the earth, so that if anyone could count the dust, then your offspring could be counted.'"**

And again,

Genesis: **I will surely bless you and make your descendants as numerous as the stars in the sky and as the sand on the seashore.**

Abraham was one man. When he was called out of the place where he lived by God and commanded to go to a completely different land where he was to be turned into the father of many nations, he didn't argue with God or hesitate to obey. He picked up and did as he was commanded. God, therefore, blessed Abraham and helped him conceptualize just how great he would become. His name would be revered, and his offspring would eventually be *"as numerous as the stars in the sky and the sand on the seashore."* I have often thought about how difficult it must have been for Abraham to conceptualize that millions and millions of people would ultimately evolve from him. In actuality, he probably couldn't grasp it; he merely acted on faith. God illustrated to him the magnitude of his family line by comparing the number of them to the stars and sand, but how could

Abraham fathom that his descendents would ultimately multiply a million fold and became inhabitants throughout the earth?

In time, Abraham had a son who he named Isaac. Many of us have heard the story of how God commanded Abraham to kill Isaac and how, as he had always done, Abraham acted in complete faith in God and proceeded to kill Isaac on an alter which he had constructed. In the last moment, while Abraham had the knife in his hand and was ready to kill his only son, God stopped him. It had been a test. God had merely been testing Abraham to see a further demonstration of his faith and fear in God. When it was evident that nothing would come between Abraham and his faith, not even the life of his only son, God knew that he was faithful and stopped the killing of Isaac. In addition, God added to his original blessing:

Genesis: **I swear by myself, declares the Lord, that because you have done this and have not withheld your son, your only son, I will surely bless you and make your descendants as numerous as the stars in the sky and as the sand on the seashore. Your descendants will take possession of the cities of their enemies, and through your offspring all nations on earth will be blessed, because you have obeyed me."**

Abraham's faith increased the blessing, which would eventually be passed on to Isaac after his death. He continued to live and prosper according to God's instructions, and after Abraham's death, Isaac received and continued on with the blessing.

During our modern times, in America and many other places in the world, it is standard procedure for an owner of real property to convey it to another party through the instrument of a recorded deed. Likewise, family members often pass their valuable properties, such as jewelry and real estate, from generation to generation by means of a Last Will and Testament, or a Trust; or again, by a recorded deed. These are legal means by which we transfer property. During Abraham's time, however, deeds and wills and trusts, if even in existence, were not the instruments of choice. During that time period, it was traditional for the father to pass his possessions and his birthrights--and in Abraham's case, his blessings--onto the eldest son by means of a brief ceremony. Generally, the ceremony consisted of the father and eldest son kneeling down before God. The father would place his right hand on his son's head and verbally announce before God and any other witnesses that the father's possessions were now being passed to the son. In this manner, the blessings and birthrights continued from generation to generation.

Abraham passed his blessings onto Isaac. Isaac had two twin sons, Esau and Jacob; and it was his intention to pass the blessings onto the eldest, Esau, who had come out of the womb first and who was, therefore, the eldest and natural owner of the birthrights and blessings. However, through a series of events discussed in Genesis 25 and 27, Jacob deceived Isaac and received the blessings instead.

Later, God changed Jacob's name to Israel, meaning *"he who struggles with God."* Eventually, upon changing his name, God continued the blessings which had been given to Abraham and Isaac:

Genesis 35: **God appeared to Jacob again and blessed him. God said to him, "Your name is Jacob, but you will no longer be called Jacob; your name will be Israel." So He named him Israel. And God said to him, "I am God Almighty ; be fruitful and increase in number. *A nation and a community of nations will come from you*, and kings will come from your body. The land I gave to Abraham and Isaac I also give to you, and I will give this land to your descendants after you."**

Just as Abraham had passed the birthright to Isaac, Isaac had passed it along to Jacob. Jacob's name was changed to Israel; and God reinforced the fact that the blessings were being passed along from generation to generation. In the same manner as He had promised Abraham, God perpetuated the blessings by passing them unto Israel and his descendants as well. This is an important fact that must be understood: Jacob received the blessings and became known as Israel. From those days forward, whenever the Bible referred to Israel, the children of Israel, or Jacob, it was referring to the direct descendents of Abraham as well. The family line was as follows: Abraham.....Isaac.....Jacob (Israel). And it continued to grow.

At this point, we must make note that God's promise stated that the seed of Abraham would become "*a nation and a community of nations*," and that the name of Jacob was changed to Israel.

Israel had 12 sons, and the one he loved the most was Joseph because he had been born to him in his old age. The other sons disliked their father's favor towards Joseph and plotted to kill their brother. Their plot failed, but served to separate the father and son--Israel and Joseph-- for several years. Here is where an interesting turn of events takes place. When Israel and Joseph finally reunited, and just prior to Israel's death, Israel bestowed the blessings, which had been handed down to him from Abraham and Isaac, upon Joseph. But, he did not give the blessings directly to Joseph. Instead, Israel passed the blessings to the *sons* of Joseph, who were named Manasseh and Ephraim.

The blessings, then, went from Abraham.....to Isaac......to Jacob (Israel).......to the *sons* of Joseph (Israel's grandsons): Manasseh and Ephraim. This is a VERY important movement to understand in the scope of identifying the United States and Great Britain in the Bible. The following passages from Genesis 48 are <u>pivotal</u> to this understanding:

Genesis 48: **When Israel saw the sons of Joseph, he asked, 'Who are these?'... 'They are the sons God has given me here,' Joseph said to his father. Then Israel said, 'Bring them to me so I may bless them.' Now Israel's eyes were failing because of old age, and he could hardly see. So Joseph brought his sons close to him, and his father kissed them and embraced them. Israel said to Joseph, 'I never expected to see your face again, and now God has allowed me to see your children too.' ...Then Joseph removed them from Israel's knees and bowed down with his face to the ground....And Joseph took both of them, Ephraim on his right toward Israel's left hand and Manasseh on his left toward Israel's right hand, and brought them close to him....But Israel reached out his right hand and put it on Ephraim's head, though he was the younger, and *crossing his arms*, he put his left hand on Manasseh's head, even though Manasseh was the firstborn....Then he blessed Joseph and said, 'May the God before whom my fathers Abraham and Isaac walked, the God who has been my shepherd all my life to this day...the Angel who has delivered me from all harm --may he bless these boys. *May they be called by my name* and the names of my fathers Abraham and Isaac, and may they increase greatly upon the earth.'**

This, again, was the standard way of passing along property and birthrights and blessings to younger generations. By placing his hands on the heads of his grandsons and declaring the words written above, Israel was passing the blessings to Manasseh and Ephraim. According to tradition, in the case of passing along birthrights to twins or to brothers, the *right* hand of the father or grandfather should be placed on the head of the eldest recipient. Joseph understood this tradition and noticed that Israel was crossing his hands instead, placing the left hand on the head of the eldest and the right hand on the head of the youngest. Joseph perceived that the blessings were being passed in error and he spoke up to correct his father's mistake:

Genesis: **When Joseph saw his father placing his right hand on Ephraim's head he was displeased; so he took hold of his father's hand to move it from Ephraim's head to Manasseh's head....Joseph said to him, 'No, my father, this one is the firstborn; put your right hand on his head.'... But his father refused and said, 'I know, my son, I know. He too will** *become a people,* **and he too will become great. Nevertheless, his younger brother will be greater than he,** *and his descendants will become a group of nations.'*......**He blessed them that day and said, 'In your name will Israel pronounce this blessing: `May God make you like Ephraim and Manasseh.' So he put Ephraim ahead of Manasseh.....Then Israel said to Joseph, 'I am about to die, but God will be with you and take you back to the land of your fathers.'**

Enter the United States and Great Britain!

Genesis 48 is extremely vital in that it concisely separates the original blessing given to Abraham into two entities. Ephraim's genetic line would become a group of nations and Manasseh's line would become a great nation. In addition, Israel's name was placed on both Ephraim and Manasseh: *"May they be called by my name."* We will follow the paths of Ephraim and Manasseh to see how they carried on this name, and how they have become to be what we know today as Great Britain (a group of nations) and the United States (a great nation). But first, very important elements of this passage which must be reinforced and understood are as follows:

1. Manessah, the oldest, was to become a great nation.
2. Ephraim, although the second born, was to be greater than Manessah and became "a group of nations."
3. Israel's name would be upon them. "**May they be called**

by my name..." They would be known as Israel.
4. They were to **"increase greatly upon the earth."**

The scenario in Genesis 48 is crucial. Manasseh and Ephraim received the original blessing that God gave to Abraham. Two brothers. One would become a great nation. One would become a group of nations. They would carry the name of Israel (or Jacob). And through them, as God promised Abraham, *all nations of the world would be blessed.*

The foundations of the United States and Great Britain had been set down. Again, Abraham received the blessing and, by means of a small ceremony, passed the blessings onto his son Isaac. Isaac, again through a brief ceremony, passed the blessings onto his son Israel. Israel, again through a brief ceremony, passed it on to his *grandsons*, Ephraim and Manasseh.

The following diagram illustrates the passing of the blessings.

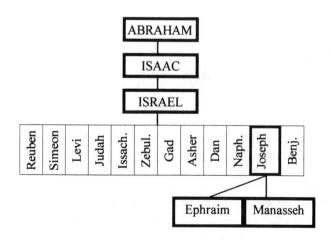

Next would come the rest of Europe. Shortly after passing the blessings onto his grandsons, Manessah and Ephraim, Israel called his 12 sons before him and prophesized to them regarding how their own genetic lines would progress:

Genesis: **Then Jacob called for his sons and said: "Gather around so I can tell you what will happen to you in days to come......Assemble and listen, sons of Jacob; listen to your father Israel:** (Again, Jacob and Israel are the same person. Jacob was the old name, Israel is the new.)

"Reuben, you are my firstborn, my might, the first sign of my strength, excelling in honor, excelling in power....Turbulent as the waters, you will no longer excel, for you went up onto your father's bed, onto my couch and defiled it...

(Reuben, the eldest of the twelve sons, had been deceitful by sleeping with Israel's concubine Bilhah. Because of this act, his father cut him off from Abraham's blessing, cursing him instead.)

"Simeon and Levi are brothers-- their swords are weapons of violence. Let me not enter their council, let me not join their assembly, for they have killed men in their anger and hamstrung oxen as they pleased....Cursed be their anger, so fierce, and their fury, so cruel! I will scatter them in Jacob and disperse them in Israel.....

A very important point here is that Israel is already referring to himself as the presence of a nation: "**I will scatter them in Jacob and disperse them in Israel.....** Both names refer to Israel. And since the name had been passed to Manasseh and Ephraim, Israel is making reference here to how he will scatter his two sons, Simeon and Levi, into the lands of Manasseh and Ephraim. Israel continued blessing his sons. The following passage is very important:

"Judah, your brothers will praise you; your hand will be on the neck of your enemies; your father's sons will bow down to you....You are a lion's cub, O Judah; you return from the prey, my son. Like a lion he crouches and lies down, like a lioness--who dares to rouse him? ....The scepter will not depart from Judah, nor the ruler's staff from between his feet, until he comes to whom it belongs and the obedience of the nations is his...He will tether his donkey to a vine, his colt to the choicest branch; he will wash his garments in wine, his robes in the blood of grapes....His eyes will be darker than wine, his teeth whiter than milk

From the name Judah the word "Jewish" was derived; there-fore, Judah became the *Jewish* bloodline of Israel from which Jesus was born. Judah was the son of Israel. Israel was the father; he had twelve sons, including Judah. Ex-tremely important in understanding our identities in the Bible is the knowledge that all Israelites are not Jews, but that all Jews are Israelites. All descendents of Judah are Israelite, but not all Israelite descendents are of Judah. To understand this relationship, it is helpful to think in terms of, say, the state of California. Not all people who live in California are from Los Angeles. But all people who live in Los Angeles are from California. Such is the case with the Jewish people and the Israelites. All Israelites are not Jews. But all Jews are Israelite, for they are the descendents of Ju-dah, one of Israel's son.

This becomes very interesting when we hear people refer-ring to the observation of Passover, for example, as a "Jewish holiday." Some may wonder why the Jewish people are generally the only ones who observe Passover, and the belief may be that it is something God commanded of the Jews. The truth is, however, that God commanded the ob-servation of the Passover to *all* of Israel, which included Ju-dah but was not limited to Judah. When God gave the people of Israel His commandments and dates of observations and festivals, He intended them to encompass *all* of Israel, which included the descendants of each of Israel's 12 sons and all of their sons and grandsons, generation after generation, throughout the ages. Historically speaking, however, due to the migration of the tribes of Israel out of the promised land and the eventual infiltration of "Christianity" into the world government under the Roman Empire, the descendents of the tribe of Judah have been the only descendents of Israel to observe God's holy days such as Passover. Judah plays an intregal part in both biblical identity and prophesy, and we will be referring to this particular tribe of Israel throughout this book.

Also, to gain further insight into Judah, Joseph, and Reuben, three of Israel's twelve sons, and to revisit the concept of *"...a little bit here, a little bit there..."* as it is used in another biblical example, the following passage from the First Book of Chronicles discusses how the birthright was withheld from Israel's firstborn, Reuben; how Judah prevailed above his brethren, and how the descendents of Joseph had received the birthright instead of either of the other sons:

1 Chronicles: **Now the sons of Reuben the firstborn of Israel...because he defiled his father's bed, his birthright was given unto the *sons* of Joseph the son of Israel: Judah prevailed above his brethren, and of him came the chief ruler; (Jesus), but the birthright was Joseph's**

"The birthright was Joseph's." That one line is paramount! The birthright originated with Abraham. It was passed to Isaac. It was then passed to Israel (Jacob). And it was then passed to Joseph when Israel blessed Joseph's sons, Ephraim and Manasseh. By passing the birthright to Joseph's sons, the birthright in essence belonged to the genetic line of Joseph. *"The birthright was Joseph's."* All that was promised to Abraham was given to Joseph and his descendants. *"Judah prevailed above his*

44

bretheren," and produced Jesus, the chief ruler; but clearly stated, *"the birthright was Joseph's."* God called out one man, Abraham, and exalted him above all men. He tested him. He continued to bless him. And all that was given to Abraham was passed on to the descendants of Joseph, through Manasseh and Ephraim.

Back to the Book of Genesis, the dying Israel continued to bless and prophesize to his sons:

Genesis: **Zebulun will live by the seashore and become a haven for ships; his border will extend toward Sidon....Issachar is a rawboned donkey lying down between two saddlebags.....When he sees how good is his resting place and how pleasant is his land, he will bend his shoulder to the burden and submit to forced labor**

Dan will provide justice for his people as one of the tribes of Israel. Dan will be a serpent by the roadside, a viper along the path, that bites the horse's heels so that its rider tumbles backward. I look for your deliverance, O LORD

Gad will be attacked by a band of raiders, but he will attack them at their heels

Asher's food will be rich; he will provide delicacies fit for a king

Naphtali is a doe set free that bears beautiful fawns

It is now time for Israel to bless Joseph specifically. Although the main blessings of Abraham, Isaac, and Israel had already been passed on to Joseph's sons, Israel moved forward and bestowed a further blessing onto Joseph:

Joseph is a fruitful vine, a fruitful vine near a spring, whose branches climb over a wall. ...With bitterness

archers attacked him; they shot at him with hostility But his bow remained steady, his strong arms stayed limber, because of the hand of the Mighty One of Jacob, because of the Shepherd, the Rock of Israel, because of your father's God, who helps you, because of the Almighty, who blesses you with blessings of the heavens above, blessings of the deep that lies below, blessings of the breast and womb.....Your father's blessings are greater than the blessings of the ancient mountains, greater than the bounty of the age-old hills. Let all these rest on the head of Joseph, on the brow of the *prince among his brothers.*

Of the twelve sons of Israel, Joseph's material blessings are clearly the greatest and most abundant. Jesus came from Judah and, in this sense, Judah received the greatest blessing. But Joseph was referred to as *"the prince among his brothers."* He not only received the blessings outlined above, he was given the greatest blessing of all: the original blessing of the promised land given by God to Abraham. Through the line of Joseph specifically, the name of Israel would be perpetuated. With one son left to receive blessings, Israel continued:

Benjamin is a ravenous wolf; in the morning he devours the prey, in the evening he divides the plunder."

All these are the twelve tribes of Israel, and this is what their father said to them when he blessed them, giving each the blessing appropriate to him.
When Jacob had finished giving instructions to his sons, he drew his feet up into the bed, breathed his last breath, and was gathered to his people.

Upon blessing his 12 sons, Israel died. And the "twelve tribes of Israel" began to grow and flourish. Ultimately, they jointly occupied the "promised land" near the Jordan River. Basically, what happened was this: the 12 sons of Israel, known as the twelve *tribes* of Israel, grew and flour-

46

ished, went into slavery, and then were led out of slavery by Moses. They eventually crossed over into the promised land, conquered all of its inhabitants, and settled into various divisions of the land. Judah was in one division, Manasseh and Ephraim in another, Asher in another, Gad in another, etc. All twelve tribes were living together as neighboring towns, or divisions, in the promised land. After several generations, God appointed King David to rule over these tribes. Solomon was David's son, and he became the ruler of Israel after David's death. But Solomon, with his 700 wives and 300 concubines, angered God because he began to follow the religious beliefs of his wives. God punished him by breaking up his kingdom and taking away his power. God took 10 tribes of Israel away from Solomon and placed them under his servant's command We see this event in the First Book of Kings. God rebuked Solomon and told him, "**I will surely rend the kingdom from thee, and will give it to thy servant**." But God also stated that He will not take away the whole kingdom, only a part of it: "**Howbeit I will not rend away *all* the kingdom**." Later in the chapter, God sends the prophet Ahijah to find Solomon's servant Jeraboam, and He gives ten tribes to the servant:

1 Kings (God to Jeraboam): : **'Behold, I will rend the kingdom out of the hand of Solomon, and will give *ten tribes* to thee.'**

The promised land became divided as God, out of anger, gave 10 tribes of Israel to the servant of Solomon; but God's blessings to Abraham and Isaac and Jacob remained with Manasseh and Ephraim, the sons of Joseph. Later, God would expel the tribes out of the land altogether; but again, the blessing would remain with Manasseh and Ephraim.

Most people of the modern world today, if shown a map of
the earth and asked where the promised land was located,
would point to the area around Jerusalem in the Middle
East. And that would be correct, if the question was stated
as follows: "Where *was* the promised land located?" The
promised land, at one time, was exactly in that location, and
it is believed to remain there even to this day. But that assumption is incorrect.

Everybody knows the infamous story of how Moses led the
Israelites out of captivity in Egypt, through the parted Red
Sea, into Sinai, and ultimately up to the edge of the
promised land. But because Moses had sinned by an act of
weakened faith towards God, Moses was not allowed to enter the promised land; he was only allowed to see it before
his death. It was the soldier and warrior Joshua, from the
tribe of Ephraim, who actually led the people into the
promised land, conquering the Canaanites and settling into
the lands both east and west of the Jordan river. It is the
place which we, throughout history and even today, identify
as "the promised land." It is where most people today believe that the Israelites remain.

If that were true, however, God's promise to Abraham and
Isaac and Jacob, which, I continue to stress, was passed on
to Ephraim and Manasseh....the promise of greatness and
abundance and citizens too numerous to count.....would
have been very short lived. It would have ended over a
thousand years ago, and it certainly would not be present in
the world today. The middle east is continually at war.
"*All nations of the earth*" are certainly no longer blessed
through that part of the world. Modern day Israel is pretty
much a third-world country. Yet, God told Abraham that
His promise would be *everlasting*. And further, God told
Israel that he would become a *group* of nations; yet we know
Israel today as a single nation.

War torn, dependent, and tumultuous Israel of the 20th century certainly does not fit the description of God's promises

to Abraham. Many nations? A group of nations? A great nation? *"All the peoples of the earth will be blessed through you."* These were all parts of God's *everlasting* promise. Yet, when we refer to Israel in modern times, these definitions simply do not apply. The one country of Israel does not appear to measure up to the blessings passed from Abraham to Isaac to Israel to Manasseh and Ephraim.

Could modern day Israel, located in the Middle East, possibly be the land promised to the one man God called out from the rest of the world? Several passages in the Bible point out that it simply is not.

First and foremost, Israel consisted of twelve tribes stemming from the twelve sons of Israel. As I have previously mentioned, Judah, from which the word "Jew" is derived, was included in this group of twelve. Judah was one of the twelve sons. When most people today think of Israel, or of Jerusalem, the word Jewish is often thought of as being synonymous or related. Jerusalem is occupied primarily by Jews. It is in the land of Israel. When Israel or Jews are referred to in general, the eyes of the world often look towards Jerusalem and Israel.

Generally, the world doesn't think of Europeans and Americans as possibly being of Israeli descent; most people in today's world believe that the country of Israel is the homeland of all Israeli/Jewish people. However, a clearer picture begins to form on this subject when, in the Second Book of Kings, God becomes infuriated with the tribes of Israel and *expels them out of the promised land:*

2Kings: **Therefore the Lord was very angry with Israel, and removed them out of his sight: there was none left** *but the tribe of Judah only.*

God became angry with the children of Israel and literally kicked all tribes except for Judah out of the promised land! He removed the tribes of Israel from his sight and left only

Judah behind. This tribe of Judah remains in the land of
Israel even today. This is why we, as a world, associate Israelites with people of Jewish descent. As the other tribes of
Israel were expelled from the area, Judah was the only one
of the twelve that remained behind. But Judah never--
NEVER!-- received the promise given to Abraham! Remember the passage sited a short time ago:

1 Chronicles: (the birthright) **was given unto the sons of
Joseph the son of Israel: Judah prevailed above his
brethren, and of him came the chief ruler;** (Jesus), *but
the birthright was Joseph's*

The promise of a great nation and many nations never went
to Judah! It went to Joseph! It went to Manasseh and
Ephraim, the sons of Joseph. The birthright *"was given
unto the sons of Joseph."* And they, Manasseh and
Ephraim, along with all the other tribes of Israel, with the
exception of Judah, were expelled out of the promised land
of old. The land of Israel, as we know it today, the place
where Judah remained, never fulfilled the promise! Judah,
tribe of the Jewish people, remained behind; but the other
tribes, including Manasseh and Ephraim, left the land of
Israel completely.

The Bible, standing on its own and providing information to
interpret itself, creates a very clear picture. Identities begin
to become clear. Judah remained in the land we now know
as Israel, and all other tribes from the children of Israel migrated outward. This is pure biblical fact. The question we
must now explore is as follows: just where in the world did
the rest of Israel go? If Judah stayed behind and all the
other tribes left the area, in which direction did they go?
And where did they ultimately end up? Nearly two
decades ago, when I first pondered this question, and when
my knowledge of the Bible was still very much embryonic, I
couldn't quite put my finger on the answer. I had taken a
large piece of poster board and outlined the entire lineage of

Abraham, following his seed out of the promised land and up into the area we now know as Europe. But my diagram fell short as to where the tribes had actually traveled. They were at first difficult to locate; after all, they have been known in history as the "lost tribes of Israel." I was perplexed for several days. But then I decided upon two avenues which broke the barrier in my mind and which helped me to further track the ultimate destinations of these lost tribes.

One, I researched theoretical and philosophical literature regarding what has been known as the "Anglo/Israeli" theory, or the "British/Israeli" theory, which dates back to the mid 19th century. These theories, in essence, adhere to the belief that the genetic line of the Germanic tribes of Europe are directly rooted in the descendents of Israel. The theories are more historically based than they are biblically based, but they help clear up a great deal of confusion as to where these lost tribes of Israel disappeared.

Two, I went back to the basics and adhered to my understanding of the "....*little bit here, little bit there...*" principle; and I searched for small passages in various parts of the Bible that would indicate for me the route and ultimate destinations of these lost tribes of Israel. As I searched the Bible and applied this principle, I made a few interesting discoveries.

First, the word "Isles" is used 25 times in the Bible: once in the book of Genesis, and 24 times after God exiled the tribes of Israel out of the promised land. In Isaiah 49, the prophet Isaiah, in speaking to Israel, addresses "the Isles" directly:

Isaiah: **Listen, O isles, unto me; and hearken, ye people, from afar; The Lord hath called me from the womb; from the bowels of my mother hath he made mention of my name....And said unto me, Thou art my servant, O Israel, in whom I will be glorified.**

In the above passage, the phrase "O isles" and the phrase "O Israel" are speaking to the same people. In a later verse of the same speech, continuing to address the Israelites, Isaiah refers to a set of directions:

Isaiah: **"Behold, these shall come from afar: and, lo, these from the _north_ and from the _west_..."**

Those two directions are significant! Isaiah was basically saying that, from where he was located, in Jerusalem, people would come to him from the north and from the west. In the Hebrew language, which is the language of the Old Testament, there is not a word for northwest. The direction is stated simply as *north and west*. As Isaiah was pointing out in the above verse, the people *"coming from afar"* would have to come from the **north** and from the **west,** or from the *northwest*. In other words, these people being addressed by Isaiah were located northwest from Jerusalem. The *Isles*, then, were **north** and **west**, or *northwest*, from the promised land.

During my research into the route of the Israelites, I placed a map of the eastern hemisphere on the table and followed a line *"north and west,"* or *northwest* from Israel to the "Isles." Bullseye! The line led directly to what is now known as the British Isles. Speaking to the children of Israel, Isaiah referred to them as a people *"from afar,"* as the *"Isles,"* and from the *"north"* and *"west."* Putting all of these pieces together, and viewing them before the backdrop of "Anglo/Israeli" and "British/Israeli" theoretical orientations, the location of the exiled tribes of Israel finally seemed very definite and very clear to me; but I did not want to base my conclusion on that simple speculation, which, of course, I now know to be true. At that time, however, I began a search for further evidence.

Within the context of the Bible, I found another verse which

I had previously overlooked, primarily because I had been following the blessings of the *fathers*, from Abraham to Joseph's sons; and I had overlooked the blessings bestowed upon the *mothers*, specifically, upon Rebekah, mother of Israel.

Rebekah's story is unique. Through the intervention of God, she was chosen as the wife of Isaac, Abraham's eldest son and recipient of God's promise. As Rebekah was preparing to leave her family to follow Abraham's servants back to Isaac and become his wife, her family bid her farewell and gave her an important blessing:

Genesis: **And they blessed Rebekah, and said unto her, Thou art our sister,** *be thou the mother of thousands of millions,* **and let thy seed** *possess the gates* **of those which hate them.**

The fact that Rebekah, as wife of Isaac and mother of Israel, did indeed become the mother of thousands of millions has already been established. Through her, the countries of Europe, Great Britain, and the United States have been ultimately populated. Her prophesy in that regard has been observably and tangibly fulfilled. The interesting part of this particular passage, however, is that Rebecka's seed would *"...possess the "gates" of those which hate them..."* This prophesy may not at first be as observable or comprehendible as the first part, until one considers the fact that, between the two of them, the United States and Great Britain (Manasseh and Ephraim) have possessed almost every port, or sea-gate, and every strategic water and land mass in the world: the British Isles, the Falkland Islands, Bermuda, the Bahamas, the Virgin Islands, San Juan, St. Lucia, St. Croix, Antigua, Barbados, the Suez, Gibraltar, the Panama Canal, Hawaii, Midway, Alexandria, the Khyber Pass, the Straits of Malaca, the Anatolian Peninsula, the

Brunei, the Aluetians, Guantanamo, Malta, the Nicobar Islands, Hong Kong, Singapore, New Guinea, Ceylon, Kenya, Wake Island.....the list continues on and on.

Then consider the fact that Great Britain has controlled, or continues to control Australia, New Zealand, Canada, South Africa....and at one time Hong Kong, India, Egypt, , Palestine, Jordan, British Honduras, Crete, and many other countries.

All of these facts together are indisputable. When Israel crossed his hands on the heads of Ephraim and Manasseh and blessed them, bestowing upon Ephraim *"a group of nations,"* and upon Manasseh, *"a great nation,"* and with Israel's mother, Rebekah, being blessed as the mother of *thousands of millions* and by her seed *"possessing the gates of those that hate them"*; and with our own historical knowledge of how the United States and Great Britain have possessed the greatest portion of the planet's wealth, including the *"group of nations"* that continue to be possessed by Great Britain; and with God's words to Abraham that his seed would be like the stars in the sky and the sands on the ocean; and with our knowledge of the fact that God kicked the entire nation of Israel--except for Judah--out of the promised land; and our common sense that says these tribes, which had at one time occupied gigantic, well-populated areas of the promised land, had to go somewhere, the picture continues to get clearer and clearer as to what became of these people and how they have evolved into our own European ancestry.

With all the facts in order, pulled together *"...a little bit here, a little bit there...,"* it becomes difficult to misunderstand the true histories of Europe and the United States. And there are many other more subtle and less obvious bits of evidence. For example, historical buffs will quickly point out that the Saxons invaded England in the 5th century A.D., and that, historically, these people had been present in parts of England, France, and Germany. The Webster's

Dictionary defines the term Anglo-Saxon as follows: *"a member of any of the Germanic peoples. A member of the English peoples. Old English."* Consider for a moment the word "Saxon." Pronounce it: Sacks-Son. Traditionally, these people were known as Saca, Sachi, Sach-sen, and Saac-sons, or the sons of Saac. If you research the word Saxon, you will find that it was derived directly from the term, "Saac-sons" or "Sons of Saac," This is by no means a coincidental name. The "Sons of Saac" were direct descendants of I*saac*. They were, in fact, "the Sons of ISAAC." By this definition alone, it is easy to see that the descendants of Abraham, the "son's of Isaac, were very present in Europe; that is, north and west from the promised land.

Further evidence, albeit subtle, can be found in the meaning of the word "British." The word *"covenant"* in the Old Testament of the Bible was derived from the Hebrew word *"berit"* or *"berith."* In fact, 280 times, when the English word "covenant" appears in the Old Testament, it has been translated from the Hebrew word "berit." Both words, of course, mean the same thing: "Berit" translated into the English language is "covenant." When one researches this word "British," one quickly discovers that it was derived from the term "Berit-ish," which, in Hebrew means "Covenant Man." The word "British" means "Covenant Man." God's promise to Abraham was a *covenant,* and God entered into several *covenants* with Israel:

Genesis: **As for me, behold, my *covenant* is with thee, and thou shalt be the father of a multitude of nations.**

Genesis: **And God said (to Abraham), '...Sarah your wife shall bear you a son; and you shall call his name Isaac: and I will establish my *covenant* with him for an *everlasting covenant* for his seed after him.'**

The descendents of Abraham--the children of Israel--are

definitely "covenant men," and it is very apparent that they carried this label with them as they migrated *north* and *west* out of the promised land into the *Isles.*

Another interesting and subtle observation to be made in following the migration of Israelites into Europe can be found in tracking the route of the tribe of Dan, one of Israel's 12 sons. It was the tradition of the tribe of Dan to leave its name upon all the places which it had conquered. We read evidence of this in the Book of Joshua "...**the children of Dan went up and fought against Leshem, and took it, and smote it with the edge of the sword, and possessed it, and dwelt therein, and called Leshem, Dan, af-**
ter the name of their father"; and in the Book of Judges, "**And they** *called* **the name of the** *city Dan***, after the name of their father, who was born unto Israel**"

In researching the history of the Danites, one discovers that versions of the name "Dan" can sometimes be found appearing as dan, don, dun, din, den, and dane. Remember Israel's blessing to Dan: *"Dan will be a serpent by the roadside, a viper along the path."* I have always envisioned this tribe of Dan moving like a serpent across the lands of Europe, slithering like a viper and leaving its track along the roadside. This reflection, of course, is neither here nor there. But as the tribe of Dan migrated out of Israel and into Europe, it left its name--or its mark--on several locations, which were indicated by the words dan, don, dun, din, den, and dane. Examples include Lon*DON*, Scan*DIN*avia, *DUN*-sidane, *DEN*mark (which means "*the mark of Dan*"), the *DAN*ube, etc. , all locations in Europe. (Incidentally, the language of Denmark is *DAN*ish.) This trail left by Dan also helps in understanding the "*north*" and "*west*" location of the "*far off people*" in the "*Isles.*" And it serves as just one more minor piece in a puzzle that, as we continue to research, forms a rather clear and indisputable picture of the location of Israel's "lost tribes."

There are two other points I want to make regarding the

identities of the United States and Europe in the Bible. The first reflects the "Dual Events" principle. The second is a truly astonishing mathematical calculation from the Bible that helps determine the timeline upon which America was founded.

In terms of the first point, consider for a moment the original promised land and how it came to be obtained, settled, and occupied. The Israelites--the children of Israel--were held captive in Egypt for generations. Under Pharaoh, these people were enslaved, oppressed, and religiously stifled. The story of the Israelites is very well known. Through a series of supernatural events bestowed upon Egypt by God, and the continual coaxing and threatening of Pharaoh by Moses, Pharaoh finally allowed the children of Israel to go free. As a tattered and torn and spiritually broken people, they migrated out of Egypt and headed towards the promised land. They eventually came to the banks of the Red Sea and found that Pharaoh had changed his mind and had sent his soldiers to pursue and kill them. Trapped, Moses relied on his faith in the power and the promise of God. He parted the Red Sea, and the entire nation of Israel passed through it and made it safely to the other side, where they truly and finally became a free people; although, at that time, they were not allowed to enter into the promised land. Because of their sins and lack of faith, God caused the Israelites to remain in the wilderness of Sinai for 40 years before entering into the promised land.

Moses himself was not allowed to enter the promised land at all! It was not until Moses' death that Joshua, who was commanded by God, took over and led the people across the Jordan River into the promised land. And like Moses did to the Red Sea, Joshua also parted the Jordan River, allowing the Israelites to pass over safely and finally enter into the promised land.

It is extremely important to understand, in putting geographical nuances into perspective, that before being attained and occupied by the children of Israel, the promised land was occupied by several other nations, namely the Canaanites, Hittites, Amorites, Perizzites, Hivites and Jebusites. These nations were not the children of Israel; they practiced both sun worship and idol worship, and God commanded the Israelites to drive these people out of the promised land and to occupy it themselves. The following excerpts are examples of the abundant passages in the Bible that detail the commission of the Israelites as they migrated to the promised land, conquered it, and ultimately settled and occupied it:

Exodus: **Then the Lord said to Moses, "Leave this place, you and the people you brought up out of Egypt, and go up to the *land I promised* on oath to Abraham, Isaac and Jacob, saying, `I will give it to your descendants.**

Exodus: **And I have promised to bring you up out of your misery in Egypt into the land of the Canaanites, Hittites, Amorites, Perizzites, Hivites and Jebusites--a land flowing with milk and honey.**

Deuteronomy: **The Lord thy God, he will go over before thee, and he will destroy these nations from before thee, and thou shalt possess them.**

Deuteronomy: **Then the Lord said to him, "This is the land I promised on oath to Abraham, Isaac and Jacob when I said, `I will give it to your descendants.' I have let you see it with your eyes, but you will not cross over into it."**

Joshua: **And these are the kings of the country which Joshua and the children of Israel smote...which Joshua gave unto the tribes of Israel for a possession according to their divisions: The king of Jericho, the king of Ai, the king of Jerusalem, the king of Hebron, the king of Jarmuth, the king of Lachish, the king of Eglon, the king**

of Gezer, the king of Debir, the king of Geder, the king of Hormah, the king of Arad.... etc. etc. etc. There were 31 defeated kings in all.

The details are very clear. The Israelites came across the sea, entered into the promised land, made war with its inhabitants, conquered the inhabitants, divided the land, and occupied the land as their own. By possessing the original promised land, the children of Israel appeared to have finally made it home. But had they? Finally?

Historically speaking, many believe that this occupation of the promised land was the realization of God's promise to Abraham; that the blessings bestowed upon Abraham and passed to Isaac, Israel, and Manasseh and Ephraim had finally been realized in full as Joshua led the Israelites into the defeat and occupation of the land of milk and honey. And rightfully so. The Bible itself points out that this was the land promised to Abraham and his descendents. The children of Israel truly had reached a promised land.

This is one example, however, of where we see the principle of "dual events" in action. The original promised land was indeed a promised land, but it was not *thee* promised land. It was merely the first manifestation of a greater promised land that was yet to come. Like all incidents of the dual events principle, it happened once on a small scale; and it happened a second time on a much greater scale....with the United States.

The United States of America is the second manifestation of the promised land! It is, in fact, *thee* promised land! It is the land that was promised to Abraham, Isaac, Israel, Manasseh, and Ephraim. Remember Israel's promises to his 12 sons? Not all of the sons received great blessings. The greatest blessings went to Joseph and Judah, with Joseph receiving the birthright. Yet, all of the children of Israel occupied the original promised land. Even Rueben, who defiled his father's bed. All of Israel was there, but the blessings were owned by Manasseh and Ephraim: *"the birthright was Joseph's."* Certainly, these two sons of Joseph were to rise to levels greater than all the rest of Israel.

The original promised land was simply not as great, not as magnificent, as the second, which is always the case with dual events in the Bible. The first event, although great, is never as magnificent as the second. America is, in actuality, the fulfillment of the blessings bestowed by Israel upon Manasseh. And it is the promised land!

America is the promised land!

Another way in which this can be illustrated, aside from all the events previously mentioned in this chapter, is by the parallel way through which the realizations of both promised lands unfolded. That is to say, the parallel ways in which both the first promised land and the second promised land, the United States, were occupied and settled. These events have been very subtle, but weighed together with all of the other pieces of evidence, they become very interesting and extremely fascinating.

Consider the two events, beginning with the first promised land . The Israelites were held captive and oppressed in Egypt. They migrated away from Egypt, came through the Red Sea, and came into a land that was pre-settled and pre-occupied by groups of idol worshipping and sun worshipping people. The Israelites were commissioned by God to overthrow these people and occupy the land in their stead, which they did. In short, the Israelites came from an oppressive land, ventured across the water, and migrated to a land in which there existed many settled inhabitants. They overthrew those inhabitants and made the land their own.

The United States was settled in very much the same way. The people were oppressed in England. They were Saxon's (**Isaac's** Sons) that ultimately migrated out of England, came across the water, and came unto a land which, at that time, was pre-settled and pre-occupied by groups of idol worshipping and sun worshipping people: the Indians. If one follows the battles of Israel against the tribes of the promised land, the Canaanites, Ammonites, etc., one can see the same type of annihilation and genocidal warfare that had taken place between the early American settlers and the Indians. In both cases, the peoples that existed first in the land were virtually wiped out. Some tribes were annihilated completely; some were allowed to live amongst the people.

Like the Israelites who came across the water into the land of Jordan, conquering its occupants and making the land of milk and honey their own, the settlers of America came across the water to a new and abundant land, conquered its inhabitants, and likewise made the land their own. These simple parallels are certainly uncanny. The two promised lands were attained and settled in much the same way. The latter promised land--the United States--however, was the greater realization of the promise. It had greater wealth and natural resources, greater military might. And its people, especially as they were combined with the other tribes of Israel, were definitely as numerous as the stars in the skies and sands in the sea. And through the United States, *"all nations of the earth"* were truly *"blessed."*

The comparisons and full contexts of God's promises manifesting through the United States are difficult to discount and ignore because they are so abundant. Where else in the world, or in the history of the world, has a *group of nations* and a *great nation* contained citizens too numerous to count, possessed the *gates* of the rest of the world, and served to bless *all the nations of the earth*? The first promised land was clearly the land near the Jordan River, but during the occupation of this land, the Israelites were not as numerous as the stars and sand. The gates of their enemies were not possessed. All nations of the earth were not blessed through this land. They did not number *thousands of millions*. The land was not nearly as abundant in crops and minerals as the United States or the possessions of Great Britain.

Through the understanding of dual events, which, as mentioned, happens repeatedly in the Bible, it becomes possible to see how the first promised land was merely a smaller-scale manifestation of the second. And the beauty and true identity of the United States and Great Britain continues to unfold and be seen in a clearer light.

Finally, there is the mathematics associated with the blessings. This subject deals directly with the issue of biblical times and systems of time-measurement in the Bible. I am not going to get too in-depth with this particular area, primarily because the subject could become a complete book unto itself; and also because it is an area of the Bible which is very vulnerable to abuse. I have seen and studied the works of *men* who have completely fabricated and miscalculated biblical timelines to satisfy and "prove" their own theories and distorted beliefs. It has become a common practice for the world's doomsday prophets to pinch and crunch numbers and apply complex, man-made mathematical theories to dates and times in the Bible to flagrantly invent and grossly miscalculate "the time of the end."

That is obviously not my objective.

There is no need to fabricate or distort the systems of time-measurement in the Bible; they are accurate, precise and self-defined within its own pages. The understanding of biblical timelines, then, is not all that complex. And for the purpose of this chapter, at a very basic level, there are simply two important terms regarding time measurements in the Bible that readers must comprehend in order to understand biblical prophesies. The first term is known as a "*year*," and the second term is known as a "*time*." Very simply, a *year* is one year, and a *time* is a *multiple* of years.

According to God's calendar, which is very different than the Roman calendar followed by the world today, a year has exactly 360 days. The term *"year"* then, in the Bible, refers to a time period of 360 days. One year equals 360 days.

A *"time,"* on the other hand, although sometimes expressed as the mathematical equivalent of a 360 day year, is actually a time period of 360 *YEARS.* One *time* equals 360 years. A *year* equals 360 days. A *time* equals 360 *years.* Shortly, we will see exactly how the measurement of a *time* was derived and can be calculated. But first, we need to understand God's principle of "a-year-for-a-day," which generally applies to prophesies and punishments. This "year-for-a-day" principle can be seen in passages such as the following:

Numbers14: **After the number of the days in which you searched the land, even forty days, _each day for a year_, shall ye bear your iniquities, even forty years, and you shall know my breach of promise.**

Ezekiel 4: **For I have laid upon you the years of their iniquity, according to the number of the days...so shall you bear the iniquity of the house of Israel......And you shall bear the iniquity of the house of Judah forty days: I have appointed thee _each day for a year_.**

It is important to keep the "day-for-a-year" concept in mind as we proceed.

Again, a measurement of *"time"* in the Bible is 360 years. One *year* equals 360 days. One *time* equals 360 years. A *time* is also referred to as a "prophetic year"; that is, 360 one year periods reflective of the "day-for-a-year" principle.

63

This is a very simple yet very important concept. Again, one year in the Bible consists of 360 days. One *time*, or *prophetic year*, in the Bible consists of 360 *YEARS*.

Here are two passages from the Book of Revelation which provide additional reflection of the measurement of a "*time*":

Revelation: **The woman was given the two wings of a great eagle, so that she might fly to the place prepared for her in the desert, where she would be taken care of for _a time, times and half a time,_ out of the serpent's reach.**

Revelation: **And the woman fled into the wilderness, where she hath a place prepared of God, that they should feed her there a thousand two hundred and threescore days.**

The first passage refers to "**a time, times and half a time,**" which is, mathematically, 360 (**a time**), 360-and-360 (**times**), and 180 (**half a time**). This is equivalent to 1260.

The second passage repeats this scenario: 1000 (**a thousand**), 200 (**two hundred**) and 60 (**threescore**). The equivalent is 1260 days. The time, times, and half a time in the first passage is the exact same thing as one thousand two hundred and threescore days in the second passage. Both equal 1260.

Also, the Book of Daniel refers to this measurement of time:

Daniel: **The saints will be handed over to him for a _time, times and half a time_.**

Daniel: **It will be for a _time, times and half a time_.**

The fact that a *"time"* is a term of *measurement* is very clear. The length of a *"time"* is also clear. As mentioned earlier, a *time* is often expressed as the mathematical equivalent of a 360 day period; however, it is in fact a *prophetic year*, adhering to the day-for-a-year principle. A *time*, then, is a 360 YEAR period. With that understanding, we can begin to see how it applies to the children of Israel, their birthrights, and the increased clarity at which we can identify the United States in the Bible.

In the Book of Leviticus, God told the children of Israel what the consequences would be if they, as a nation, would turn away from Him and cease to follow His laws:

Leviticus: **If after all this you will not listen to me, I will punish you *seven times* for your sins.**

Leviticus: **And if ye will not yet for all this hearken unto me, then I will punish you *seven times* more for your sins.**

Leviticus: **Then will I also walk contrary unto you, and will punish you yet *seven times* for your sins.**

Leviticus: **Then I will walk contrary unto you also in fury; and I, even I, will chastise you *seven times* for your sins.**

Again, a *time* is 360 years. Two *times* would be 720 years (360 years x 2). Seven *times*, as it is mentioned in God's warnings of punishment to Israel, is 2520 years (360 years x 7). In short, what God was warning the Israelites in the four above passages is as follows: "...if you do not listen to me and follow my laws, I will punish you for a period of 7 *times*, or for 2520 years." If Israel would not follow God and adhere to His laws and statutes, a period of punishment—with a beginning and an end— would certainly be handed to their nation. God repeated this warning to the

Israelites on four occasions; it was definitely a point He was attempting to drive into their heads. And with that statement, God was also asserting something unspoken. By threatening a definite period of punishment for Israel, God was also saying, in essence, "I won't annihilate you. I won't wipe you off the face of the planet. I won't kill you. But I will punish you for a definite period of time. I will punish you for 7 *times*. I will allow 7 *times*--or 2520 years-- to pass before you are *un*punished. Israel would be punished for 2520 years and then be released from punishment.

Once this time period is understood, we can go back to the Second Book of Kings and see a very clear indication of God's punishment upon Israel.

2 Kings: **Therefore the Lord was very angry with Israel, and removed them out of his sight: there was none left but the tribe of Judah only.**

Although the two Books of Kings are very tightly written in terms of chronology, there exists a slight bit of historical confusion surrounding the actual time period in the Second Book of Kings regarding when, *exactly*, God sent all tribes except for Judah out of the promised land, thus beginning Israel's time period of punishment. The chapter which discusses this exile, Chapter 17, begins with the following time statement: **"In the 12th year of Ahaz, King of Judah.."** This is where the slight bit of confusion exists. History is a bit hazy as to the exact date and time when the reign of Ahaz, King of Judah, began. There is about a 20 year period of time that is in question, a 20 year window, which really isn't all that off the mark. Some historians agree on 744 B.C. Others agree on 765 B.C. Still others agree on time periods somewhere in between those two dates. For our purposes, the *exact* dates are irrelevant. We know that, in the 12th year of the king's reign, Israel was punished and booted out of the promised land. Using the 20 year window that exists, time possibilities for the actual date which begins Israel's exile--and punishment-- range from 732 B.C to 753 B.C. The three dates that are most often agreed upon for this exile are B.C 745, 747, and 752. We can pick any one of those dates, or simply use the two extremes of the 20 year range, and we will surely understand the significance of what we are looking at....once we do the math.

When God sent Israel out of the promised land, leaving only Judah behind, He was fulfilling the warning He gave to them regarding their punishment for turning away from His commandments; specifically, that He would punish them *7 times* (or 2520 years) for their sins. Using the high end of the range discussed above, 753 B.C, and calculating the 2520 years of punishment, we arrive at the *end date* of that punishment: <u>1767</u>. If we use the low end of the 20 year range, 732 B.C, and calculate the 2520 years of punishment, we arrive at this date: <u>1788.</u>

There is an obvious correlation here! Somewhere between 1767 and 1788, the 2520 year punishment of Israel was lifted, and they were allowed to become *un*punished and to realize the fruits of their promises and blessings. Is it merely coincidental that the birth of the United States is considered to be 1776?

Obviously, there is enough material in following the lineage of the United States back to its roots in the seed of Abraham to write an entire book, maybe an entire series of books. And a single chapter, like I have offered up here, simply cannot do it justice. I am aware of this fact, and also aware of the fact that, in condensing the study and the collective bulk of information down to the confines of a single chapter, a great deal of that material had to be either written in a highly condensed manner or merely left out altogether. And much of it was, in the end, left out. But that is okay. Enough biblical passages and background information has been provided to create, I believe, an excellent starting point for those who wish to study further and research this particular subject both in the Bible and in the annals of documentation regarding the Anglo/Israeli and British/Israeli theories. It's an amazing subject; and the deeper one gets into it, the more fascinating it unfolds. And the more crystal clear it becomes as to the true identities of the United States, Great Britain, and the children of Israel.

My reason for including the material in this book is because, as I have mentioned previously, I am a firm believer that, in order to understand biblical prophesies, one must first understand his or her biblical and national identity. If we know who the United States, Europe, Great Britain, Israel, and Judah are in the Bible; and if we understand how the name of Israel has been placed upon these people, we can comprehend who the Bible is referring to when it speaks to Israel, the children of Israel, Jacob, the seed of Abraham, or any other number of references that are used to refer directly to the modern day people of the United States, Europe, and Great Britain. And when we understand this fact, the Bible suddenly becomes more significant, more personalized, and more comprehendible. No longer do we see it as an outdated book referring only to a nation of people several thousand years in the past. We begin to see it for what it is: a book of contemporary significance speaking directly to the nations of the world today. Guiding them. Detailing their histories to them. Pointing out to them what they need to do today in order to achieve health and happiness. And showing them, in no uncertain terms, what will become of their entire world in the relatively near future.

Once we understand who we are and where we have come from, we can understand what the Bible is saying to us when it is revealing our futures through its abundant prophesies. Darkness becomes light. Confusion becomes understanding. And prophesies become clear and comprehendible: *"....a little bit here, a little bit there...."*

Chapter 3

God's 7000 Year Plan (4000 BC to 3000 AD)

When God created Adam and Eve, He also, at the same time, implemented a 7000 year plan for mankind that would be subdivided into two specific time periods: a 6000 year period, during which time man would be allowed to control and govern the earth, followed by a 1000 year time period of rest, which would include abundant peace and prosperity under a world government headed by Jesus. We are currently nearing the end of the 6000 years, and what will follow will be a 1000 year period of absolute peace on earth. And then, after the 1000 years are finished, the earth as we know it will end; and God will create a new heaven and a new earth. This is all clearly documented in the Bible.

I, at first, had great reservations as I set out to write this chapter because I felt that by doing so, and laying out specific time periods such as "7000 years," I might be instantly categorized into the sad ranks of the doomsday prophets, who continually throw these arbitrary, man-made conclusions out into the wind to predict "the end time" or "the end of the world." And this book is certainly not about the end of the world; it's about the prophesies that reflect the end of a dark age and the beginning of a newer, more peaceful, and more productive time period on Earth. It is not about jumping onto the bandwagon of the negative and fearful doomsday people and trying to predict dates and end times that even Jesus Himself told us He doesn't know. It is about looking at prophesies and understanding that we are currently nearing the end of a 6000 year period in God's 7000 year plan. This book is about hope, not fear.

The Bible clearly and repeatedly states that the world will not end until the final days of the 7000th year of God's plan. We will examine specific passages throughout this chapter, and in following chapters, which detail the plan and its related concepts. After such an examination, we can then begin to piece together the prophesies which reveal how this plan has unfolded and will continue to unfold before our collective eyes.

Remember in Chapter 1, I discussed the Sign of Jonah and suggested that we use it as a sort of litmus test to apply towards the beliefs and doctrines of modern day church teachings, to test those beliefs and teachings for their validity and connectedness to God's desires. I basically asked you to challenge, if ever so slightly, the accepted beliefs and traditions of the church and to research those beliefs further to determine which are accurate and which are merely *"....the traditions of men...."*

Well, there are two additional beliefs I would like you to please challenge for a moment. The first is that the earth was created by God. And the second is that it was created around the time of Adam.

Oh no, I am starting to sound like a fanatic, right? Of course the earth was created by God. Right? And of course it was created around the time of Adam. Right? Well, let's move away from what the churches teach for a moment, and let's look at what the Bible actually says about these things. Let's first take the issue of who created the earth and how it was created. Everybody knows that in Genesis 1, the creation of the earth is explained in the following manner:

Genesis: **In the beginning God created the heaven and the earth. Now the earth was without form, and void; and darkness was upon the face of the deep. And the Spirit of God moved upon the face of the waters. And God said, Let there be light: and there was light.**

This seems very cut and dried. *"In the beginning, God created the heaven and the earth."* Looking at this one statement, who can dispute the fact that God created the heaven and the earth? It says so right here in no uncertain terms. *"God created the heaven and the earth."* Period! In Genesis 1, it appears very plain and very simple.

But then, maybe that good ol' principle of *"...a little bit here, a little bit there...."* can be applied. And maybe we can start by asking these questions: "Where else in the Bible does it talk about the creation of the earth? Does the New Testament mention it? If so, what does it have to say about it? The fact is that the New Testament *does* talk about it. In the Book of John, the fourth Gospel in the New Testament, John opens up with an extremely detailed statement concerning the involvement of Jesus in the creation of the earth:

John: **In the beginning was the Word, and the Word was with God, and the Word was God. The same was in the** beginning with God. *All things were made by Him; and without Him was not any thing made that was made*.....In Him was life; and the life was the light of men.... And the light shineth in darkness; and the darkness comprehended it not....There was a man sent from God, whose name was John. The same came for a witness, to bear witness of the Light, that all men through him might believe....He was not that Light, but was sent to bear witness of that Light....That was the true Light, which lighteth every man that cometh into the world.....*He was in the world, and the world was made by Him,* and the world knew him not....He came unto his own, and His own received Him not....But as many as received Him, to them gave he power to become the sons of God, even to them that believe on His name: Which were born, not of blood, nor of the will of the flesh, nor of the will of man, but of God. *And the Word was made flesh, and dwelt among us....John bare witness of him...*

This verse talks very specifically about Jesus. Jesus was "The Word." In the beginning, Jesus (the Word) was with God and *was* God. Notice the next verse: *All things were made by Him; and without Him was not any thing made that was made.* This is referring to "*The Word,*" who in a later verse, John points out "*...was made flesh and dwelt among us.*" And further, that "*...John bare witness of Him.*" As readers of the Bible, we know that John did not bare witness to God, but he *did* bare witness to Jesus; he lived with Jesus and saw Him and spoke with Him. John is talking about Jesus in these verses. Jesus was The Word, and John very clearly indicates that "*He was in the world, and the world was made by Him.*" The world was made by Him, by The Word. By Jesus.

In the beginning, God and Jesus existed together in the same family, father and son in a God family. They were, in essence, one and the same. Jesus was "*The Word,*" the logos, the physical representation of both God and Jesus. God and Jesus formed a sort of God "family." They were one and the same, a God *duo* or a God *team*. God was there, but Jesus was the manifestation, the Word. Jesus created the earth. We see this again in the New Testament in the Book of Ephesians:

Ephesians 3: ...which from the beginning of the world hath been hid in God, who created all things by Jesus Christ:

In the beginning, God was there. So was Jesus. And God created all things *through* Jesus. It was God's will but it was Jesus' *doing.* If we continue reading the book of Genesis, during the creation of man, we can see further evidence of the presence of both God and Jesus:

And God said, Let us make man in _our_ image, after _our_ likeness.

Jesus and God were together in the beginning, and it was, again, Jesus who created the earth and, according to the will of God, made man in *"our"* image; that is, in the image of both God and Jesus. This is the first challenge to traditional doctrine that we can make in this chapter; as a world, we have learned that God made the earth when, in fact, it was Jesus' *doing.* The second challenge is that Jesus did not merely create the world as mentioned in Genesis one, but that he _re_created it. That the world, in a different state, possibly existed prior to the events of Genesis 1, and that God, through the works of Jesus, *re*created it into the world as we know it today. Check out the following passage:

In the beginning, God created the heavens and the earth. _Now_ the earth was without form, and void; and darkness was _upon the face of the deep._ And the Spirit of God moved _upon the face of the waters_. And God said, "Let

there be light": and there was light.

This passage is very interesting and revealing. First, the word *"Now"* in the second sentence is often translated as *"and,"* but many modern Bible translations, such as the NIV, correctly translate it as *"now."* The first two sentences of Genesis, then, indicate two specific and very different occurrences of time: *"In the beginning,"* and *"Now."* On the surface, there is no indication as to how much time may have elapsed from the *"beginning"* to the *"now,"* but future passages, as we will see, suggest that it may have been a very significant movement of time, possibly hundreds of millions of years.

Secondly, the words *"void"* and *"form"* must be examined. In our modern day dictionary the word *"void"* means *"empty space, unoccupied, vacant."* The word from which *"void"* was translated in the Hebrew language was *"bohuw"* which means *"emptiness."* It's the same word which is used in Isaiah 34 **"...upon it the line of confusion, and the stones of emptiness..."**

The word *"form"* was translated from the Hebrew word *"tohuw,"* which meant emptiness, wasteland, confusion, empty space. It is used in Jeremiah 4 **"I beheld the earth, and, lo, it was without form and void.."** and in other locations of the Old Testament to mean *wilderness* and *chaos.*

So, In Genesis 1, where it states *"....And the earth was without form, and void...,"* it is basically saying, by Hebrew definition, that *"...the earth was unoccupied, empty, desolate, an empty space, a wasteland."* These definitions suggest that, by the second sentence in the Bible, the Earth was not just air in the middle of space. It existed. It was there. It was *"beheld"* by Jeremiah. It was an *unoccupied wasteland* or *empty space.* A wilderness of sorts. The opening lines of Genesis seem to be saying, *"In the beginning,* **God created the heavens and the earth.** *NOW,* **the earth was**

without form, and void." In the beginning it was created, but *now* it was a wasteland, desolate, unoccupied, and empty.

Further along in the passage, there is additional information which suggests the earth was there, that it existed. Consider these lines: **"darkness was *upon the face of the deep.*"** and **"...God moved *upon the face of the waters*."** These passages are generally read over quickly without much consideration; and rightfully so. When a person sits down to read the Bible, he or she generally begins in the Book of Genesis; and with this huge book to tackle sitting in front of someone, it is understandable that the first few lines, which are generally taken for granted and thought to be universally understood, are lightly read over to get into the more "meaty" sections of this intense book. But consider what these first few lines in Genesis are telling us. *"In the beginning.....Now..." "...and darkness was upon the deep. And the Spirit of God moved across the face of the waters."* In order for darkness to be upon the face of the deep, the deep had to be there. In order for God to move upon the *"face of the waters,"* the waters had to be there. And they were! The first thing God—through Jesus—brought upon these waters, and upon this place without form, was light. He brought light to the wasteland, or to the void.

Incidentally, the word *"deep"* was translated from the Hebrew word *"tehome,"* which meant *"depths, deep places, the sea, and the grave."* The word "grave" is interesting because there are further suggestions throughout the Bible that indicate the earth was, indeed, a grave prior to its recreation in Genesis 1, that the earth may have been a desolate place before the creation of light and of man. And there is also evidence that this desolation may have existed because of the corruption of the angels, who, as we will see, were cast to earth *prior* to the creation of man.

We know the following facts: the Book of Genesis opens up

with the creation of the heavens and earth. Then, in the next sentence, the earth was without form and void, and darkness was upon the face of the deep. And the first thing created in the new world was light, followed by the creation of all the other elements of the new world. Soon afterwards, we know that there were two presences--God and Jesus-- who decided between *them* to create man in "*our*" image. So as the Bible opens up, in Genesis 1 and 2, we see the creation of heaven and earth, of all living things, and ultimately of man. But we need to be very conscious of what happens next. In Genesis 3, soon after man is created, he is tempted and deceived by a much slicker Satan. It is very evident then, by this chronology alone, that Satan existed on the earth *prior* to the creation of man. Sometime between "***in the beginning***" and the creation of man, Satan was created. As we examine Satan, who is also called Lucifer in the Old Testament, we'll see that he was actually a perfect angel created by God; and that he was cast to earth because of his corruption. God created Satan in absolute perfection; but as he eventually grew corrupt and caught up in his own beauty and perfection, he was cast to earth along with the angels which he also corrupted. We will see Bible passages talking specifically about this event.

But first, back to the verses in Genesis 1, we know this: the deep existed. The waters existed. God said, "***Let there be light.***" And there was light. And soon after, there was the creation of man. Man was immediately corrupted by Satan, a fallen angel, who was on earth prior to man. The chronology was "***in the beginning***," followed by "***now***," followed by the presence of Satan, followed by the creation of man. Several biblical books later, in the Book of Job, there is further suggestion that the angels existed prior to the creation of man and prior to the events of Genesis 1:2. The Book of Job shows how the angels, referred to as the *morning stars*, actually celebrated and sang together as the earth was being created:

Job: **Where were you when I laid the foundations of the earth?... Or who laid the corner stone thereof; when** *the morning stars sang together, and all the sons of God shouted for joy?*

The term "morning star" here refers to angels, as it does in the Book of Isaiah in reference to Satan, who was a God-created angel prior to his rebellion and exile down to earth:

Issaiah: **How you have fallen from heaven, O morning star, son of the dawn! You have been cast down to the earth, you who once laid low the nations!**

Another translation reads: **How art thou fallen from heaven, O Lucifer, son of the morning!**

Also, in some translations of the Bible, the term "*sons of God*" in the Book of Job is written "*angels of God.*" The point is that, in the Book of Job, there is indication that the angels were already created, that they were singing together and shouting for joy during the creation, or re-creation, of the earth.

In Genesis, during the 7 days in which God was creating the earth, the creation of Satan and the angels is never mentioned. However, in later verses, there are quite detailed descriptions indicating that Satan was indeed created as the perfect angel and the "*anointed cherub.*" Consider the following passages from the Book of Ezekiel:

Ezekiel (God speaking to Lucifer): **You have been in Eden the garden of God; every precious stone was your covering....in** *the day that you were created.....***You are the anointed cherub that covereth; and I have set you so: you were upon the holy mountain of God....***You were perfect in your ways from the day that you were created,* **till iniquity was found in you....**

...you haved sinned: therefore I will cast you as profane out of the mountain of God: and I will destroy you, O covering cherub,....Your heart was lifted up because of your beauty, you have corrupted your wisdom by reason of your brightness: I will *cast you to the ground...*

Satan was created by God as a beautiful angel, perfect in his ways. Wise. Anointed. But at some point, iniquity was found in him, and he was removed from heaven and cast down into the earth. In terms of Biblical chronology, this all had to happen sometime prior to Genesis 3, because that chapter is when Satan was present in the Garden of Eden to tempt Eve. Satan had already been cast out of heaven and sent down to the earth *prior* to Adam and Eve's falling away in the Garden of Eden. Long before Eve was tempted into eating the forbidden fruit, Satan had already been created in beauty and perfection; he had grown wise, and he had become corrupt to the extent that *"iniquity was found"* in him, and he had sinned and was cast to earth. He had already been cast to earth, and he was already here and waiting when he seized the opportunity to deceive Eve.

The Book of Revelation suggests that both Satan and a host of angels were cast down to earth together:

Revelation: **The great dragon was hurled down--that ancient serpent called the devil, or Satan, who leads the whole world astray. He was hurled to the earth, and his angels with him**.

Revelation: **And his tail drew the third part of the stars** (angels) **of heaven, and did cast them to the earth:**

The Book of Jude and the Second Book of Peter also makes reference to these other angels being cast out of heaven for their sins:

Jude: **And the angels which kept not their first estate, but left their own habitation**

2 Peter: **For if God spared not the angels that sinned, but cast them down...**

All of this activity--the creation, corruption, and casting down of Satan and the angels-- had to take place prior to Genesis 3 and the corruption of Adam and Eve because, again, as we know, Satan was present in the Garden of Eden to lead Eve astray.

It is not my intention to get into the depths of this particular discussion. There are thousands and thousands of pages written on the argument of whether or not God created or *re*created the earth in Genesis 1. These, of course, are the arguments of men; and although there are strong cases on both sides of the debate, the Bible, which was written not to examine pre-creation but only to serve as a source of infor-mation and instruction during the 7000 year plan of God, offers very little in terms of an account of a pre-creation, pre-mankind world. The entire subject is actually covered in only two lines: the first two lines of Genesis: *"In the be-ginning..."* and *"Now..."*

My intention for mentioning this material here is merely to indicate that there is a very clear starting point for God's plan; and that starting point is at the creation of Adam and Eve. It is not important whether or not we adhere or under-stand all the nuances of a pre-creation world; what *is* impor-tant is that we understand the starting point of God's plan, which is at the point of creation of Adam and Eve. This starting point is extremely significant and important because God's plan is 7000 years long; and this time line is signifi-cant to us now as we experience the new millenium, 2000 years after the death of Jesus and nearing the end of the first 6000 years of the plan.

And further, there are scientists and geologists and archeol-ogists all over the world who are quick to point out signs from the earth itself that indicate the planet is much older than 7000 years.

I personally have no dispute with that fact. I believe that the earth existed possibly millions of years before Adam and Eve. Jesus clearly created the earth. When? We don't know. And the angels were clearly cast down onto the earth. When? Again, we don't know; but we *do* know that it happened sometime before the creation of Adam and Eve, because Satan was present in the Garden of Eden.

My belief, based on years and years of intense study into the Bible and all of its details and references, is that Satan and the corrupt angels were cast down to the earth prior to Genesis 1:2, where we learn the world was *"without form, and void."* These angels, and their leader, Satan, who were all immortal beings; that is, beings that could not die nor be destroyed like the beings of man which were to follow, corrupted the earth with sins of such grotesque magnitude that God destroyed the earth of old and rendered it a desolate wasteland. The earth became *"without form, and void."* Or, as the original Hebrew words meant, " *unoccupied, empty, desolate, an empty space, a wasteland."* And after God silenced the corrupt and sinful earth, His spirit *"...moved upon the face of the waters. And he said, "Let there be light: and there was light."* The light was the dawning of a new age. The age of man.

The Book of Psalms, 104, makes reference to this advent of renewal: **"Thou sendest forth thy spirit, they are created: and thou *renewest* the face of the earth."**

Like the sun coming up in the calm of morning after a dark and stormy night, God cast light upon the old earth and started everything anew. And He made everything beautiful and plentiful and good. And then God, through Jesus, created man.

This was the beginning of God's 7000 year plan.

In terms of this plan, it was intricately structured from the very beginning. God does everything in sevens. He created the heavens and earth in seven days (actually in six days, then He rested on the seventh). As we studied earlier, he punished Israel 7 *times* for their sins. He created the 7 day calendar week: six days of which are meant for the works of man, and a seventh day which is set aside for a day of rest. He gave us seven holy days (which we as a planet no longer follow!). Seven is a number that represents completion and perfection to God throughout the Bible.

Right from the very beginning, the number seven was a significant number in the workings of God. The first week of creation was seven days long. God worked for six days and rested on the seventh. This is by no means a small or coincidental occurrence; the structure of this first week was extremely significant, and it was created in such a way as to become an eternal sign between God and man. God repeats its significance in the 10 Commandments given to Moses in Exodus 20:

Exodus: **Remember the Sabbath day, to keep it holy. Six days shall you labor, and do all your work. But the seventh day is the Sabbath of the Lord your God: in it you shall not do any work.....For in six days the Lord made heaven and earth,...and rested the seventh day: therefore, the Lord blessed the Sabbath day.**

God made the earth in six days and rested on the seventh. The structure of the week was so significant to God that He incorporated its observance into the 10 Commandments. Ranked in the same list of basic commandments as *"thou shalt not murder," "thou shalt not covet thy neighbors goods,"* etc. the fourth commandment rings loud and clear: *Remember the Sabbath day and keep it holy."* But please note that merely keeping the Sabbath holy is not the complete fourth commandment; it is only part of it. The entire commandment *commands* to the Israelites "...**six days shall you labor and do all *your* work, but the seventh day is a Sabbath to the Lord, and in it you shall not do any work...**"

The commandment is very specific. For six days, man was allowed--*commanded*--to do his work; but on the seventh day, he was not allowed to do any work; that is, he was commanded to cease from working. Six days of man's work. A seventh day of man's rest for God. Both parts of the same commandment, and both structured to reflect the foundation of God's plan. Man was commanded to work for the first six days of the week and rest on the seventh day; and God explains in the same commandment why He is enforcing this rule.

The fact that God created the earth in six days and rested on the seventh was not just some happenchance, coincidental event. It was significant. It had a purpose! It was not just an arbitrary number. God chose seven days because they were pivotal to His purpose and to His plan: Work for six days and rest on the seventh. And the observation of those seven days in that manner were so crucial and so important to God, that He incorporated their observance in the 10 Commandments and equated them to the importance of "thou shalt not murder," and the other Commandments. And note what both Jesus and his brother James say about observance of the 10 Commandments:

Jesus in Matthew 5 : **Whosoever therefore *shall break one of these least commandments*, and shall teach men to do likewise, he shall be called least in the kingdom of heaven: but whosoever shall do these commandments and teach them, he shall be called great in the kingdom of heaven.**

James: **For whosoever shall keep the whole law, and yet stumble in one, he is guilty of them all. For He that said,**

Do not commit adultery, said also, Do not kill. Now if you do not commit adultery, but you do kill, you are a transgressor of the whole law.

In other words, if a person breaks one commandment, that person is guilty of breaking them all. In the eyes of God, observing the fourth commandment--six days of work and one day of rest--is as important as not killing another human being; and the breaking of the fourth commandment is the same as committing murder or adultery or any of the other commandments. We can see the importance of observing the seven days again in Exodus 31:

Exodus: **And the Lord spoke to Moses, saying, 'Speak to the children of Israel, saying, Verily my Sabbaths you shall keep: for it is a sign between me and you throughout your generations; that you may know that I am the Lord....You shall keep the Sabbath therefore, for it is holy unto you: every one that defiles it shall surely be put to death: for whosoever does any work therein, that soul shall be cut off from among his people. Six days may work be done, but the seventh day is the Sabbath of rest, holy to the Lord. Whoever does any work in the Sabbath day, he shall surely be put to death....The children of Israel shall keep the Sabbath throughout their generations for a perpetual covenant. It is a sign between me and the children of Israel *forever*: for in six days the Lord made heaven and earth, and on the seventh day He rested, and was refreshed.'**

The degree of importance that God placed on the seven day week is as clear as anything written in the Bible or anywhere else. The observance of seven days is part of the 10 Commandments. The breaking of it is punishable by death. It is a sign between God and the children of Israel. It is a *perpetual covenant*; an everlasting agreement between God and His people, the children of Israel (who, as we have discussed, have become Great Britain and the United States!). It is very clear throughout the Bible that the seven day week,

6 days of work and 1 day of rest, is of absolute importance in the eyes of God. And here is why: it replicated God's plan. It represented, on a weekly basis, the 7000 year plan for civilization that God put into motion with the creation of Adam and Eve.

Now, to sidestep for a brief moment, I would like to discuss a certain theory in counseling and psychotherapy that has been made famous by the behavioral scientist, B.F. Skinner, who is most widely known for his work in behavioral psychology. Skinner, building on a Pavlovian foundation, worked specifically in the areas of behavior modification through the application of both operant and classical conditioning techniques, using stimulus, enforcement, and reinforcement to modify the behaviors and thought patterns of animals and human beings. To briefly visualize an approach of behavior modification used by Skinner to modify the behaviors of human beings, let's consider his use of positive and negative reinforcement on a laboratory rat. Placed in a big cage with two buttons and one door, the rat soon learns that Button A provides an electric shock, but Button B opens the door to a dish of food. After a few attempts, the rat gets pretty smart; he avoids Button A but pushes Button B whenever he gets the urge to eat.

To view another example of the principles of behavior modification at work in circumstances outside the experimental lab, consider the noontime feeding of a patient in the hospital. If lunch is served every day at noon, the patient's body will eventually adapt and become hungry and expectant of food as noon approaches. And as the patient hears the food trays rattling in the hallways before being served, actual physiological changes begin to occur in the patient's body, such as a growling stomach or a salivating mouth. This is just a mere snapshot of the basic principles and practices of behavior modification as presented in the modern world by B.F. Skinner. And in both of the above scenarios, behavior is modified through the process of *conditioning;* changes are made by providing the same stimulus and the same form of reinforcement over and over again, repeatedly, until the behavior becomes a natural response, at which point, the subject is said to be "*conditioned.*"

On a much larger and more significant scale, one can see how God used very much the same behavior modification type approach in modifying and conditioning the behavior of the Israelites throughout the Bible, especially where observance of the seven day week was concerned. A small example of this occurring is in Exodus 16, where the Israelites have crossed the Red Sea and are in the wilderness in need of food. God feeds them by placing manna on the ground each morning, which they are to gather up and eat. He places manna on the ground for six days, but instructs the Israelites to gather twice as much on the sixth day; for there would not be manna placed on the ground on the seventh day because it was the day of rest, the Sabbath. The passage is very revealing in terms of the approach God used to condition the Israelites into observing the six days of work and the seventh day of rest:

Exodus 16: **Then the Lord said to Moses, 'Behold, I will rain bread from heaven for you; and the people shall go out and gather a certain rate every day...And it shall come to pass that on the sixth day they shall prepare that which they bring in; and it shall be twice as much as they gather daily'..... And it came to pass.....and when the children of Israel saw it, they said it is manna.....And Moses said to them, 'This is the bread which the Lord hath given you to eat....gather of it every man according to his eating'...And the children of Israel gathered the manna, some more, some less.**

And they gathered it every morning....And it came to pass that on the sixth day they gathered twice as much bread....And Moses said to them, 'Tomorrow is the day of rest, the holy Sabbath of the Lord. Bake what you will bake today, and eat what you will eat. And that which

**remains and is left over, lay up for you to be kept until
the morning'.....And they laid it up till the morning.....And Moses said, 'Eat that today; for today is a
Sabbath unto the Lord: today you won't find any manna
in the field. Six days you shall gather the manna from
the fields; but on the seventh day, which is the Sabbath,
in the fields there shall be none.....And it came to pass
that some of the people went out anyway on the seventh
day to gather manna, and they found none.**

The six days of work and seventh day of rest was so important to God, that He conditioned the Israelites to observe the
days in such a manner by feeding them. They worked to
gather the manna each morning for six days; and on the
sixth day, they were told to gather enough for 2 days because, since the seventh day was a day of rest, God would
not provide the manna on that day. For six days, the children of Israel were fed with manna which they would find
on the ground every morning; but on the seventh day, there
was no manna because it was a day of rest, not a day for going out and collecting their food. This was a clear process
of behavior modification, of conditioning: six days of food,
one day of rest. Six days of work, one day of rest. Over and
over again until the children of Israel were conditioned, psy-
chologically and physiologically, to follow the seven day
week as it was designed by God. And this routine did not
just happen for one week, or two, or a month. It went on
for 40 years! The children of Israel were conditioned for
forty years, as a generation and as a nation, to observe the
important six days of work and one day of rest. The importance of this seven day week cannot be discounted, and I
have been repeating it here to stress its importance. It is
paramount to the entire plan of God.

Again, the seven day week was important in the scheme of
God's plan because it _replicated_ the plan. On a small,
weekly scale, God was creating for man a prototype or symbol of His grand plan for humanity. As we will see, six days

of work and one day of rest served as a weekly example of the greater picture, which was 6000 years of work followed by 1000 years of rest. The six-days-and-one-day parallel the 6000 years and 1000 years. God created Adam, the first man, and allocated 6000 years during which man would be allowed to conduct *his* works. At the end of those 6000 years, God would intervene in man's works with His own works; that is, with the second coming of Jesus and a 1000 year period of rest. God would cut off man's works on earth and replace it with His 1000 years of peace. The week, then, was structured to consist of 6 days of man's work and 1 day of rest, consistant to God's plan.

One may wonder why God would have given man 6000 years to act out his works upon the earth, but the answer is actually pretty evident. It is God's desire that all men come to salvation and the acceptance of His truth, but He is wise in knowing that, in order to be truly believed and accepted, such salvation and truth cannot be forced upon man's carnal mind. It appears that Satan exemplified this experience. Satan challenged God in His authority and knowledge and, in so doing, became eternally caught up in his own corruption and, ultimately, cast out of God's favor.

Unlike Satan, however, who is immortal, God made man mortal; that is, perishable. He gave man a free will to choose between God's way or man's way. And he placed before us 6000 years to experience the peaks and valleys and the general dynamics of man's way. Through 6000 years of civilization, man has followed his own way and has, consequently, experienced wars, diseases, disasters, atrocities, death, genocide, and, in general, absolute corruption. Within those darker consequences, man has also experienced love and beauty and peace and moments of great joy and happiness; but these events have been, in general, short lived and incomplete. Times of peace have been interrupted with times of war. Times of love have been diluted with times of grief. Man's way does not work, but we need to see and understand that as a race. Later on, we will see how man's way will lead up to the near destruction of the planet, but how God will intervene before this total destruction actually occurs. But this point remains: man's way, if allowed to perpetuate in its current state of disorder and corruption, will ultimately lead to the complete destruction of mankind. And this is possibly the lesson God has placed before us all. Through 6000 years of trials and tribulations, mankind has been able to experience the ways of man. Since the days of Adam, it has been a time of man's works. But at the end, God will intervene and put away the works of man, placing before us 1000 years of rest and peace. Just like the seven day work week, which involves six days of man's work and one day of God's rest, so shall the ages be: 6000 years of man's works and 1000 years of God's rest.

Throughout the Bible, God lays before mankind His ongoing plan, which began with the creation of Adam and Eve and will end with the complete alteration of earth as we know it, actually in the creation of a *new* earth. Whereas the plan of God began in Genesis when God, through Jesus, created Adam and Eve, it ends in the Book of Revelation, at the beginning of Chapter 21:

Revelation: **And I saw a *new* heaven and a *new* earth: for the first heaven and the first earth were passed away; and there was no more sea. And I, John, saw the holy city, new Jerusalem, coming down from God out of heaven, prepared as a bride adorned for her husband.**

This is an event that will happen at the very end of the 7000 years. It is the point in time where God's plan has been fully completed. It is the point where all of mankind is guided out of the old earth and out of their old ways of life and into a whole new dimension of existence. It is the final episode in God's plan for mankind, an event that has been referred to repeatedly throughout the Bible and one that serves to culminate what God had intended for man and for earth from the very beginning.

And this is why the seven day week is so important to God. It is a small scale replica, a weekly reminder of God's 7000 year plan. It is a weekly form of behavior modification-- 6 days of work, 1 day of rest, over and over and over again. It was designed to help all of our generations recognize God's plan and to simulate it week after week in our own lives.

This concept may at first be hard to grasp, but we will examine Bible passages that will enable it to become very clear. God placed 7 days in our week and, in addition, he gave us 7 holy days to further reinforce his 7000 year plan. This was all done to *condition* us, just like God did to the Israelites with the manna, to follow a pattern consistent to the plan. And it was so important for us to follow this pattern that it was ranked in the 10 Commandments with murder, adultery, theft, and false witness; and the punishment for deviating from its observance was, at one point, death. Six days of our work, one day of rest for God; it is our week, our sign, our weekly dose of behavior modification. It is the process through which we are conditioned, on a weekly basis, towards the ways and the will of God.

Six *days*. One *day*. On the outset, they may seem to stand all alone without connection to God's plan. But let's look at *"...a little bit here, a little bit there..."* and analyze just how they so perfectly connect.

The apostle Peter, as he explained God's plan to his followers, told them of how, in the end times, scoffers would come and question God's honesty, wondering when the end of the world would come and when Jesus would return. Peter predicted that they would scoff and say sarcastically, **"Where is this `coming' he promised? Ever since our fathers died, everything goes on as it has since the beginning of creation."** In other words, these people would doubt God and the second coming of Jesus because, as far as they could observe, everything was the same generation after generation without any sign of His coming. But regarding these scoffers, Peter told his followers: **"But they deliberately** forget that long ago by God's *word* the heavens existed and the earth was formed... by the same word the present heavens and earth are reserved for fire, being kept for the day of judgment and destruction of ungodly men.....But do not forget this one thing, dear friends: *With the Lord a day is like a thousand years, and a thousand years are like a day.*"

This one line speaks volumes! With the Lord, one day is equivalent to one thousand years. Seven days in a week? Seven Thousand Years in God's Plan? The parallel comes a little closer together. The scoffers Peter talked about would be speaking out against the honesty of God, wondering whether or not Jesus would really be coming back as promised. They would be doubting God's word, and confronting, in absolute ignorance, His timeline. And Peter reminded them very clearly:

But forget not this one thing, beloved, that one day is with the Lord as a thousand years, and a thousand years as one day.

Now, let's look once again at the way God structured his seven day week from the very beginning. Six days of work, one day of rest. It is worded in the 10 Commandments as follows: "...**six days shall you labor and do all _your_ work, but the seventh day is a Sabbath to the Lord, and in it you shall not do any work...**" When we understand Peter's statement regarding *"one day is with the Lord as a thousand years,"* we can begin to understand how, in the same manner, God has structured His 7000 year plan: 6000 years for mankind to do *man's* work. 1000 years of rest mandated by God.

Just as the Sabbath was allocated as a day of rest in the seven day week, God's 7000 year plan has a "day of rest" as well: a 1000 year period of time in which peace and rest are present throughout the world. Like the one day of rest God instructed us to follow each week, God's 1000 year period of rest will be refreshing and filled with peace. And the Bible is very specific as to what will happen during these 1000 years: The stubborn and rebellious doings of man will no longer be at work, Satan will be bound up and unable to corrupt the world, and Jesus will be present on earth ensuring peace and rest for 1000 years.

It's a perfect plan! And it's a perfect parallel to the 7 day week. Six days of work, one day of rest. 6000 years of work. 1000 years of rest. *"One day is with the Lord as a thousand years.."* The picture comes together tightly and makes beautiful sense, and we can see how it has been manifested through our daily work week since the beginning of time. Regarding this "day" of rest, or the 1000 year period of peace on the earth, the Bible states as follows:

Revelation: **...And he laid hold of the dragon, the old serpent, which is the Devil and Satan, and bound him for *a thousand years*...and cast him into the abyss, and shut it, and sealed it over him, that he should deceive the nations no more, until the *thousand years* should be finished: after this he must be loosed for a little time.**

Revelation (speaking of the followers of God): **...they lived, and reigned with Christ a *thousand years*. The rest of the dead lived not until the *thousand years* should be finished.**

Revelation: **And when the *thousand years* are finished, Satan shall be loosed out of his prison.**

These passages from the Book of Revelation refer to a 1000 year time period on earth when Satan is bound by God and unable to deceive the nations. It is a time when the followers of Jesus are actually allowed to live and reign with Him on earth for 1000 years of peace. This particular period of peace, an entire millenium of peace, will be discussed in greater detail in Chapter 4; but for now, I am mentioning it to serve as a sort of marker from which we can measure the 7000 year length of God's plan.

We already know that, like the 7 day week, and with the echo of Peter's words that *"...one day is with the Lord as a thousand years, and a thousand years as one day,"* there will be a definite 1000 year period of rest on earth. This millenium of peace is a Sabbath-- a day of rest--equivalent to the weekly Sabbath which God mandated as a day of weekly rest. As we begin to understand the 1000 year period of peace and rest, we can also begin to understand the "6 days of man's work," or the 6000 year period of time leading up to this peaceful millenium. We merely need to look at the other 6000 years of history; the 6 days of man's work prior to the seventh day Sabbath.

Of all the books in the Bible, the First Book of Chronicles is one of the most difficult to read. It is merely a chronicle of the generations that grew out of Adam, leading to Noah, to Abraham, through the line of David, and beyond. Reading and studying the book involves a great deal of counting and the tracing of genealogies, but by comparing the First Book of Chronicles to the histories of the Mesopotamian and Egyptian dynasty chronologies, the end result helps us divide the history of Israel into three distinct passages of time: (1) The time period from Adam to Abraham, which is calculated at approximately 2000 years. (2) The time period from Abraham, through the line of David, and up to the birth of Jesus, which is approximately another 2000 years. And (3) the time period from Jesus to the year 2000 A.D., our current day and age, which of course is calculated at another 2000 years. The total number of years, from Adam to the present, is approximately 6000 years. We are nearing the end of the first 6000 years of God's 7000 year plan.

Here is where we need to put the pieces of the puzzle together. We know that God implemented a 7 day week in
which 6 days were allocated for man's work, and one day
was allocated for God's day of peace. We know that Peter,
in addressing man's impatience with the second coming of
Jesus and referencing the end time scoffers as well, said that
each day with God is 1000 years. We know that there will
be a 1000 year period of peace and rest on earth, when Satan
will no longer be allowed to deceive mankind. And we
know that approximately 6000 years have passed from the
creation of Adam to the present day. 2000 from Adam to
Abraham, 2000 from Abraham to Jesus, and as the year
2000 A.D. is upon us, all inhabitants of the earth know that
we live in a time period which has been calculated as 2000
years after the death of Jesus. The following diagram illustrates the time span of civilization from the creation of
Adam and Eve to the present time:

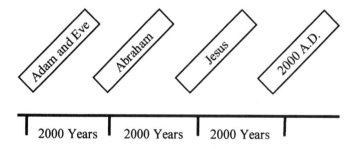

| | 2000 Years | | 2000 Years | | 2000 Years | |

The end of the 6000 year period of "man's work" on earth is
known as the end time, or the "time of the end." It is the
time when Jesus Christ will return and overthrow the governments of the world to establish His own government of
truth and the 1000 year millenium of peace. Concerning
this particular period of time, the confusing part for most
people who study prophesy is the way in which the Bible
speaks of two distinct end times. There is mention of a first

resurrection, a second resurrection, the second death, etc. And at times it can seem trying to differentiate and understand these specific events. However, the Bible continues to answer all questions within itself.

The Bible shows how the 6000 years of man's works on earth will climax in the near destruction of the planet. Nation will rise up against nation, and a period of great tribulation will befall mankind. The earth will be in utter chaos. Jesus Himself talks about this period of time in the Book of Matthew:

Matthew: "...**for then shall be great tribulation, such as was not since the beginning of the world to this time, no, nor ever shall be. And except those days should be shortened, there should no flesh be saved: but for the elect's sake those days shall be shortened.**"

This comes at the end of the 6000 years. Great tribulation and chaos will be upon the world. Governments will be rising up against governments. And, as Jesus states, if God were not to intervene and shorten those days, no flesh would be saved. But God will intervene and *those days shall be shortened.* And then Jesus will return to overthrow the world governments and establish his own throne *on earth.* This is at the beginning of the 1000 year period of rest, the "Sabbath" so to speak. Remember the previous passages from the Book of Revelation concerning God's people:

Revelation: ...**they lived, and reigned with Christ a *thousand years*. The rest of the dead lived not until the *thousand years* should be finished.**

Revelation: **And when the *thousand years* are finished, Satan shall be loosed out of his prison.**

After the 6000 years of man's works ends in great tribulation and destruction and the terrible wrath of God, Jesus will
come to bring in the 1000 years of peace. At His coming,
those who are dead in Christ and who have lived and believed according to the ways of God and Jesus will rise to
meet Him and will *"live and reign with Christ a 1000
years."* This is known as the first resurrection.

The 1000 years or peace and rest will happen and eventually
pass; and then, as it mentions above, two things will happen: (1) Satan will be loosed from his prison. And (2) the
rest of the dead who were not resurrected at the beginning of
the 1000 years will then be resurrected for a final judgement
(known as the White Throne Judgement).

We explore all of this in greater detail in later chapters. The
point I want to clarify now is that the Bible speaks of two
end periods of time. The first being the end of the 6000
years, and the second being the end of the 1000 years. The
first resurrection takes place at the beginning of the 1000
years with the coming of Jesus. The second resurrection
takes place at the end of the 1000 years.

It's important at this point just to understand that there are
two periods of time referred to in terms of the end.: the end
of the 6000 years and the end of the 1000 years. Later, we
will explore the details of both ends, and we will discuss the
events that will take place *during* the 1000 years.

The prophet Daniel spoke abundantly regarding the end of
the 6000 year period of time. We will explore his prophesies in Chapters 5, 6,7, and 8. But one brief glimpse into
what has been written in the Book of Daniel may shed light
onto the significance of the time period we are in today, as
the 6000 years from Adam to the present slowly wind down
to an end. One of the things Daniel recorded was something
God told him regarding the end time. This information may
be more familiar to us now than it has been throughout his-

tory:

Daniel: ...but you, O Daniel, shut up the words and seal the book until the time of the end: many shall go to and fro, and knowledge shall be increased.

This passage can, in part, help us identify our place in the 6000 years. Never before in the history of the world, in all of the 6000 years of man's works, has knowledge been increased to the extent that it has in just the past 20 years, even moreso in the past 10. We live in an era that we widely acknowledge as "the information age." Children, with a few keystrokes on their family-room computers, have access to more knowledge than wordly scholars did only 50 years ago. Computers are nearly as common as TVs, and through them we are able to tap into information sources around the world. Knowledge has most definitely increased. And speaking in terms of *"going to and fro,"* consider the roads, the highways, the railways, and the airlines. Never before in the history of man have more people gone to and fro. I heard a statistic once stating that, on any given day, there are more than 60,000 airline passengers flying over the skies of America at the same time. Add this to the many millions who travel our roads and highways each and every day, and that is a lot of people *"going to and fro!"*

And yes, knowledge has increased steadily throughout the ages, and men have gone to and fro on horses and ships for centuries. So, the statement in Daniel can be viewed as relative; it could be said to apply to all stages of knowledge and transportation throughout history. But looking at the 6000 years from Adam until now, and knowing that the end time of the 6000 years will climax before the 1000 years of peace begin, which is consistent to our understanding of God's 7 day week; it seems a little bit easier to place Daniel's statement into the time we are living in today. And there are so many other prophesies and biblical events concerning this end time.

Which leads us into a discussion of God's holy days. Just as
God set forth a 7 day week to condition us repeatedly
throughout the ages, He also established seven holy days to
remind us annually about His plan. Early in the history of
the Israelites, when Moses led them across the Red Sea into
Sinai, God began to condition them towards the manifestation of his 7000 year plan by implementing both weekly and
annual conditioning activities. Like the establishment of the
seven day week, God established 7 holy days that were to be
observed throughout the year. These seven holy days were
designed to outline God's 7000 year plan in a clear, step-by-
step manner. The observation of the holy days throughout
the year allows mankind to experience and understand the
various phases of God's plan, including the second coming
of Jesus, the 1000 year millenium of peace, and the final
resurrection at the end of the 1000 years.

God established His seven holy days to allow each day to
represent a certain phase, a certain aspect, of His plan. So
as a human race, we can experience the structure of God's
plan in two different ways: we can experience it through
our six day work week and a single day of rest; and we can
experience it in greater detail, year after year, with the observance of God's established holy days.

Let's take a look at how this works: In the Book of Leviticus 23, and later in Deuteronomy, God instructs Moses to
implement a series of Sabbaths and feasts which were to become God's seven holy days. These holy days were to occur
in the first seven months of God's calendar, which, incidentally, began in what we now know as April, but which the
Israelites named Abib. Unlike the Roman calendar, which
begins on January 1 in the dead of winter, God's calendar
begins in the spring when plant life is young and there is a
sense of newness or *renew*edness on the planet. Beginning
in God's first month, which is our 4th month of April, the

holy days begin and God's plan is gradually revealed. In
succession, in various months, seven very significant Sabbaths and feasts are to be observed annually to detail the
various phases in God's plan.

Taking the information we know already, let's examine
God's seven holy days and see how they parallel the unfolding of God's 7000 year plan.

The first holy day implemented by God is **Passover**, which
occurs in the middle of what we know as April. The purpose
of Passover is to remember God's intervention into Israel's
captivity in Egypt. During the first Passover, the Israelites
marked their doorposts with lamb's blood; and death *passed
over* them and killed all of the first born in Egypt. It was
the beginning of the time when Moses led the Israelites out
of captivity, across the Red Sea, and into the area near the
promised land.

Dueteronomy: **Honor the Lord your God by celebrating
Passover in the month of Abib; it was on a night in that
month that He rescued you from Egypt.**

There are so many metaphors present with Passover. Egypt
is often seen as a state of sin, in which the lamb's blood, like
Jesus' blood later on, saved the people from death and led
them out of sin. It can also be seen as a sort of evoluiton out
of desolation and emptiness, much like the world described
in Genesis 1. And with the intervention of God and Jesus,
the old world was left behind and a new world was to begin.
In any case, the observation of Passover is the observation of
God's deliverance from sin and death and destruction.

And remember, Passover is not merely a "Jewish Holiday."
It is a holy day commanded by God to be observed by ALL
tribes of Israel, not just the tribe of Judah. Passover should
be observed, to this day, by all citizens of the United States,
Great Britain, Europe, and the Middle East. Each of Israel's

twelve sons were given the commandment of Passover. All the sons, and grandsons (Ephraim and Manasseh), and all generations to follow *forever* were to observe the Passover. And the same holds true for the other holy days of God.

The second holy day is the **Feast of Unleavened Bread,** which occurs one day after Passover in the month of "April." Leaven is symbolic of sin in the Bible. And during this feast, the Israelites eat bread without leaven, representative of humility and the absence of sin. It is also representative of God establishment of Law with the Israelites and man's connectedness to God through the absence of sin.

The third holy day is known as the **Day of Pentecost or the Feast of Weeks (also known as the Day of First Fruits.),** and it occurs in the third month from Abib, which is what we know as June and July. This holy day originally celebrated God's blessings and abundance to Israel; but later, in Acts 2, Jesus established His church on the Day of Pentecost. Consistent to God's plan, this day of observance represents the establishment of salvation through Jesus in the world.

So, up to this point, we have three holy days Passover, Unleavened Bread, and Pentecost, which are symbolic of Deliverence, the Law, and Salvation. God delivered mankind, established His laws, and later gave the world Jesus, in the flesh, through which a church was formed and salvation can be obtained. Shortly, we will see how this all ties in together.

The fourth holy day is **The Feast of Trumpets**, in which a blast of trumpets ushers in a day of rest. Like all of the other holy days, the principle of dual events is present in the Feast of Trumpets. The original feast began with a trumpet and was followed by a period of rest. In terms of God's plan, the feast represents the second coming of Jesus to bring in the 1000 year millenium of peace; and it can seen moreso when it is compared to Paul's account of the end of the 6000 years, and subsequent beginning of the 1000 years of peace, in 1 Corinthians.

1 Corinthians: **"...in a moment, in the twinkling of an eye, at the last trump:** *for the trumpet shall sound,* **and the dead shall be raised incorruptible, and we shall be changed."**

Like the Feast of Trumpets, which consists of a day of rest, the 1000 years of peace will begin, as Paul said, *"...at the last trump: for a trumpet shall sound..."* As we look at all the holy days organized in a timeline, we will see how perfectly the Feast of Trumpets fits into the scheme of things. It is also interesting to read what God wrote about the way in which the day was to be observed: **"...in the seventh month, on the** *first day* **of the seventh month, you are to have a** *day of rest,* **a sacred assembly commemorated with trumpet blasts."** First day of the seventh month. A day of rest. The parallel to the 1000 years of peace begins to manifest. God's holy days begin to show purpose other than mere celebrations.

As mentioned earlier, the 1000 years of peace will begin with the second coming of Jesus. When Jesus is on earth, peace will prevail. And those who *"live and reign with Him for 1000 years"* will be at one with Him. The 1000 years of peace are characterized by mankind being *at one* with Jesus. Consequently, the fifth holy day, which occurs in the 7th month after the Feast of Trumpets, is the **Day of Atonement**. Examine the word: At-one-ment. As a feast, it is a celebration of oneness with God. In God's plan, there are 6000 years of man's basic separation from God, and a 1000 year period of time in which Jesus lives on earth with mankind. God's 1000 year period of rest will be exactly what this Day of Atonement represents in its symbolic sense, a day of AT-ONE-MENT with God. In His description to Moses of this particular holy day, God stresses the importance of rest.

Leviticus: **And you shall do no work in that same day: for it is a day of atonement....And whatsoever soul it be that does any work in that day I will destroy from among his people. You shall do no manner of work: it shall be a statute forever throughout your generations in all your dwellings....it shall be unto you a *Sabbath of rest.***

In God's plan, the 1000 years of rest is a time when man's work is over. Man's rule is allowed for 6000 years only. And as the 1000 years of rest are brought forth by the second coming of Jesus, man's rule is no longer valid. It's over. As we are *at one* with Jesus, man's work and manipulation of the planet is done. The Day of Atonement reflects this day, this 1000 year "day," of rest.

The sixth holy day is the **Feast of Tabernacles**, which also appears in the seventh month. It is a 7 day celebration in which work is prohibited on the first and last days. Originally reflective of the Israelites who lived in humble dwellings and grew prosperous in the promised land under God's guidance, it is also representative of mankind's prosperity in spiritual growth under Jesus' rule in the millenium of peace. The word *"tabernacle"* means *"a home, a dwelling, and the sacred house of God."* The Feast of Tabernacles, then, reflects a time of dwelling with God and Jesus, **"living and reigning with Him for 1000 years."** Unlike the Day of Atonement, which is a single day celebrating the initial *at-one-ment* with Jesus, the Feast of Tabernacles is a 7 day celebration of actually living and prospering with Jesus. It is also a reflection of living humbly, happily, and without sin under the rule of Jesus.

The second coming of Jesus is a celebration. It is, at last, after 6000 years of virtual separation, a time of man's at-one-ment with God. This is reflected in the Day of Atonement. Living on earth under the rule of Jesus is also a time of celebration. It will be a time in which Satan is imprisoned and no longer able to deceive the nations, a time during which both earth and man will rest and flourish for 1000 years with Jesus. This is reflected in the week long celebration of the Feast of Tabernacles.

The seventh holy day is known as the **Final Day** (or the **Last Day** or the **Last Great Day**). Occurring in the day immediately following the Feast of Tabernacles, the Final Day is a celebration of the end of the festival year. The next festival would be Passover as the new year begins. The Final Day is a celebration in which rest occurs and great joy is observed. It is parallel to the final days of God's plan, when the 1000 years of peace are over and the plan is thereby complete. As mentioned earlier, there are two ends spoken of in the Bible. The end of the 6000 years and the end of the 1000 years. In terms of the holy dates, the first is represented and celebrated through the Feast of Trumpets. And the second is celebrated in the Final Day. After this final celebration, the festival year is complete. Or, true to its parallel, God's 7000 year plan is complete.

By studying and observing the holy days of God, one can see the manifestation of God's plan celebrated year after year. Each holy day represents a phase in God's plan: creation and deliverance, the Law, the birth of Jesus, the second coming of Jesus, the 1000 year reign of Jesus with man, and the final day (the second resurrection and the final judgement). Turn to the Book of Leviticus and read about these holy days. They are truly representative of God's master plan.

On the following page, the holy days are outlined in accordance to their respective months. Please note that the two holy days representing deliverance and the law are at the beginning of the year, the establishment of Jesus and His church are in the third month, and the other three holy days appear in the seventh month, in the order they will appear in the end time: a trumpet blast, Jesus' coming, life with Jesus on earth for 1000 years, and the final judgement day.

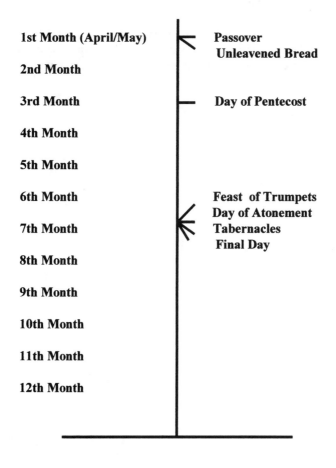

1st Month (April/May)	Passover Unleavened Bread
2nd Month	
3rd Month	Day of Pentecost
4th Month	
5th Month	
6th Month	Feast of Trumpets Day of Atonement
7th Month	Tabernacles Final Day
8th Month	
9th Month	
10th Month	
11th Month	
12th Month	

Through the establishment of the seven day week and the seven holy days, God presented us with a weekly and annual symbol of His plan, a regular opportunity to get to know and understand His timeline. As we approach the end of the first 6000 years, we can look forward to our sabbath of rest, the 1000 year sabbath to follow; a time that will allow us to live at one with Jesus, and with each other, in an earthly kingdom established by Jesus, free from Satan and free from the pain and sadness of the modern day world.

The time is rapidly approaching when we will let go of the old world and embrace the new one. And if we are believers and followers of Jesus, we will be able to live and reign with Him, as priests and teachers, for 1000 years.

Chapter 4

The Millenium to Follow

As we have discussed, the millenium of peace will immediately follow the end of man's 6000 years of control of the earth. The "6 day work week," which began with Adam, will culminate with great destruction and *tribulation* the likes of which have never been known to mankind *"..since the beginning of the world to this time, no, nor ever shall be.."* Absolute chaos will climax and the earth will be on the brink of utter destruction. As Jesus foretold it, *" except those days should be shortened, there should no flesh be saved: but for the elect's sake those days shall be shortened."* The good news, of course, is that those days *"shall be shortened."* As man's 6000 year rule winds to a halt and results in the near annihilation of the entire planet and all of its inhabitants, possibly as the world stands in wait of a final nuclear attack between all the world powers of the earth, God will intervene and prevent utter desolation. At that time, before the destruction of the planet and all of its flesh, the second coming of Jesus will occur.

The second coming of Jesus will be a true event, and it will usher in the new millenium of peace. It will mark the end of the old world and the beginning of the new. Just as the Feast of Trumpets and the Day of Atonement were celebrated at the beginning of the 7th month in God's calendar, creating a parallel to the coming of Jesus and the *at-one-ment* between man and God, Jesus will come to put away the old and initiate the new, ending the 6000 years of man's *separation* from God and beginning an era of man's *togetherness* with God. Jesus will come and begin the new millenium, the 1000 years of peace.

The particular day upon which Jesus descends to earth will be a day unlike any other event in the history of civilization. It will occur at a time when most of the world will not be expecting it, at the brink of mankind's total destruction of the earth coupled with the furious wrath of God. It will come like lightening and with the sounding of trumpets. Every eye on earth will see Jesus descending from the clouds. The dead will be resurrected. And the old ways of the world's man-made chaos and heartache and destruction will be put to an end. Immediately. It will be a glorious and magical day that will begin a 1000 year period of peace and happiness. But first, just prior to that time, mankind's violence and hatred toward one another will have gotten so great that the earth and all of its inhabitants will be teetering close to total annihilation. Man will be just a short time away from wiping out all of mankind. In addition, God will unleash His wrath and anger upon the corrupted world. Then Jesus will come to earth and the planet will be saved from utter destruction. Bible passages reveal that Jesus will come down from the heavens in triumph! Then, as He descends to the earth, the dead *in Christ* will be resurrected. Graves all over the earth will open up and new human bodies will ascend upwards from these graves to meet Jesus in the air. Those of us who haven't died but are alive on this particular day will change instantly into immortal beings. And the entire old ways of earth will no longer be valid.

The new millenium of peace will begin.

The events surrounding Jesus' second coming to earth will be so phenomenal and supernatural, they are hard to even fathom as we reflect upon them today. Graves opening up. Live bodies coming from those graves to meet Jesus. Those of us who are alive changing into immortal beings. It is magical, and seems almost too good to believe, or maybe even too far fetched to comprehend. But here are just two of the many excerpts from the New Testament that tell of these events on the day when Jesus returns to earth:

1 Thessalonians: **"...we which are alive and remain unto the coming of the Lord shall not prevent them which are asleep (dead).....For the Lord himself shall descend from heaven with a shout, with the voice of the archangel, and with the *trump* of God: and the dead in Christ shall rise first.....Then we which are alive and remain shall be caught up together with them in the clouds, to meet the Lord in the air: and so shall we ever be with the Lord....."**

1 Corinthians: **"...for since by man came death, by man came also the resurrection of the dead....For as in Adam all die, even so in Christ all shall be made alive....But every man in his own order: First, Christ...afterward they that are Christ's at His coming...Then cometh the end.... when He shall have put down all rule and all authority and power.....Behold, I show you a mystery; We shall not all sleep (die), but we shall all be changed,.....In a moment, in the twinkling of an eye, at the last trump: for *the trumpet shall sound*, and the dead shall be raised incorruptible, and we shall be changed....For this corruptible must put on incorruption, and this mortal must put on immortality......**

In the *twinkling of an eye*: all the people on earth at that time who are alive and believe in Jesus will be changed *in*

107

the twinkling of an eye. They won't die, they will just change into incorruptible, immortal beings. And those who are dead will come to life and also be immortal and incorruptible. Together, all people resurrected and changed will ascend up into the air to meet Jesus as he descends to earth. It will be an event that will mark the change of the entire universe. All that is old will be put away, and all that is new will begin. It will be a day that separates the 6000 years of man's control and the 1000 years of peace under Jesus' control. It will be the long awaited second coming of Jesus Christ. The dead who have believed in Jesus during their lifetimes will be resurrected. Those who are alive and have believed upon Him will be changed. And together, all will live *at one* with Jesus and with each other for 1000 years. **On earth**!

I emphasize *"on earth"* here because I want to immediately discount the infamous "rapture" theory that prevails among many of the churches in existence today. In short, followers of the rapture theory believe that, in the end time, men will secretly be swept up into the air with Jesus and be whisked away to live with Him *in heaven* for 1000 years. The theory is based, primarily, on the passage just quoted from 1 Thessalonians: **"Then we which are alive and remain shall be *caught up together with them in the clouds*, to meet the Lord in the air: and so shall we ever be with the Lord....."** It is generally paired with this passage from Matthew 24 : **"...so shall also the coming of the Son of man be. Then shall two be in the field; the one shall be taken, and the other left. Two women shall be grinding at the mill; the one shall be taken, and the other left. Watch therefore: for you do not know what hour your Lord does come.**

At first glance, of course, these two passages seem to make a strong argument for the rapture theory. Two women will be grinding at the mill, one is taken, the other left. We *"shall meet the Lord in the air: and so shall we ever be with the*

Lord." Without looking further, one might see how a secret rapture is being discussed here, where one person, standing at the mill with another person, seemingly vanishes to meet the Lord in the air and be with Him forever. These two verses, isolated with each other, have been used to build and entire religious belief system within many of today's churches. However, those who believe in the rapture theory and rely on the excerpts in Matthew 24 to validate their claim, pay absolutely no attention to the other verses in Matthew 24, appearing just two or three paragraphs earlier:

Matthew 24:26-27: **Wherefore if they shall say unto you, Behold, He is in the desert; go not forth: behold, He is in the *secret* chambers; believe it not. For as the lightning cometh out of the east, and shineth even unto the west; so shall also the coming of the Son of man be.**

There is nothing secret about lightening. And Jesus purposely uses the image of lightening coming out of the east and *shining* to the west to illustrate His point that His second coming will not be secret by any means. Instead, it will be very visual. It will be like lightening coming out of the east and shining in the west. It will be observable! Matthew continues:

Matthew 24:31: **And then _shall appear_ the sign of the Son of man in heaven: and then shall all the tribes of the earth mourn, and they _shall see_ the Son of man coming in the clouds of heaven with power and great glory. And He shall send His angels with _a great sound of a trumpet_, and they shall gather together His elect from the four winds, from one end of heaven to the other.**

Another verse regarding Jesus' return can be found in the Book of Acts:

Acts: **And when Jesus had said these things, as they were looking, He was taken up; and a cloud received him out of their sight.** And while they were looking into heaven as He went, behold, two stood beside them dressed in white who also said, 'You men of Galilee, why do you stand looking into heaven? This Jesus, who was received up from you into heaven, *shall also come in a like manner as you saw Him going into heaven.*

The second coming of Jesus will be both visual and audible. Jesus *shall appear* in heaven, and all tribes of the earth *shall see* Him. He shall come with a *great sound* of a trumpet. This is in direct conflict with what the man-contrived "rapture" theory teaches, that men will be secretly taken from the earth. We can see that the Bible states in no uncertain terms that there simply will not be a secret coming of Jesus, no secret rapture of the elect. The coming of Jesus will not be secret; it will be a world wide spectacle. All the tribes of the earth *shall see* Him coming. It shall be accompanied by *a great sound of a trumpet.* It will be like lightening, seen in both the east and the west. The Book of Revelation states that, **"...behold, He comes with clouds, and every eye shall see Him.."** The second coming of Jesus will be a visual and audible event for the entire world. And Jesus Himself specifically warns against beliefs of a secret, hidden coming. Right here, in Matthew 24, in the same verse that is used to create a belief around this secret coming, Jesus states, **"if they say, behold, he is in the desert; go not forth: behold, he is in the** *secret* **chambers; believe it not..."** In other words, don't believe people if they say that Jesus came to earth without you knowing about it. Don't believe He's in a secret place somewhere, or off in the desert somewhere. Because, as Jesus states, " *as the lightning comes out of the east, and shines even unto the west; so shall also the coming of the Son of man be.* " Don't believe people if they say Jesus is off in some secret place; because when Jesus comes to earth, it will be a very visible and audible event, a worldwide spectacle. Like lightening.

With a great sound of a trumpet. He will come and sweep across the entire earth, gathering His elect--the dead who will be resurrected and the living who will be changed *"in the twinkling of an eye."* And together, they will all descend down upon the earth in glory. Together, *on earth,* they will establish the government of Jesus:

Isaiah: **...for unto us a child is born, unto us a son is given: and the *government* shall be upon His shoulder: and His name shall be called Wonderful, Counsellor, The mighty God, The everlasting Father, The Prince of Peace....of the increase of His *government* and peace there shall be no end..**

As Jesus descends to earth to establish His government of rest and peace, the era of man's 6000 year rule will have finally ended. Man's kingdoms and governments will be overthrown, and the new 1000 years of peace on earth will have finally arrived. It will be a day of visible and audible glory! Not a secret rapture. Not a whisking away of the elect. But a loud and visual display of triumph! Jesus will gather his elect and descend to the earth to establish His government. And the Bible is specific about where Jesus and His elect will come down as they descend on that day:

Zechariah: **And His feet shall stand in that day upon the Mount of Olives, which is before Jerusalem on the east....**

This particular location, the Mount of Olives, is unique and significant in the scope of end time prophesies. In the first three of the four Gospels--Matthew 24, Mark 13, and Luke 21--the account of Jesus' return to earth is given to His disciples. Not coincidentally, this is done while Jesus is sitting on the Mount of Olives. With His disciples on hand, there at the Mount of Olives, Jesus talks specifically about the end time events, stating that, ultimately, He would come back to earth in the clouds: *"...and they shall see the Son of man coming in the clouds of heaven with power and great glory."* Jesus was talking to His disciples about His return

111

on the exact place and at the exact location where He will ultimately descend: the Mount of Olives. And never once did He mention a secret rapture; instead, He talked of a visible return while, at the same time, providing this information on the exact location of His second coming. He spoke of the end time while on the Mount of Olives. And, in the end time, *"His feet shall stand in that day upon the Mount of Olives..."* There is nothing secret about any of this!

The reason for Jesus' second coming is to do away with the old and establish the new, to abolish all the kingdoms and governments of the earth and to establish a new government under Jesus' absolute authority. It is to implement the 1000 year Sabbath in God's 7000 year plan. It's not about a secret gathering of the elect. It's about a period of 1000 years *on earth* during which time the government of Jesus rules all mankind and enables the world to flourish and experience unparallelled rest and peace. It is a time when Satan is not even present on earth to cause chaos:

Revelation: **...And he laid hold of the dragon...Satan... and bound him for a thousand years...that he should deceive the nations no more until the thousand years should be finished:**

Satan has been present on earth since the time before Adam and Eve, and he has served to corrupt and deceive mankind for 6000 years. But as man's 6000 year period of time grinds to a halt in destruction and tumult, and God's 1000 years of peace prevails, Satan will be bound and gagged and prevented from deceiving the nations for the entire span of Jesus' earthly government.

Revelation: **And when the *thousand years* are finished, Satan shall be loosed out of his prison.**

As we continue to examine passages in the Bible, we come

to understand that Jesus' government will be established on earth, and that it will consist of Jesus as the supreme ruler and head of the hierarchy. Under Jesus, all of those people who were resurrected from the dead or who were changed at His coming will also reign. They will all reign and rule together as one perfect, worldwide government under Jesus.

Revelation: **...they lived, and *reigned* with Christ a *thousand years*. The rest of the dead lived not until the *thousand years* should be finished.**

The above passage summarizes two very important points. One, that the resurrected dead--and those who changed--will live and *reign* with Jesus for 1000 years. And two, that the *rest* of the dead, those who died without following or believing on Jesus during their lifetimes, would not be resurrected at the second coming of Jesus. Instead, they would remain dead for the 1000 years of peace and *then* be resurrected. These facts are helpful in understanding the beginning and end events of the 1000 year period of time. At the beginning, the first resurrection of the dead occurs. During the 1000 years, men will leave in peace and prosperity. At the end, the second resurrection of the dead will occur. And again, nothing is done in secret.

There is a definite beginning and end to the 1000 year period of peace. At the beginning, Jesus comes with sound and fury and establishes His government on earth. At the end, Satan is loosed for a short time from his prison: **"...he should deceive the nations no more, until the *thousand years* should be finished: after this he must be loosed for a little time."** This is very important! At the beginning of the peaceful millenium, Jesus will come to earth and establishes His government. The nations will be present, but they will no longer be deceived by Satan. At the end of the millenium, Jesus' earthly government, and the 1000 year Sabbath, will be finished and Satan will be released from his prison for a short time. And during this short period of time, Satan will jump on the opportunity to deceive the nations once again. Upon his release, Satan will rush to the four corners of the earth and gather the peaceful nations to battle against the government of Jesus, trying once again, as he did with Adam and as he did during Jesus' first presence on earth, to overthrow the ways of God and establish his own satanic plan throughout the world. The book of Revelation discusses this short period of time at the end of the 1000 years of peace under Jesus:

Revelation: **When the thousand years are over, Satan will be released from his prison and will go out to deceive the nations in the four corners of the earth....to gather them for battle. They will march across the breadth of the earth and surround the camp of God's people, the city He loves. But fire will come down from heaven and devour them. And the devil who deceived them will be thrown into the lake of burning sulfur where the beast and the false prophet had been thrown. And they will be tormented day and night for ever and ever.**

The next few verses in the Book of Revelation discuss what will happen immediately following this event, once the thousand years are ended and Satan has been released to cause one final battle on the earth. After Satan's defeat and destruction, the rest of the dead will be resurrected for judgement and a new heaven and new earth will be created:

Revelation 20:11: **"Then I saw a great white throne.....and I saw the dead, great and small, standing before the throne.....The dead were judged according to what they had done..."**

Revelation 21:1: **Then I saw a new heaven and a new earth, for the first heaven and the first earth had passed away..."**

We need to revisit God's 7 holy days for a moment. In the seventh month of God's calendar, there are actually four of the seven holy days. In order of their observation, again, they are The Feast of Trumpets, The Day of Atonement, the Feast of Tabernacles, and the Final Day. We discussed the way in which the Feast of Trumpets and the Day of Atonement parallels Jesus' second coming and man's *at-one-ment* with God. And we have also discussed the parallel between mankind's dwelling on earth with Jesus and the Feast of Tabernacles. The final holy day, The Final Day, is likewise in direct parallel to the events mentioned in the above passages from Revelation. At the end of the 1000 years of peace, after Satan is loosed from his prison and ultimately destroyed, the last great day of God's 7000 year plan for mankind will occur. This is known as "the Great White Throne Judgement," in which all of the dead who have not yet been resurrected or changed will stand before the great white throne of God to be judged. And immediately afterwards, a new heaven and a new earth will be created as the old heaven and the old earth are permanently destroyed. This particular event marks the absolute end of God's 7000 year plan.

Notice also the way in which Revelation 20 discusses the two definite events that mark the beginning and the end of the 1000 year period of peace and, likewise, makes reference to what will become of the people who are raised from the dead--or changed--at the second coming of Jesus and who will enter the millenium of peace with Him:

Revelation 20: **I saw the souls of them that were beheaded for the witness of Jesus, and for the word of God, and which had not worshipped the beast....and they lived and reigned with Christ a thousand years....But the rest of the dead lived not again until the thousand years were finished. This is the first resurrection. Blessed and holy is he that has part in the first resurrection: on such the second death has no power, but they shall be priests of God and of Christ.**

At the beginning of the peaceful millenium, there will be a first resurrection. Jesus will return, and a portion of the dead will be resurrected to reign with Him for 1000 years. At the end of the millenium, after Satan gathers the nation for battle and is defeated, a second resurrection will occur, at which time all of the remaining dead will be raised to stand before the great white throne and be judged. The first resurrection marks the beginning of the millenium. The second resurrection marks its end. And in between, for 1000 years, Jesus will rule the nations; and those who have been resurrected or changed at His coming will serve as priests and teachers in His name. This is reflected in Revelation 1 and 5:

Revelation: ...**and from Jesus Christ, who is....the first begotten of the dead, Him that loved us and...has made us kings and priests unto God...**

Revelation: ...**and hast made us unto our God kings and priests: and we shall *reign on the earth.***

For 1000 years, the earth will be at peace under the government of Jesus. A large portion of the Bible is dedicated specifically towards a discussion of this particular time period in God's plan. The entire book of Isaiah, for example, is filled with allusions toward the peaceful period of Jesus' rule.

Now, maybe it would be wise to pause for a moment and reflect on the magnitude of what is being discussed here in this chapter. I realize that, because of the way in which traditional religious doctrines have spoken of Jesus in such heavenly and humble terms, it is unusual to visualize Him coming to earth to head a government with absolute authority. Very often, we think of Jesus as sitting in heaven, walking among the human beings who have died and gone there (a subject to dispute in a whole different book!); or we see

Jesus as the meek and mild-mannered prophet, walking about the earth 2000 years ago, with long hair and a beard, humbly carrying out the miracles and the will and manifestations of God. And in one sense, that is true. Jesus did exercise humility and a humble heart during His first presence on earth. But His second coming will not be such a humble event. When Jesus descends to the earth, His purpose will be to overturn the governments present at that time. It will be somewhat of a hosile takeover. An actual battle. A shaking of the earth. Jesus will return and shatter the governments and the kings of the earth as they stand, replacing their corrupt rule with His own authority of truth and justice:

Daniel: **And in the days of these kings shall the God of heaven set up a kingdom, which shall never be destroyed: and the kingdom shall not be left to other people, but it shall break in pieces and consume all these kingdoms, and it shall stand** *forever.*

Daniel: **...but the saints of the most High shall take the kingdom, and possess the kingdom for ever, even for ever and ever.**

Revelation: **And I saw the beast, and the** *kings* **of the earth, and their armies, gathered together to make war against Him that sat on the horse, and against His army...**

Revelation: **...And he that overcometh, and keepeth my works unto the end, to him will I give power over the nations: And he shall rule them with a rod of iron...**

The Book of Zechariah discusses Jesus fighting two battles, one at the beginning of the millenium and one at the end. **"Then shall the Lord go forth, and fight against those nations, as when He fought in the day of battle....."** We know that Jesus never fought in any battle; yet here, in

Zechariah, we see Him going forth and fighting a second battle against the nations. This is the battle at the end of the millenium when Satan, loosed from his prison, gathers the nations for war. And Zechariah makes reference that this would be similar to **"when He fought in the *day* of battle...."** Of course, the day of battle, as represented by God's holy day, the Day of Atonement, is the day of Jesus' second coming, the day in which Jesus returns to earth and overthrows the acting kingdoms and governments of that time. It will be a hostile takeover, a grand scale replication of the scene in which Jesus threw the money-changers out of God's temple. In this new scene, he will be throwing the decision-makers out of their controlling positions throughout God's earth. And he will replace them all with Himself. And after Jesus removes these governments and establishes His own kingdom, allowing all the peoples of the earth to live in peace and prosperity and freedom, as mentioned in the Book of Micah...*the Lord shall reign over them in mount Zion.*

After the first battle and the tossing out of all worldly governments, absolute peace will exist throughout the earth. Those people who died in Christ throughout the ages and were resurrected at Jesus' return will be made of incorruptible flesh and will never again experience death. The same holds true for those who will be alive during the time of Jesus' return and who will be, in the *twinkling of an eye,* changed from corruptible to incorruptible. To these individuals, death will never again occur. However, what about the people who are non-believers? What will become of those individuals in the world who do not believe in Jesus or who do not act upon what little belief they do have? What about those people from the overthrown governments?

This gets back to what we were discussing regarding the two women grinding at the mill: one will be taken, the other will remain. The one taken will be the believer and the follower of Christ. She will be taken to meet Him in the air and descend to the earth with Him. She will be the one changed to incorruptible flesh in the twinkling of an eye. The other woman, the non-believer, will remain as she is: mortal flesh. And she will become a subject in the earthly kingdom of Jesus. The woman taken will become a member of Jesus' government, a priest or teacher, guiding the others into the ways of the Lord. Remember what the Book of Revelation says about those who will be changed or resurrected from the dead: **"...they lived, and *reigned* with Christ a thousand years..."**

The word *"reigned"* was translated from the Greek word *"basileuo,"* which means *"to be king, to exercise kingly power, to exercise the highest influence or control."* Those who have followed Jesus throughout the ages, or who are following Him at the time of His return, will be changed into incorruptible flesh to be kings and to exercise kingly powers and high influence and control over the entire earth. This control and power and influence will be over those who were *not* changed and who are still living in corruptible flesh after Christ's return.   Those who have been resurrected or changed will be rulers and priests and teachers, reigning with Jesus for 1000 years over the entire earth. They will be guiding those who have not changed, teaching them the ways of God and Jesus. Together with Jesus, they will lead nations for 1000 years. Here is some of what the Bible says about it:

Revelation: **And he that overcometh, and he that keepeth my works unto the end, to him will I give authority over the nations:**

Jeremiah: **...the son of man, who is to rule all the nations with a rod of iron...**

Revelation: **And out of his mouth proceedeth a sharp sword which he should smite the nations: and he shall rule them with a rod of iron**

119

Isaiah: **And it shall come to pass in the latter days, that the mountain of God's house shall be established on the top of the mountains, and shall be exalted above the hills; and** *all nations shall flow unto it.*

Isaiah: **For I know their works and their thoughts: the time cometh, that I will gather all nations and tongues; and they shall come, and shall see my glory.**

Jeremiah: **At that time they shall call Jerusalem the throne of Jehovah (God); and all the nations shall be gathered unto it....neither shall they walk any more after the stubbornness of their evil heart.**

These passages indicate that Jesus will set up his throne on earth and, with his followers, will rule the nations *ON EARTH.* This is so very important to know and understand. With the year 2000 A.D. and the start of a new millenium, there have been dozens and dozens of people coming to the forefront of the media, and in books, and in the churches, all continuing to make great noise about the "secret rapture," the great whisking away of God's people to heaven. As I have been writing this book, I have heard the rapture discussed at least 20 times on TV. There is a church down the street from where I live that has placed a sign out in its front lawn. One side reads: "Where Will You Be During The Rapture?" The other side reads, "Will You Be Taken in the Rapture?" And I get frustrated when I drive by the sign because I know around which passages they have been constructing their incorrect beliefs, and I secretly wish that they would just open their Bibles and read all of the other verses. Verses like these:

Micah: **But in the last days it shall come to pass, that the mountain of the house of the Lord shall be established in the top of the mountains, and it shall be exalted above the hills; and people shall flow unto it. ....And** *many nations* **shall come, and say, 'Come, and let us go up to the moun-**

tain of the Lord, and to the house of the God of Jacob; and He will teach us of His ways, and we will walk in His paths'..... And He shall judge among many people, and rebuke strong *nations afar off*; and they shall beat their swords into plowshares, and their spears into pruninghooks: *nation shall not lift up a sword against nation, neither shall they learn war any more*.....But they shall sit *every man under his vine* and under his fig tree; and none shall make them afraid: for the mouth of the Lord of hosts has spoken it......For all people will walk every one in the name of his god, and we will walk in the name of the Lord our God for ever and ever...

.....in that day, saith the Lord, I will assemble her that halteth, and I will gather her that is driven out, and her that I have afflicted;....And I will make her that halted a remnant, and her that was cast far off *a strong nation*: *and the Lord shall reign over them in mount Zion* from henceforth, even forever.

Zepphaniah: **For then will I return to the people a pure language, that they may all call upon the name of the Lord to serve Him with one consent.**

Zechariah: **...And the Lord shall be king over all the earth: in that day shall there be one Lord, and His name one. ....All the land shall be turned as a plain... and it shall be lifted up, and *inhabited*....And men shall dwell in it, and there shall be no more utter destruction...**

This all takes place after the second coming of Jesus and during the 1000 years of peace on earth. Jesus will assign positions of authority to all His followers and appoint them to rule the nations with Him, to *reign* with Him *on earth*. There is nothing here about a secret rapture or about God's people being whisked away in secret. This is the time of the Tabernacles, the 1000 year long Sabbath day. The day of rest on earth. A time without the presence of Satan in which all the earth is allowed to rest and grow abundant. This will be a time in which the earth grows as beautiful as what is generally visualized as the Garden of Eden.

Jesus will return to earth as He pointed out in the parable recorded by Luke. The story behind the parable parallels Jesus' resurrection and ascension into heaven and His ultimate return:

Luke: **A nobleman went into a far country to receive for himself a kingdom, *and to return*.....**

At the time when Jesus returns, the earth will be in shambles. As Jesus stated Himself, if those particular days were allowed to continue, no flesh would be saved. But Jesus will return at that time and save the earth from destruction. Then, when His government is founded on earth and His followers are appointed positions of power and authority over all nations, He will restore all things and the earth will be allowed to flourish and prosper and become more beautiful than ever before. Jesus will restore the entire earth:

Acts: ...**Jesus Christ, whom the heavens must receive until the time of *restitution of all things*...**

As Jesus establishes His 1000 year long government on earth, everything will be restored and will, in fact, flourish beyond any measurement of the past. There will no longer be wars or violence or murders or diseases. The sick will be healed. People inflicted with physical and mental impairments will be made whole again. There will be absolute peace and beauty and wellness throughout the world. It will be a time of the *restitution of all things*. Deserts will blossom and bring forth water and beauty. Animals will be gentle. People will be gentle. It will be a time of unsurpassed peace and beauty, of Paradise on earth!

Isaiah: ...The wolf and the lamb shall feed together, and the lion shall eat straw like the ox... They shall not hurt nor destroy in all my holy mountain....And the nursing child will play by the hole of the cobra, and the weaned child will put his hand on the viper's den.

Isaiah: Then the eyes of the blind shall be opened, and the ears of the deaf shall be unstopped. ....Then shall the lame man leap...and the tongue of the dumb sing: for in the wilderness shall waters break out, and streams in the desert.....

Isaiah: The wilderness and the solitary place shall be glad for them; and the desert shall rejoice, and blossom as the rose....It shall blossom abundantly...

Isaiah: ...In that day shall the branch of the Lord be beautiful and glorious, and the fruit of the earth shall be excellent...

Isaiah: ...And the parched ground shall become a pool, and the thirsty land springs of water...And a highway shall be there, and a way, and it shall be called The way of holiness; the unclean shall not pass over it; but it shall be for those: the wayfaring men......No lion shall be there, nor any ravenous beast shall go up thereon, it shall not be found there; but the redeemed shall walk there.....

Isaiah: ...And the ransomed of the Lord shall return and come to Zion with songs and everlasting joy upon their heads: they shall obtain joy and gladness, and sorrow and sighing shall flee away......And it shall come to pass in the last days, that the mountain of the Lord's house shall be established in the top of the mountains, and shall be exalted above the hills; and all nations shall flow unto it.....And many people shall go and say, Come ye, and let us go up to the mountain of the Lord, to the house of the God of Jacob; and he will teach us of his ways, and we

**will walk in his paths: for out of Zion shall go forth the
law, and the word of the Lord from Jerusalem.**

Isaiah: ....**And he shall judge among the nations, and
shall rebuke many people: and they shall beat their
swords into plowshares, and their spears into pruninghooks: nation shall not lift up sword against nation,
neither shall they learn war any more......**

The new millenium will be one of pure peace, tranquility,
and happiness. It will be a time of rest. And we have been
given the opportunity to glimpse into this time of rest and
peacefulness well in advance: our weekly Sabbath, the 7th
day of each week, has been established as a symbol to help
us understand the spirit of this peaceful time period. Work
for 6 days; rest for 1. Rule civilization for 6 milleniums;
rest for 1. Each week, we can rest and rejoice in the 1000
years to come. It will begin with the coming of Jesus, and
it will end with Satan's release from his prison and the gathering of the nations to battle against Jesus and the saints at
Jerusalem, a battle in which Jesus will conquer Satan and
abolish him for eternity, and which will mark the last moments of God's 7000 year plan. After it is over, the old
earth and the old heaven will pass away, and there will be a
new heaven and a new earth and an eternity in front of us to
do whatever else God has planned.

Chapter 5

Signs of the End Time

So much has been written and speculated upon throughout history regarding the time of the end. Each generation from Jesus' time on earth to the present day has guessed that the end would come during their lifetimes. The apostles thought that they would live to see it. Citizens of 14th century Europe felt that they were about to witness it as the bubonic plague (black death) swept across the land. The two centuries of Christian crusades were certainly fueled by an observable degree of end time zeal. As Hitler's troops invaded Poland in 1939, pangs of fear regarding the end time swept around the planet. The turn of the first millenium after Christ's death brought about a high level of speculation, and the approach of the turn of the second millenium--2000 A.D.--has also been accompanied by speculation.

I have made a diligent attempt to avoid speculation in this book; it is just too easy and too unfounded. I have not relied on any conjured up wivestales of man, nor made mention of the false prophesies of well-known false prophets like Nostradamus and Edgar Cayce. Instead, I have brought forth only biblical references and have invited all readers of this book to open their own Bibles and explore what God has given to us for undisputed answers. And this approach continues to be my intention as we discuss the signs of the end time as foretold by Jesus and many other prophets throughout the Bible.

By the biblical references we have examined so far, we have learned that, starting with the creation of Adam and Eve, God has set forth before mankind a 7000 year plan. The first six thousand of these years would be allocated to man to do *his* works, and the final one thousand years would be allocated to Jesus to do *His* works. We have seen that approximately 2000 years have passed between Adam and Abraham, another 2000 between Abraham and Jesus, and another 2000 from Jesus to the present day. We can conclude that we are, therefore, close to the end of the first 6000 years of the plan. We have also learned that God established a seven day week and seven annual holy days to condition us and help us understand His plan as it unfolds. These were also present for all the generations prior to us that speculated on the end time; however, during our present age of information and increased knowledge, and our 2000 years of additional perspective, we can better understand the parallels designed between the week, the holy days, and the plan.

We have also learned by examining the Bible that Jesus will return at the end of the 6000 years to set up a government on earth that will last 1000 years. It will be a government of justice and righteousness and of peace and restitution. The other man-made governments will topple at His coming. Jesus will come in glory and triumph, overthrowing world governments and policies of corruption and chaos; and establishing His own reign of absolute authority, assigning positions of power and responsibility to the resurrected dead and those of the living who changed *in a twinkling of an eye* at His coming. Satan will be thrown into prison for 1000 years, and pure beauty and tranquility will exist on earth for the entire span of Jesus' reign.

This information is not man-made fantasy or tall tales told by an idiot. It doesn't come from the annals of the occult, or from the false-prophetic verses of Nostradamus. It's not a Hollywood movie script. It's not fiction. It comes from the words of Jesus and the prophets and has been written down and available for centuries in the Bible.

And such is the case with the signs of the end time. Much of the Bible, I would estimate approximately one quarter of it, speaks directly to the events surrounding the time of the end. It is often referred to as just that: the time of the end. Or the end time. Or the Day of the Lord. Or the Ancient of Days. Almost all of the prophets refer to it in some capacity. Read the Books of Isaiah, Jeremiah, Ezekiel, Daniel, Joel, Amos, Obadiah, Micah, Zephaniah, Zechariah, and Malachi. Read the 4 Gospels in the New Testament and the Book of Revelation. These books are filled with prophesies concerning the end time.   And once a reader understands the concepts of dual events and *"...a little bit here, a little bit there...,"* these prophesies become much clearer to understand. We will examine some of these prophesies in this chapter.

The best place to start when seeking signs of the end time and the second coming of Jesus is with the words of Jesus Himself. As most readers of the Bible know, the four Gospels--Matthew, Mark, Luke, and John-- are very inclusive of Jesus words. In most Bibles, those words appear in red. The Book of Revelation is also inclusive of Jesus' words; in fact, the Book of Revelation, although written by John, was actually "...**the revelation *of* Jesus Christ....**" And in both places, the Gospels and the Book of Revelation, much is revealed in terms of what will occur throughout the world in the time of the end.

The best way for us to begin is to first examine passages in three of the four Gospels--Matthew, Mark, and Luke--which are known as the synoptic Gospels, meaning that they are very similar to one another in their content. As mentioned earlier, Matthew 24, Mark 13, and Luke 21 all tell of the same event which occurred on the Mount of Olives when Jesus addressed His disciples concerning the end time and Jesus' second coming. The three passages are presented here in their entirety:

Matthew 24: **And as He sat upon the mount of Olives, the disciples came unto him privately, saying, Tell us, when shall these things be? and what shall be the sign of thy coming, and of the end of the world? And Jesus answered and said unto them, Take heed that no man deceive you. For many shall come in my name, saying, I am Christ; and shall deceive many. And ye shall hear of wars and rumours of wars: see that ye be not troubled: for all these things must come to pass, but the end is not yet. For nation shall rise against nation, and kingdom against kingdom: and there shall be famines, and pestilences, and earthquakes, in divers places. All these are the beginning of sorrows. Then shall they deliver you up to be afflicted, and shall kill you: and ye shall be hated of all nations for my name's sake. And then shall many be offended, and shall betray one another, and shall hate one another. And many false prophets shall rise, and shall deceive many. And because iniquity shall abound, the love of many shall wax cold. But he that shall endure unto the end, the same shall be saved. And this gospel of the kingdom shall be preached in all the world for a witness unto all nations; and then shall the end come. When ye therefore shall see the abomination of desolation, spoken of by Daniel the prophet, stand in the holy place, (whoso readeth, let him understand:) Then let them which be in Judaea flee into the mountains: Let him**

which is on the housetop not come down to take any
thing out of his house: Neither let him which is in the
field return back to take his clothes. And woe unto them
that are with child, and to them that give suck in those
days! But pray ye that your flight be not in the winter,
neither on the Sabbath day: For then shall be great
tribulation, such as was not since the beginning of the
world to this time, no, nor ever shall be. And except
those days should be shortened, there should no flesh be
saved: but for the elect's sake those days shall be shortened. Then if any man shall say unto you, Lo, here s
Christ, or there; believe it not. For there shall arise false
Christs, and false prophets, and shall shew great signs
and wonders; insomuch that, if it were possible, they
shall deceive the very elect. Behold, I have told you before. Wherefore if they shall say unto you, Behold, he is
in the desert; go not forth: behold, he is in the secret
chambers; believe it not. For as the lightning cometh out
of the east, and shineth even unto the west; so shall also
the coming of the Son of man be.......Immediately after
the tribulation of those days shall the sun be darkened,
and the moon shall not give her light, and the stars shall
fall from heaven, and the powers of the heavens shall be
shaken: And then shall appear the sign of the Son of
man in heaven: and then shall all the tribes of the earth
mourn, and they shall see the Son of man coming in the
clouds of heaven with power and great glory. And he
shall send his angels with a great sound of a trumpet, and
they shall gather together his elect from the fou winds,
from one end of heaven to the other. Now learn a parable
of the fig tree; When his branch is yet tender, and putteth forth leaves, ye know that summer is nigh: So likewise ye, when ye shall see all these things, know that it is
near, even at the doors.

Mark 13: And as He sat upon the mount of Olives over
against the temple, Peter and James and John and An-

drew asked him privately, Tell us, when shall these things be? and what shall be the sign when all these things shall be fulfilled? And Jesus answering them began to say, Take heed lest any man deceive you: For many shall come in my name, saying, I am Christ; and shall deceive many. And when ye shall hear of wars and rumours of wars, be ye not troubled: for such things must needs be; but the end shall not be yet. For nation shall rise against nation, and kingdom against kingdom: and there shall be earthquakes in divers places, and there shall be famines and troubles: these are the beginnings of sorrows. But take heed to yourselves: for they shall deliver you up to councils; and in the synagogues ye shall be beaten: and ye shall be brought before rulers and kings for my sake, for a testimony against them. And the gospel must first be published among all nations. But when they shall lead you, and deliver you up, take no thought beforehand what ye shall speak, neither do ye premeditate: but whatsoever shall be given you in that hour, that speak ye: for it is not ye that speak, but the Holy Ghost. Now the brother shall betray the broher to death, and the father the son; and children shall rise up against their parents, and shall cause them to be put to death. And ye shall be hated of all men for my name's sake: but he that shall endure unto the end, the same shall be saved. But when ye shall see the abomination of desolation, spoken of by Daniel the prophet, standing where it ought not, (let him that readeth understand,) then let them that be in Judaea flee to the mountains: And let him that is on the housetop not go down into the house, neither enter therein, to take any thing out of his house: And let him that is in the field not turn back again for to take up his garment. But woe to them that are with child, and to them that give suck in those days! And pray ye that your flight be not in the winter. For in those days shall be affliction, such as was not from the beginning of the creation which God created unto this time, neither shall be. And except that the Lord had

shortened those days, no flesh should be saved: but for th
elect's sake, whom he hath chosen, he hath shortened the
days. And then if any man shall say to you, Lo, here is
Christ; or, lo, he is there; believe him not: For false
Christs and false prophets shall rise, and shall shew signs
and wonders, to seduce, if it were possible, even the elect.
But take ye heed: behold, I have foretold you all things.
But in those days, after that tribulation, the sun shall be
darkened, and the moon shall not give her light, And the
stars of heaven shall fall, and the powers that are in
heaven shall be shaken. And then shall they see the Son
of man coming in the clouds with great power and glory.
And then shall he send his angels, and shall gather together his elect from the four winds, from the uttermost
part of the earth to the uttermost part of heaven. Now
learn a parable of the fig tree; When her branch is yet
tender, and putteth forth leaves, ye know that summer is
near: So ye in like manner, when ye shall see these things
come to pass, know that it is nigh, even at te doors.

Luke 21: And they asked him, saying, 'Master, but when
shall these things be? and what sign will there be when
these things shall come to pass?' And he said, Take heed
that ye be not deceived: for many shall come in my name,
saying, I am Christ; and the time draweth near: go ye
not therefore after them. But when ye shall hear of wars
and commotions, be not terrified: for these things must
first come to pass; but the end is not by and by. Then
said he unto them, Nation shall rise against nation, and
kingdom against kingdom: And great earthquakes shall
be in divers places, and famines, and pestilences; and
fearful sights and great signs shall there be from heaven.
But before all these, they shall lay their hands on you,
and persecute you, delivering you up to the synagogues,
and into prisons, being brought before kings and rulers
for my name's sake. And it shall turn to you for a testimony. Settle it therefore in your hearts, not to meditate

before what ye shall answer: For I will give you a mouth
and wisdom, whic all your adversaries shall not be able
to gainsay nor resist. And ye shall be betrayed both by
parents, and brethren, and kinsfolks, and friends; and
some of you shall they cause to be put to death. And ye
shall be hated of all men for my name's sake. But there
shall not an hair of your head perish. In your patience
possess ye your souls. And when ye shall see Jerusalem
compassed with armies, then know that the desolation
thereof is nigh. Then let them which are in Judaea flee
to the mountains; and let them which are in the midst of
it depart out; and let not them that are in the countries
enter thereinto. For these be the days of vengeance, that
all things which are written may be fulfilled. But woe
unto them that are with child, and to them that give
suck, in those days! for there shall be great distress in
the land, and wrath upon this people. And they shall fall
by the edge of the sword, and shall be led away captive
into all nations: and Jerusalem shall be trodden down of
the Gentiles, until the imes of the Gentiles be fulfilled.
And there shall be signs in the sun, and in the moon, and
in the stars; and upon the earth distress of nations, with
perplexity; the sea and the waves roaring; Men's hearts
failing them for fear, and for looking after those things
which are coming on the earth: for the powers of heaven
shall be shaken. And then shall they see the Son of man
coming in a cloud with power and great glory. And
when these things begin to come to pass, then look up,
and lift up your heads; for your redemption draweth
nigh. And he spake to them a parable; Behold the fig
tree, and all the trees; When they now shoot forth, ye
see and know of your own selves that summer is now nigh
at hand. So likewise ye, when ye see these things come to
pass, know ye that the kingdom of God is nigh at hand.

Through these three similar Gospel chapters, Jesus has indicated some very specific signs that will assist His followers in knowing that His second coming--and the beginning of His kingdom--are about to occur. In addition, He sets up somewhat of a chronological timeline that will serve as further assistance. And in each Gospel, with the parable of the fig tree, the message is clear that the signs will be able to be observed and that, when we see them unfolding, we can rest assured that the end is right at the door.

By combining the three Gospels regarding Jesus own words, we can make a list of the signs that will immediately precede the second coming of Jesus. These signs are as follows:

1. Wars and rumors of wars

2. Nations rising against nation

3. Famines

4. Pestilences (defined as "*destructive, infectious, swiftly spreading disease.*")

5. Earthquakes in various places

THEN

6. The martyrdom of saints

7. The coming of false prophets and people claiming to be Jesus

8. Intensified cold heartedness in the world

9. Betrayal of one another and discord between children and parents

10. The Gospel preached in all the world

11. The abomination of desolation (which is discussed in the Book of Daniel)

12.*" Jerusalem compassed with armies,"* at which time we can *" then know that the desolation thereof is nigh..."*

12. More False Christs

THEN....*After* the Above Tribulation

13. Signs in the sun and moon and stars. The sun and moon darkened and the stars falling off. Heaven shaken.

THEN

14. The second coming of Jesus.

With a quick glance at the list, one can see an outline of gradual deterioration in the conditions of the world. First of all, there will be *wars and rumors of wars*, which have been prevalent throughout history and which will continue in greater proportions. As we look around the world today, we can see wars and skirmishes and "**commotions**" occurring in many regions. We will continue to see "*nation rising against nation*" as the end of our 6000 years draws nearer. Next, there will be famines: agricultural and sociological conditions which serve to perpetrate great hunger and death; and pestilences: infectious, swiftly spreading diseases that will cause worldwide sickness and death. The Book of Revelation discusses all three of the above conditions of the earth as the end approaches.

Revelation: **And I looked, and behold a pale horse: and his name that sat on him was Death.....and power was given unto them over the fourth part of the earth, to kill with *sword*, and with *hunger*, and with *plague*...**

The wars and famines and pestilences that Jesus spoke of in the three Gospels will cause death to one quarter of the earth. As we look back on the wars of the past, or on the black death in fourteenth century Europe, we know that those events did not kill off one fourth of the world's population. But as the end time approaches, and conditions grow continually worse, the likes of which have not been seen "...*since the beginning of the world to this time, no, nor ever shall be...*" wars and starvation and diseases will start to take a global toll, wiping out billions of people in a relatively short time.

It is hard to imagine a time period on earth that will be filled with such devastation and disaster. One quarter of the world's population will be destroyed by wars and starvation and infectious diseases. The resulting social tumultuousness will most likely provoke global panic. People will be dying off around the world. Millions and millions of people will starve to death, or becoming infected with diseases that medicine can no longer cure. Wars and bombings will claim the lives of millions more. The world at that time will, mostly likely and understandably, begin looking for some type of supernatural intervention, turning to God and seeking His help and guidance in the face of all the chaos. It would be a world very vulernable to religious zealotry. Debates and wars may rise up over appropriate religious practices and beliefs.. And, without understanding the way in which Jesus will return to earth, many of these people may fall pray to false prophets and individuals claiming to be Jesus Himself.

Looking back at the list, we can see that all three Gospels tell of the martyrdom of the saints; that is, people who believe in the ways and commandments of Jesus being put to death for their convictions. And as we read this, we may wonder how it could possibly happen that the people in the world today could be put to death, or stand back and watch the executions of believers in Jesus who are being executed solely on the grounds of their religious beliefs. Would we not, as a society, step forward to stop such absurdity? Would we not understand that prophesies were being fulfilled right before our eyes and step forward to bring about

the salvation of our culture? A few comments on this:
first, the execution of saints has taken place throughout history; but most importantly to remember is that Jesus Himself
was stoned and persecuted when He spoke out against the
world religions of His day. It seems logical that a world in
utter chaos would be even more susceptible to the persecution of opposing voices of traditional religiou beliefs. A
world in tribulation and chaos may turn to religious doctrine
for an answer. It may look for signs or for leaders to come
forward and make sense of all the despair and disasters run-
ning rampant throughout the earth.. But, as Jesus foretold,
there would be a martyrdom of all the saints *and* the coming
of false prophets and people claiming to be Jesus:

*...For false Christs and false prophets shall rise, and shall
show signs and wonders, to seduce, if it were possible,
even the elect...*

*...for many shall come in my name, saying, I am Christ;
and the time is drawing near: therefore, do not go after
them...*

As death and disease and wars and hunger begin to run
rampant throughout the world, false Christs and false
prophets will arise and *seduce* the world into believing in
them. Millions and millions of people without knowledge of
Jesus' own words regarding these false prophets will fall
prey to them. Through great signs and wonders, these false
prophets will be believable enough to seduce *"even the
elect"* if it were possible. World conditions will be such
that the minds of mankind will be fair game to such great
deceit. The Apostle Paul describes this deception clearly in
The Second Book of Corinthians and The Second Book of
Thessalonians:

2 Corinthians: **I am afraid that your minds will be corrupted and that you will abandon your full and pure de-
votion to Christ, in the same way that Eve was deceived
by the serpent's clever lies. For you gladly tolerate any-**

one who comes to you and preaches a different Jesus...and you accept a spirit and a gospel completely different from the Spirit and the gospel you received from
us... well, no wonder! Even Satan can disguise himself to
look like an angel of light! So it is no great thing if his
servants disguise themselves to look like servants of righteousness.

2 Thessalonian: ...Concerning the coming of our Lord
Jesus Christ and our being gathered together to be with
Him: I beg you, my friends, not to be so easily confused
in your thinking or upset by the claim that the Day of the
Lord has come..... do not let anyone deceive you in any
way....for the Day will not come until the final rebellion
takes place and the wicked one appears, who is destined
to hell. He will oppose every so-called god or object of
worship and will put himself above them all. He will even
go in and sit down in God's Temple and claim to be
God.... At the proper time, then, he will come with the
power of Satan and perform all kinds of false miracles
and wonders, and use every kind of wicked deceit on
those who will perish. They will perish because they did
not welcome and love the truth so as to be saved. And so
God sends the powerful deception to work in them so
that they believe what is false....

Satan, who cleverly and quickly deceived Eve in the Garden
of Eden will, as the above passage states, "*use every kind of
wicked deceit*" to deceive the people's of the earth during
the time of the end. And it will be successful! He will lend
his power to the "wicked one" who will "*perform all kinds
of false miracles and wonders.*" A world in awe will believe in the miracles and follow the "wicked one" and his
powersource, Satan.

As individuals of an intellectual society living in the information age, we may wonder how one person could deceive

an entire world into turning away from God and following after false miracles and wonders created of an earthly presence. On the surface, it seems we would know enough as a culture to analyze the big picture, make sound conclusions, and figure out that we were, in reality, being deceived. But note this statement: *He will even go in and sit down in God's Temple and claim to be God....* The world may be openly deceived and led away from God because the presence creating all the miracles and wonders is *claiming to be God.*

Think for a moment of some ways in which Satan has practiced deception in the past. To Eve, who had been given everything, he promised wisdom and knowledge and the opportunity to be *like* God. When Jesus came up from His baptism and went into the wilderness for 40 days knowing full well of his earthly mission, Satan came to Him with verses of scripture and promises of power. Jesus, as a human, had been fasting for 40 days and was weak and hungry. Satan tried to seize upon His moment of weakness by scrambling God's words in ways that would be beneficial to Jesus at the moment. Satan basically said, "Hey, look, you're the Son of God, you haven't eaten for 40 days and you're hungry; here are some stones, turn them to bread." He also offered Jesus all the kingdoms of the world; which both Jesus and Satan knew that Jesus would eventually receive anyway.

The point is that Satan approached both Eve and Jesus with crafty salesmanship, catering to their hungers and their human instincts. Eve didn't have the knowledge of God; Satan deceived her in going against God's word by promising her such knowledge. Jesus, as a human being, was hungry and famished; Satan promised Him fulfillment and worldly power for giving into His human weakness. Eve was defeated. Jesus prevailed.

In a world in which wars and famines and earthquakes and diseases have rocked the very foundation of every human being on the planet, the need for spiritual intervention and earthly miracles would be very great. The people of the world would be extremely empty and spiritually famished inside, seeking help and salvation and an end to all the madness. They would be calling out for God. The stage would be set for the appearance of someone claiming to be God. The human spirit is weak in its relationship to God in the first place. Think of how the Israelites under Moses, after having the Red Sea part in front of them and bread appear on the ground for food in the desert, so easily turned into constructing a golden calf to replicate their version of what God would look like. How much greater would the falling away from truth be in the midst of world chaos and confusion. It is, in reality, not such a large step to understand the way in which the world could follow after a false god, especially one who is filled with the power of Satan and who is performing miracles and wonders and claiming to *be* God.

Jesus' prophecies regarding the end time are clear. Wars, Famine, Hunger, and Earthquakes. Rapidly speeding, deadly diseases. The coming forth of false prophets and false Christs . The martyrdom of the saints. Children and parents betraying one another. Cold heartedness in the world. Chaos and confusion and deceitfulness. A picture is painted of a world civilization in rapid decline. With one glimmer of hope: "**...the gospel of the kingdom shall be preached in all the world for a witness unto all nations...**" or as it was recorded by Mark: "**...the gospel must first be** *published* **among all nations...**"

There is an age old argument regarding just what this gospel is that will be preached and published throughout the nations. The word "*gospel*" is translated from the Greek word "*eujaggevlion,*" which means "*good news*" or "*good tidings.*" So, in Jesus' foretelling of the end time, He states, in essence, that the "*good news of the kingdom*" shall be preached and published unto all nations. The "good news" that Jesus Himself preached was just that: the "**good news**

of the kingdom" of God. The age old argument regarding this "*good news*" looks something like this: One school of thought believes that the publishing of the Gospels of Matthew, Mark, Luke, and John has fulfilled this prophesy. The other school of thought believes that those 4 particular Gospels were merely reflections of the "good news" about Jesus Himself and not of the kingdom of God.

Throughout the New Testament, the gospel is referred to as "the gospel of Jesus Christ (14 times)," "the gospel of God (6 times)" "the gospel of the kingdom (4 times)," the gospel of the grace of God (once)." "the gospel of His son (once)" "the gospel of peace (once)," and a few other assorted references such as "the gospel unto Abraham" and "the gospel of uncircumcision."

The main argument is focused primarily on the belief that the Gospels of Matthew, Mark, Luke, and John were merely gospels *about* Jesus, "good news" about Jesus; whereas the gospel which would be preached unto all nations would be the gospel *of* Jesus; that is, the "good news" that Jesus Himself preached regarding the kingdom of God.

In one case, the prophesy has been fulfilled. In the other case, the prophesy *has not* been fulfilled because the gospel of the "kingdom," which relates to the coming kingdom of God manifested through the 1000 year government of Jesus on earth, has been pretty much diluted and distorted--and oppressed--through traditional religious doctrines and rapture theories. The "good news" *about* Jesus is widely published and known. But the "good news" of the kingdom of God, although as equally and as widely published, is not thoroughly preached nor understood. So the debate continues to teeter between the two factions.

I am not taking the side of either argument here; I feel it is an unnecessary higgling of semantics that only serves to confuse sincere seekers of the truth who get sucked into it. The point I see Jesus making is that, amidst the chaos and deterioration of the world through the compilation of wars and diseases and disasters, the "good news" will continue to flourish and be presented to all nations of the earth. And all of mankind will have the opportunity to hear and either accept or reject the good news. Therefore, the second coming of Jesus and the end of the world as we know it will be fair. *ALL NATIONS* will have had the opportunity to hear the good news; so, at the end time, there won't be some estranged continent of people standing there in awe saying, "what's this all about? Jesus who?" The gospel will be preached **...in all the world for a *witness* unto all nations; and then shall the end come.**"

It should be noted here that the word "*witness*" in this statement was translated from the Greek word "*maturvrion,*" which means "*testimony.*" And the English definition of the word "testimony" means "a solemn declaration" or "evidence." So basically, Jesus is stating that the good news will be preached in all the world as a *testimony* (solemn declaration and evidence) "**... unto all nations; and *then* shall the end come.**" It is pointless to get caught up in the "gospel *about* Jesus or the gospel *of* Jesus argument." The point is that all nations will have the opportunity to hear and read the declaration of the good news and decide upon whether or not they accept or reject it based on their own system of beliefs. All peoples of the earth will have a fair chance to believe in Jesus and follow His ways, and then the end will come. And those who have accepted the good news and have believed in Jesus and have lived according to His ways will "*...live and reign with Him for 1000 years.*"

Although the first part of Jesus' words to His disciples on the Mount of Olives cannot necessarily be attached to any certain chronology in terms of which happens first and second and third etc., they can all collectively be acknowledged as occurring before the events in the second and third parts of His prophesy. In other words, we can determine which *group* of events will happen at the *beginning* of the end, which will happen in *the middle*, and which will happen *in the closing moments* of the end. Jesus outlines this chronology very clearly for us. Worldwide wars and famines and diseases, which are said to be "*the beginning of sorrows*," or as interpreted in some translations, "*the beginning of birth pains,*" will happen first. After these events, the martyrdom of the saints together with the appearances of false prophets and the worldwide preaching of the gospel will happen, as will the ***abomination of desolation,*** which we will discuss shortly. After those events, there will be signs in heaven such as the blackening of the sun and moon and the falling off of the stars. Immediately following those events in the heavens, Jesus will return.

So, we have discussed the beginning of sorrows: wars and rumors of wars, famines, earthquakes, and diseases. After those horrors upon the earth, the surgence of false prophets and the martyrdom of the saints, which we have also briefly discussed, will be prevalent. The next very visible sign, and one about which Jesus gives extensive warning, is... "***the abomination of desolation, spoken of by Daniel the prophet.***" To understand this sign, we need to first go to the Book of Daniel and see what the prophet says about an "*abomination of desolation*":

Daniel 9: **...and to the end there shall be war; desolations are decreed.... and on the wing of the temple (the ruler) shall set up an abomination that causes desolation, until the end that is decreed is poured out on him....**

Daniel 11: **...forces from him (the ruler) shall appear and profane the temple and fortress...and they shall set up the abomination that causes desolation...**

By reviewing the above two passages, we know that the *abomination of desolation* will be something that is *set up* by a *ruler.*

The Book of Daniel was written in Hebrew, and the word *"abomination"* was translated from the Hebrew word *"shiqquwts,"* which means *"detestable things"* and *"detestable idols."* The root word of *"shiqquwts"* generally referred directly to an idol which God detests, something that is placed as an object of worship instead of God. The word *"abomination"* was translated from the Hebrew word *"shamem,"* which means *"astonished, wasted, ruined, appalled."* So, in speaking of the *"**abomination of desolation**,"* Daniel was speaking of *"detestable things or idols"* which cause *"ruin"* or *"astonishment."*

The Gospels were written in Greek. The word *"abomination"* there was translated from the Greek word *"bdelugma,"* meaning *"a foul thing"* or *"a detestable thing."* The word *"desolation"* was translated from the Greek word *"eremosis,"* which means *"ruined,"* or *"wasted."* So, in essence, when Jesus mentioned the *"**abomination of desolation**,"* He was talking about the *"detestable thing"* that causes *"ruin"* as mentioned by Daniel, the prophet. This detestable thing that causes ruin will be, as recorded in the Gospel of Mark: *"**standing where it ought not.**"* And this will be a sign of the end time. Let's look at the phrase from Mark once again:

...But when you shall see the abomination of desolation, spoken of by Daniel the prophet, *standing where it ought not*, (let him that readeth understand,)...

When speaking of the abomination that causes desolation, the detestible thing to God which causes ruin, Daniel was discussing the building and the destruction of a temple in Jerusalem, and primarily of the *restoration* of a temple in Jerusalem. He was speaking of a ruler with forces who will set up a *"detestable thing"* that causes *"ruin"* in relation to a temple. This ruler--and the temple--are also spoken of in the Second Book of Thessalonians:

2 Thessalonians: **He** (the ruler) **will even go in and sit down in God's Temple and claim to be God.**

In another book I wrote simultaneous to this one, entitled **666: The Beast Revealed**, I thoroughly examine the beasts and the horns and the "*little horn*" discussed in Daniel 7 along with its counterpart, the "*lamb/dragon horn*" in Revelation 13. I briefly discuss the same in Chapter's 6,7, and 8 of *this* book, **The Signs.** To avoid being redundant by reexplaining the "*little horn*" and the "*lamb/dragon horn*" and all of their implications here, please allow me to just suffice it by saying now that both of these symbols relate to a false religion--a false "Christianity"--through which world governments have been dominated and influenced in the past, and through which governments of the future will also be dominated. From this false "Christianity," a ruler will arise, an antichrist or, as it is defined by its Greek root-word, an "*adversary of Christ.*" He will occupy a temple and *set up* an abomination of desolation where it ought not be. He will, as we just read in First Thessalonians, "*even go in and sit down in God's Temple and claim to be God.*"

The place in which God's temple has always been established is in Jerusalem. When the *ruler*--or antichrist--sets up the abomination of desolation, it will be in Jerusalem. As we read earlier, "**...on the wing of the temple (the ruler) shall set up an abomination that causes desolation...**" This is speaking of God's temple, in which the ruler will "*even go in and sit down in God's Temple and claim to be God.*" And an interesting statement regarding this temple and the abomination of desolation that should not go overlooked is the line stating that it will be "*standing where it ought not.*"

Think of this one statement for a moment. If a person is standing, say, on a new carpet while wearing muddy shoes, one might say, *"you're standing where you ought not."* The implication is that the person is standing in the wrong place and that there is a different place to stand. If Joe is standing atop a painted X on the sidewalk, and Mary knows that a piano is about to drop out of the sky onto that X, Mary could say, "you ought not stand there," implying that the X is the wrong place to stand and that another place would be more suitable. The point here is that the phrase *"standing where it ought not"* implies that there is a *different* place to stand. And since this statement was given to us as a sign, it stands to reason that this abomination of desolation, this idol and temple, would be standing in a place that we would recognize as being out of place; that is, that the temple and idol "ought not be there" but somewhere else..... "over there."

To use another comparison, suppose we trekked to Alaska one day and saw the Statue of Liberty standing out in the middle of a snow covered pasture. We would immediately recognize, of course, that this statue was *"standing where it ought not."* We know that it is supposed to be standing in New York Harbor. Or to put it another way, suppose we had been told to go to Alaska and look around for something *"standing where it ought not."* We could go there and walk around the entire state for months upon months and never see anything unusual. But the instant we saw the Statue of Liberty standing out in the middle of that snowy pasture, we would go, "Ah HA!" and know immediately that we found what we were looking for. Because we know that the Statue of Liberty is *"standing where it ought not,"* that it should be standing back in New York Harbor.

Jesus gave us this particular sign of the abomination of desolation, and He was very careful to bring it to our attention: **"...you shall see the abomination of desolation, spoken of by Daniel the prophet, standing where it ought not, *(let him that readeth understand)...*** In other words, *"you will see this detestable thing--this temple and idol-- standing in a place where you know it doesn't belong. (if you are read-*

ing this, understand)... "

We know by reading other biblical verses that the abomination of desolation--the temple and idol--will be standing in Jerusalem; and *readers* throughout the world who *understand* will know that it ought not be standing there, that it should be standing somewhere else. And when we see this, Jesus instructs us as to what to do next. **"then let them that be in Judaea flee to the mountains."** In other words, when you recognize this thing that's out of place, *standing where it ought not*, those that are in Judea should flee to the mountains and, basically, head for the hills because **"...for in those days shall be affliction, such as was not from the beginning of the creation unto this time, nor ever shall be..."**

Remember the tribe of Judah? They were the only ones left behind in the promised land when the other tribes of Israel were booted out. In their land, even to this day, Jerusalem remains. And that is why they are told directly to flee when they see this abomination of desolation. It's right in their back yard! The temple and idol will be set up right in Jerusalem, where it will be out of place and *"standing where it ought not."* The readers that understand will know that it's *standing where it ought not*, that it should be standing somewhere else and is therefore out of place; and when they recognize this they are instructed to head for the hills because great, unparalleled affliction is about to be unleashed upon the area.

Now, let's go back to discuss the *"little horn"* and the *"lamb/dragon horn"* from which the "ruler" or antichrist will arise. As I mentioned, and as we will discuss in later chapters and in my book **666: The Beast Revealed**, the *little horn* and the *lamb/dragon horn* are both the same thing, which is the powerful, government-controlling religion that will be present during the end time, and which has actually been present on earth for centuries.

Think for a moment. Which religion in the world today would we recognize as being out of place or *"standing where it ought not"* if it were to build a temple in Jerusalem? Remember, the phrase standing *where it ought not"* implies that it should be standing somewhere else, that we would recognize it as being out of place if it stood in Jerusalem. Like the Statue of Liberty whose home is recognized as New York Harbor, and which would be out of place anywhere else in the world, which powerful world religion has its own home and would be recognized as out of place if it were housed in any other place in the world?

A world religion? Powerful? Exercised authority of government in the past? Recognized worldwide as having it's own home-base or temple? Would be out of place and *"standing where it ought not"* if relocated to Jerusalem? Very likely to construct an idol in this new temple?

Only one religion fits that description, and that's the Catholic religion, the papacy which has forever been established in Rome. The "desolation of abomination" is the establishment of a Catholic temple--or a Christian temple under the papacy's control--in Jerusalem. It will be a Catholic/Christian temple *"standing where it ought not"* in Jerusalem instead of, or in addition to, Rome. The Roman Empire has historically been known as a "divided empire" because of its east and west presence in the region. This division will continue as the *desolation of abomination* will involve the extended presence of Rome in the east—in Jerusalem— through the establishment of a "Christian" temple in which an idol will be set up. The ruler--antichrist--will *"sit down in God's Temple and claim to be God."* It will be a time of great anarchy in the world. A time when famine and diseases and wars have shaken the very foundation of the earth. When false prophets and false Christs will arise. A time that will get progressively worse as disastrous events continue to unfold, one after another.

The Gospel of Luke also speaks of the time during the abomination of desolation:

"...And when ye shall see Jerusalem compassed with armies, then know that the desolation thereof is near..."

The temple and idol set up in Jerusalem will *cause* desolation. Jesus talked of the *"abomination of desolation spoken of by Daniel the prophet,."* and Daniel spoke of *"the abomination that causes desolation"* It is a detestable thing before God, an idol, which causes desolation. And in his Gospel, Luke records Jesus' words that tell us *"...when you see Jerusalem compassed with armies, then know that the desolation thereof is near..."* In other words, when this sign is present, when we see armies surrounding Jerusalem, we should know that the destruction of that area is very near. And from that point, the Gospels are very concise as to what the people in that area should do next:

Matthew: **...Then let them which be in Judaea flee into the mountains: Let him which is on the housetop not come down to take any thing out of his house:** (in other words, move quickly!) **Neither let him which is in the field return back to take his clothes. And woe unto them that are with child, and to them that give suck in those days! But pray ye that your flight be not in the winter, neither on the Sabbath day: For then shall be great tribulation, such as was not since the beginning of the world to this time, no, nor ever shall be. And except those days should be shortened, there should no flesh be saved: but for the elect's sake those days shall be shortened.**

Luke: **...And when you shall see Jerusalem compassed with armies, then know that the desolation thereof is nigh. Then let them which are in Judaea flee to the mountains; and let them which are in the midst of it depart out; and let not them that are in the countries enter**

thereinto. For these be the days of vengeance, that all things which are written may be fulfilled. But woe unto them that are with child, and to them that give suck in those days! For there shall be great distress in the land and wrath upon this people. And they shall fall by the edge of the sword, and shall be led away captive into all nations: and Jerusalem shall be trodden down of the Gentiles, until the times of the Gentiles be fulfilled.

Jerusalem will be trodden down and turned desolate by the *Gentiles*. It will be a *time* of the Gentiles. The word *"Gentile"* is defined as *"heathen"* and *"pagan"* and most accurately as *"those who are not of Israeli descent."* Many believe that this definition includes the United States and Great Britain; but as we have seen earlier, the United States and Great Britain *are* of Israeli descent. Jerusalem will not be trodden down by these countries. Note that the word *"pagan"* is also found in this definition of Gentiles, a term which is most readily associated with "pagan Rome." The armies that will surround Jerusalem may be of Roman origin. Or Rome may occupy Jerusalem and other Gentile armies will surround the city. The point is this: if Rome is involved, and if the temple and the idol are set up in Jerusalem. And if Gentile armies are surrounding the city, it's time for those in the area to flee. *Because the desolation thereof is nigh.*

Now it's time to revisit the rest of the signs offered by Jesus on the Mount of Olives. As the abomination of desolation is sitting in Jerusalem as a gigantic symbol for all those who understand, and more false Christs arise, the utter desolation of Jerusalem is at hand. People are told to flee because those people of that area are going to be trodden and killed (*"fall by the sword"*). Then, after that destruction and annihilation of the peoples of Judaea, all three gospels are specific about what will happen next:

Matthew: **But in those days, *after that tribulation*, the sun**

shall be darkened, and the moon shall not give her light,
And the stars of heaven shall fall, and the powers that
are in heaven shall be shaken. And then shall they see
the Son of man coming in the clouds with great power
and glory

Mark: **But in those days, after that tribulation, the sun
shall be darkened, and the moon shall not give her light,
And the stars of heaven shall fall, and the powers that
are in heaven shall be shaken. And then shall they see
the Son of man coming in the clouds with great power
and glory.**

Luke: **...And there shall be signs in the sun, and in the
moon, and in the stars; and upon the earth distress of
nations, with perplexity; the sea and the waves roaring;
Men's hearts failing them for fear and for looking after
those things which are coming on the earth: for the powers of heaven shall be shaken. And *then* shall they see
the Son of man coming in a cloud with power and great
glory**

After the tribulation of that time, during the time of the
Gentiles, when the Gentile troops surrounding Jerusalem
devastate the city, and inhabitants of that place are told to
flee to the mountains in a hurry;, and mere anarchy is loosed
upon the entire world as men's hearts fail for fear, THEN
will there be signs in heaven: changes in the moon and the
sun and the stars. And THEN, "*shall they see the Son of
man coming in a cloud with power and great glory.*" That
is the moment when Jesus will return to earth.

The Bible has provided the world with many detailed signs
concerning the time of the end. Through the words of Jesus
and the prophets, the signs are extremely comprehensive.
When they are read in tandem with other prophesies in the
Bible, and when they are approached with the "*little bit*

here, little bit there" principle, the entirety of God's plan and the ways in which the end time will unfold--and why-- becomes easier to see and understand. Jesus shows us the temple and the idol and instructs us to understand.

My hope is that all readers of this book will merely use the words and passages I have presented here as a springboard into a more detailed study of the Bible. The signs and the truths are all there; and it is simply not necessary to be in the dark regarding the time of the end. The Bible offers extensive detail regarding the chaotic climax that will accompany the end of mankind's 6000 year rule. Listen to the teachings of Jesus. Study the words of the prophets. Together they give us all of the answers; and as world events begin to unfold before our very eyes, we can all rely on these words and teachings for understanding. And we can be relieved to know the truth, and stand ready to act on that truth.

Chapter 6

Important: The Books of Daniel and Revelation

In the study of biblical prophesy, the two most important and pivotal books are the Book of Daniel and the Book of Revelation. The Book of Daniel, appearing in the Old Testament, was written by the prophet Daniel, a descendent of the tribe of Judah who was held in captivity after Babylon's seize of Jerusalem. The Book of Revelation is the final book of the New Testament and was written by the apostle John through visions that were revealed to him by Jesus. Both books offer up independent prophesies; however, both must be read in tandem with each other to interpret each other's symbols. Whereas the Book of Revelation presents prophesy in a very symbolic and abstract manner, Daniel's primary prophetic mission was to interpret dreams and their symbols as they related to prophesy and to clarify them. Revelation serves up symbolism; Daniel defines symbolism and brings it into clearer focus and definition. Consequently, many of the symbols offered in Revelation are interpreted and defined in the Book of Daniel, which was written approximately 600 years earlier. In fact, some of the symbols in

Revelation cannot be interpreted *without* the Book of Daniel. It is only through the use of *both* of these books that interpretations can be found and symbols in Revelation can be understood.

The Book of Daniel and the Book of Revelation should be read together, flip-flopping back and forth to connect images and create a clear understanding of the symbols used in both books. In this chapter, we will do just that: look at the Book of Daniel and the Book of Revelation together and arrive at clear interpretations of some pivotal and important symbols in each.

Beginning in the second chapter of Daniel, an extremely vital prophesy is offered that gives a clear picture of the kingdoms that would exist on earth between the time of the Babylonian empire and the coming of Jesus. The chapter begins with King Nebuchadnezzar calling upon his magicians and wise men to interpret a dream that he had. The catch was, however, that he would not tell the wise men the dream; instead, they were to tell him what he had dreamed and then interpret it. The magicians simply could not do it, and Nebuchadnezzar grew so enraged that he ordered the execution of all the wise men in Babylon. This order of execution included Daniel who, although imprisoned, had established himself as a wise man who could understand visions and dreams of all kinds. Upon hearing of his ordered execution, Daniel asked for time to interpret the dream, which he was granted. He then prayed to God for understanding and was indeed given understanding of the dream. The next day he went to Nebuchadnezzar, told him what he had dreamed, and proceeded to interpret the king's dream:

Daniel: **Your Majesty, in your dream you saw standing before you a giant statue, bright and shining, and terrifying to look at. Its head was made of the finest gold; its chest and arms were made of silver; its waist and hips of bronze, its legs of iron, and its feet partly of iron and** partly of clay. While you were looking at it, a great stone broke loose from a cliff without anyone touching it, and it struck the iron and clay feet of the statue, and shattered them.

At once the iron, clay, bronze, silver, and gold crumbled and became like the dust on a threshing place in summer. The wind carried it all away, leaving not a trace. But the stone grew to be a mountain that covered the whole earth.

This was the dream. Now I will tell Your Majesty what it means.

Your Majesty, you are the greatest of all kings. The God of heaven has made you emperor and given you power, might, and honor. He has made you ruler of all the inhabited earth and ruler over all the animals and birds. *You are the head of gold.*

After you there will be another empire, not as great as yours, and after that a third, an empire of bronze, which will rule the whole earth. And then there will be a fourth empire, as strong as iron, which shatters and breaks everything. And just as iron shatters everything, it will shatter and crush all the earlier empires.

You also saw that the feet and the toes were partly clay and partly iron. This means that it will be a divided empire. It will have something of the strength of iron, because there was iron mixed with the clay. The toes—partly iron and partly clay—mean that part of the empire will be strong and part of it weak.

You also saw that the iron was mixed with the clay. This means that the rulers of that empire will try to unite their families by intermarriage, but they will not be able to, any more than iron can mix with clay.

At the time of those rulers the God of heaven will establish a kingdom that will never end. It will never be conquered, but will completely destroy all those empires and then last forever. You saw how a stone broke loose from a cliff without anyone touching it and how it struck the statue made of iron, bronze, clay, silver, and gold. The great God is telling Your Majesty what will happen in the future.

The king said, "Your God is the greatest of all gods, the Lord over kings, and the one who reveals mysteries. I know this because you have been able to explain this mystery."

Daniel not only told Nebuchadnezzar an accurate account of what the king had dreamed, he interpreted it. He outlined the nature of the image which the king had visualized in his dream: *"...a giant statue.... Its head of the finest gold; its chest and arms of silver; its waist and hips of bronze, its legs of iron, and its feet partly of iron and partly of clay..."* and then Daniel went on to tell the king the most pivotal element of the dream. Daniel told Nebbuchadnezzar, *"You are the head of gold."*

Through the interpretation of the king's dream, Daniel told Nebuchadnezzar of the 4 great kingdoms that would rule on the earth, beginning with the king's own empire, Babylon. *"You are the head of gold."* The head of gold symbolized Babylon, and it was followed by the other parts of the body, other kingdoms. History shows that Babylon fell to Medo-Persia in 539 B.C., and that the Medo-Persian empire was then consumed by the Greek empire established by Alexander the Great. After Babylon, Medo-Persia, and Greece came a fourth empire which consumed all remnants of the other three: *" And then there will be a fourth empire, as strong as iron, which shatters and breaks everything. And just as iron shatters everything, it will shatter and crush*

all the earlier empires. "
History shows that this prophesy was fulfilled by Rome in 63
B.C. So the four empires represented by the tall statue in
Nebuchadnezzer's dream were: Babylon...... Medo-
Persia.........Greece.........and Rome.

Now, the perplexing thing is that Daniel tells of how "...*at
the time of those rulers the God of heaven will establish a
kingdom that will never end...*" and that God's kingdom
would *"destroy all those empires and then last forever...*"
As we have already discussed, Jesus will return and overthrow the existing kingdoms and governments present during the end time. But here, in Daniel 2, by outlining the 4
successive kingdoms beginning with Babylon, Daniel alludes to Babylon, Medo-Persia, Greece, and finally to the
Roman Empire, which would consume all three kingdoms
but which would also be present when the God of Heaven
established His kingdom.

We know today that the Roman Empire does not exist during our time. But here, once again, is where the principle of
"dual events" is clearly at work. Jesus first came to earth as
a human being during the time of the Roman Empire. It
was in existence at that time! Therefore, in a small sense,
Daniel's prophesy has already been fulfilled: when Jesus
came out of his 40 days of fasting, after defeating the deceitful temptation of Satan, he proclaimed, *"the kingdom of
God is at hand!"* Jesus was the victor against Satan and
therefore was in a position to establish the kingdom of God.
The Roman Empire was in existence; the kingdom was established. These two predictions had, in a small sense, been
fulfilled; however, the kingdom of God, at that time, did not
yet destroy all of the other empires. In fact, the Roman Empire eventually crucified Jesus. The "dual" aspect--the 2nd,
greater fulfillment of the prophesy--had not yet come. It *is*
yet to come.

We will later discuss how the Roman Empire will be in existence again on the earth during the second coming of Jesus. But first, let's look at some additional prophesies of Daniel to gain further understanding and insight into the world empires as the relate to the past and the future. Whereas in Daniel 2 the dream of Nebuchadnezzar was interpreted, in Daniel 7, the prophet Daniel himself had his own vision. In a dream, he saw:

Daniel 7: ...Four huge beasts came up out of the ocean, each one different from the others. The first one looked like a lion, but had wings like an eagle. While I was watching, the wings were torn off. The beast was lifted up and made to stand up straight. And then a human mind was given to it.

The second beast looked like a bear standing on its hind legs. It was holding three ribs between its teeth, and a voice said to it, "Go on, eat your fill of flesh!"

While I was watching, another beast appeared. It looked like a leopard, but on its back there were four wings, like the wings of a bird, and it had four heads. It had a look of authority about it.

As I was watching, a fourth beast appeared. It was powerful, horrible, terrifying. With its huge iron teeth it crushed its victims, and then it trampled on them. Unlike the other beasts, it had ten horns.

While I was thinking about the horns, I saw a little horn coming up among the others. It tore out three of the horns that were already there. This horn had human eyes and a mouth that was boasting proudly.

While I was looking, thrones were put in place. One who had been living forever sat down on one of the thrones. His clothes were white as snow, and his hair was like pure wool. His throne, mounted on fiery wheels, was blazing with fire, and a stream of fire was pouring out from it. There were many thousands of people there to serve him, and millions of people stood before him. The court began its session, and the books were opened.

While I was looking, I could still hear the little horn bragging and boasting. As I watched, the fourth beast was killed, and its body was thrown into the flames and destroyed. The other beasts had their power taken away, but they were permitted to go on living for a limited time.

During this vision in the night, I saw what looked like a son of man. He was coming with the clouds of heaven. He approached the Ancient of Days and was led into his presence. He was given authority, honor, and sovereign power, so that the people of all nations, races, and languages would serve him. His authority would last forever, and his kingdom would never end.

In this vision, Daniel saw four beasts: the first like a lion with wings of an eagle. The second a bear with ribs between his teeth. The third was like a leopard with four wings on its back. And the fourth beast had ten horns and iron teeth that crushed its enemy; it was unlike the other beasts. And among its horns a little horn arose. Daniel was confused by the vision and asked God for help in interpreting it:

Daniel: **I went up to one of those standing there and asked him to explain it all. So he told me the meaning. He said, 'These four huge beasts are *four empires* which will arise on earth. But the saints of the Most High will receive the kingdom and possess it forever and ever.'**

We have already read Daniel 2 and know that the head of the image dreamed by Nebuchadnezzar was a symbol of Babylon, after which three other kingdoms would arise, we can begin to see similarities in the beasts of Daniel 7 and the image in Daniel 2. The fact is that both visions are identical. The head of gold in Daniel 2 is the lion in Daniel 7 (Babylon). The chest of silver in Daniel 2 is the bear in Daniel 7 (Medo-Persia). The belly of bronze in Daniel 2 is the leopard in Daniel 7 (Greece). And the legs of iron in Daniel 2 is the terrifying beast in Daniel 7 (Rome). If you flip-flop between the chapters, you can note the similarities in both visions. Daniel 2 and Daniel 7 are talking about the same kingdoms that will arise on earth. Daniel 7 is more explicit in that it describes the fourth beast as having ten horns and a "*little horn*." Daniel wants to know more about the fourth beast and the horns and the little horn. Daniel 7 continues:

Daniel 7: ...**Then I wanted to know more about the fourth beast, which was not like any of the others—the terrifying beast which crushed its victims with its bronze claws and iron teeth and then trampled on them. And I wanted to know about the ten horns on its head and the horn that had come up afterward and had made three of the horns fall. It had eyes and a mouth and was boasting proudly. It was more terrifying than any of the others. While I was looking, that horn made war on God's people and conquered them. Until the Ancient of Days came and pronounced judgement in favor of the saints of the Most High, and the time came when they possessed the kingdom.**

This is the explanation I was given:

"The fourth beast is a fourth empire that will be on the earth and will be different from all other empires. It will crush the whole earth and trample it down. The ten horns are ten kings who will rule that empire. Then another king will appear; he will be very different from the earlier ones and will overthrow three kings. He will speak against the Supreme God and oppress God's peo-

ple. He will try to change their religious laws and festivals, and God's people will be under his power for three and a half years. Then the heavenly court will sit in judgment, take away his power, and destroy him completely. The power and greatness of all the kingdoms on earth will be given to the saints of the Most High. Their sovereign power will never end and all rulers on earth will serve and obey them."

The fourth beast is a fourth empire upon the earth. The ten horns are ten kings who will rule that empire. Our knowledge of history tells us that never in the history of the world has ten kings ruled one kingdom simultaneously; therefore, the ten kings must be ten successive kings, kings which come one after another throughout history.

We know from Daniel 2 that the fourth kingdom is Rome because, as Daniel told Nebuchadnezzer, "*You are that head of gold,*" referring to Babylon, after which three other kingdoms would follow in succession: Medo-Persia, Greece, and Rome, each one devouring the preceding kingdoms. As we look at the beasts in Daniel 7, we see the same scenario: four kingdoms, the fourth of which is destroyed by Jesus' kingdom; however, in Daniel 7 we learn that the fourth beast will have 10 successive kings.

So, by reading Daniel 2 and Daniel 7 together, we understand that there will be 4 empires upon the earth beginning with Babylon. Daniel 7 gives us these kingdoms in the form of beasts, the fourth of which has 10 horns, or 10 successive kingdoms. And note again, the beasts in Daniel 7. A lion, a bear, a leopard, and a terrifying beast with ten horns. Now, before we go further, let's jump ahead to the Book of Revelation for a moment, to Chapter 13:

Revelation 13: **And I saw a beast coming up out of the sea, having *ten horns*, and seven heads, and on his horns ten crowns, and upon his heads names of blasphemy.**

161

And the beast which I saw was like unto a _leopard_, and his feet were as the feet of a _bear_, and his mouth as the mouth of a _lion_, and the dragon gave him his power, and his throne, and great authority.

The beast in Revelation 13, the infamous beast with the mark 666, is the exact same beast as described in Daniel 7. The lion, the bear, the leopard, and the ten horns are all present. But note that Daniel 7 described 4 beasts, whereas Revelation 13 describes one; and it happens to be the one with the ten horns, the fourth beast. Remember, the four beasts in Daniel 7 came one after another, devouring the ones before them. Medo-Persia consumed Babylon. Greece consumed Medo-Persia. And Rome devoured Greece. It actually crushed and devoured the remnants of the other three empires, which we see in Daniel 2 as well: "_.it will shatter and crush all the earlier empires._"

So, in Revelation 13, we see this fourth beast, with characteristics of the other three (like a leopard with the mouth like a lion and feet like a bear). But just as Daniel 2 and Daniel 7, through their linear description of the beast, point to the fourth empire as the Roman Empire, the beast in Revelation 13 is depicting just that: the Roman Empire. It is the empire from which 10 successive kings will arrive, the one which 10 horns are present.

The Bible is amazing in that it so neatly works "..._a little bit here, a little bit there...._" to offer a crystal clear interpretation of itself. Revelation 13 read alone, without references to Daniel 2 and 7, might lead one to believe the beast is some enraged animal loosed upon the earth in the end time. Or a deformed man. Or something else completely off base. But once it is mirrored with Daniel 7, we know it is a kingdom. And once we read them both with Daniel 2, where we are oriented to Babylon and 3 kingdoms which will follow in succession, we know that the beast in Revelation 13 is talking about Rome, or more specifically, the Roman Empire.

Now we can read the remainder of Revelation 13 and find out more about the Roman Empire. In fact, as you read the following passage, substitute the word "beast" or the word "him," both of which I have underlined, with the word "Roman Empire" and see if this passage begins to make more sense to you:

Revelation 13: **And I saw one of his heads as though it had been smitten unto death; and his deadly wound was healed: and the whole earth wondered after the beast; and they worshipped the dragon, because he gave his authority unto the beast; and they worshipped the beast, saying, Who is like unto the beast? And who is able to war with him?**

And there was given to him a mouth speaking great things and blasphemies; and there was given to him authority to continue forty and two months. And he opened his mouth for blasphemies against God, to blaspheme His name, and His tabernacle, even them that dwell in the heaven. And it was given unto him to make war with the saints, and to overcome them: and there was given to him authority over every tribe and people and tongue and nation. And all that dwell on the earth shall worship him, every one whose name hath not been written from the foundation of the world in the book of life of the Lamb that hath been slain. If any man hath an ear, let him hear. If any man is destined for captivity, into captivity he shall go: if any man shall kill with the sword, with the sword must he be killed. Here is the patience and the faith of the saints.

And I saw another beast coming up out of the earth; and he had two horns like unto lamb, and he spake as a dragon. And he exerciseth all the authority of the first beast in his sight. And he maketh the earth and them

dwell therein to worship the first <u>beast</u>, whose deadly blow had been healed. And he does great signs, that he should even make fire to come down out of heaven upon the earth in the sight of men.

And he deceives them that dwell on the earth by reason of the signs which it was given him to do in the sight of <u>the beast</u>; saying to them that dwell on the earth, that they should make an image to <u>the beast</u> who hath the *stroke of the sword* and lived. And it was given unto him to give breath to it, even to the image of <u>the beast</u>, that the image of <u>the beast</u> should both speak, and cause that as many as should not worship the image of <u>the beast</u> should be killed.

And he causeth all, the small and the great, and the rich and the poor, and the free and the bond, to receive a mark on their right hand, or upon their forehead; and that no man should be able to buy or to sell, unless he that has the mark, or the name of <u>the beast</u> or the number of <u>his</u> name.

Here is wisdom. He that has understanding, let him count the number of <u>the beast</u>; for it is the number of a man: and <u>his</u> number is six hundred and sixty and six.

Still confused? That is understandable, and exactly why I have dedicated a single chapter in this book and an entire other book (**666: The Beast Revealed**) to an in-depth look at the beast. It is truly a fascinating journey as one begins to unravel the mystery of the beast. But for our purpose right now, in this chapter, we need to understand that by all accounts the beast mentioned in Daniel 7 and Revelation 13 is the Roman Empire.

Notice one item before we move on. In the above passage, in reference to "the beast" or "the Roman Empire," we learn that the beast had a deadly wound and was healed. We are shown *"the beast who had the <u>stroke of the sword</u> and lived."* The Bible often uses the term *"sword"* or the phrase *"fall by the sword"* to depict a battle or a war. "Falling by the sword," means "losing a battle" or "losing a war" or "being conquered." We learn that the beast had *"the stroke of the sword,"* or that it *"lost a war"* or *"was conquered,"* but that it lived. This gives us further insight into the beast, or the Roman Empire. In 476 A.D., the Roman Empire was conquered in what has been known throughout history as the fall of Rome. It was restored, however, 78 years later, in 554 A.D., under the emperor Justinian. The beast did, indeed, receive *"the stroke of the sword and lived."* For over three-quarters of a century, the Roman Empire, after its defeat and subsequent fall, found itself under the ruling government of three successive barbarian entities: the Vandals, the Heruli, and the Ostrogoths. When the Empire was finally resurrected and placed back in control under Justinian, the words of Revelation 13 are echoed loud and clear:

"...and he (the second beast) **makes the earth and them that dwell therein to worship the** *first beast***, whose deadly blow had been healed."**

"...the beast who had the *stroke of the sword* **and lived..."**

These are only two of many strong indications that the beast mentioned in both Daniel and Revelation is, in fact, the Roman Empire. Many more pieces of evidence can be found, examined, and analyzed throughout the pages of th Bible.

Let's go back to Daniel 7 and look at one more characteristic of the beast: *"...He will speak against the Supreme God and oppress God's people. <u>He will try to change their religious laws and festivals</u>."* (In some Bibles, this is read "change laws and times," which means the very same thing.) Remember God's festivals? His holy days? His calendar? These were all changed by the Roman Empire. As a culture, we don't celebrate the Passover, the Feast of Un-leavened Bread, The Feast of Tabernacles, the Day of Atonement, etc. Those were God's festivals, but they have been *changed* for us. Instead of celebrating those God-given festivals, our culture now celebrates Christmas, Easter, etc., all celebrations rising out of the pagan-based Roman Empire. God's laws and festivals were changed to Roman laws and festivals. Likewise, God's calendar began in the month of March/April with the month of Abib. The Roman/Julian calendar, which the whole world follows, begins in the middle of winter, in January. God's Sabbath was celebrated on the last day of the week, on Saturday, the 7th day. Under the Roman Empire, the day of worship was *changed* to Sunday, the 1st day of the week.

Look at the churches of today; look at the "Roman Catholic" church. The largest percentage of these churches (excluding only a few) hold services on Sunday, acknowledging it as the day of worship. And remember also, the observation of the Sabbath was not a mere festival or day of worship: it was the LAW of God. It was written as the 4th commandment: *"Remember the Sabbath...."* No other empire in the history of the world has changed God's laws and festivals like the Roman Empire.

So, to put it into perspective: Daniel 2 and 7 talk about 4 empires that will rule on earth: Babylon, Medo-Persia, Greece, and Rome. The fourth empire will not be like the other three. It will change God's laws and festivals and have 10 successive kings--or kingdoms-- that will spring out of it. We know this empire to be Rome. In Revelation 13, we see the same fourth beast, the Roman Empire, which, again, has 10 successive kings that rise out of it. These three books--Daniel 2, Daniel 7, and Revelation 13-- reviewed together paint a very clear picture. The Roman Empire is the beast of Revelation 13, the beast whose number is 666. We must read "...*a little bit here, a little bit there*..." to understand this.

Let's jump forward to Revelation 17 in which we see further evidence of the beast and kings and horn. This time, however, a prostitute is added to the picture:

Revelation 17: **Then one of the seven angels...came to me and said, "Come, and I will show you how the famous prostitute is to be punished, that great city that is built near many rivers. The kings of the earth fornicated with her, and the people of the world became drunk from drinking the wine of her immorality."**

The Spirit took control of me, and the angel carried me to a desert. There I saw a woman sitting on a red beast that had names insulting to God written all over it; the *beast had seven heads and ten horns*. The woman was dressed in purple and scarlet, and covered with gold ornaments, precious stones, and pearls. In her hand she held a gold cup full of obscene and filthy things, the result of her immorality. On her forehead was written a name that has a secret meaning: "Great Babylon, the mother of all prostitutes and the abominations of the earth."

And I saw that the woman was drunk with the blood of the saints and the blood of those who were killed because they had been loyal to Jesus. When I saw her, I was completely amazed. "Why are you amazed?" the angel asked me. "I will tell you the secret meaning of the woman and of the *beast* that carries her, *the beast with seven heads and ten horns.*

That beast was once alive, but lives no longer; it is about to come up from the abyss and will go off to be destroyed. (This references a period in the end time when "the beast," or the Roman Empire, will once again be resurrected and will go off to be destroyed by Jesus at His second coming.) **The people living on earth whose names have not been**

167

written before the creation of the world in the book of
the living, will all be amazed as they look at the beast. It
was once alive; now it no longer lives, but it will reap-
pear.

This calls for wisdom and understanding. The seven
heads are seven hills, on which the woman sits. They are
also *seven kings*: five of them have fallen, one still rules,
and the other one has not yet come; when he comes, he
must rule only a little while. And the beast that was
once alive, but lives no longer, is itself an eighth king
who is one of the seven and is going off to be destroyed.

"The *ten horns you saw are ten kings who have not yet
begun to rule, but who will be given authority to rule as
kings for one hour with the beast.* These ten all have the
same purpose, and they give their power and authority to
the beast. They will fight against the Lamb; but the
Lamb, together with His called, chosen, and faithful followers, will defeat them, because He is Lord of lords and
King of kings."

The angel also said to me, 'The waters you saw, on which
the prostitute sits, are nations, peoples, races, and languages. The ten horns you saw and the beast will hate
the prostitute; they will take away everything she has
and leave her naked; they will eat her flesh and destroy
her with fire......"The woman you saw is the great city
that rules over the kings of the earth.'

The recurring theme in the Books of Daniel and Revelation
is the beast, with 10 horns, seven heads; and now, in Revelation 17, a woman sits on the beast and becomes *"drunk
with the blood of the saints."* The Roman Empire executed
millions of "saints" because of their refusal to submit to its
official religion. In the Bible, a prostitute, or sometimes just
a woman, is often symbolic of a church or a religion. The
prostitute riding the beast is a religion which had become a

part of the beast. Understanding this, terms such as "Roman Catholic" and "Holy Roman Empire" start to have a clearer, more crystallized meaning. And the fact that the beast is the Roman Empire begins to become more and more evident.

Back to the Book of Daniel, in the 8th chapter we see references to the Medo-Persian and Greek empires. Daniel has a vision of a ram and a goat. The ram made war with the west and north and south. After great destruction, the goat made war against the ram and was victorious. Daniel asked for understanding of the vision, and a being named Gabriel gave him the interpretation:

Daniel 8: **And it came to pass, when I, even I Daniel, had seen the vision, that I sought to understand it; and, behold, there stood before me as the appearance of a man. And I heard a man's voice.....which called and said, 'Gabriel, make this man understand the vision.' So he came near where I stood....and said.....'Behold, the ram which you saw that had two horns, they are *the kings of Media and Persia*. And the rough he-goat is the *king of Greece*: and the great horn that is between his eyes is the first king...."**

In the 11th chapter of Daniel, we actually hear of Medo-Persia and Greece. We have seen Babylon, under Neb-uchadnezzer, as the first empire. Now we see Medo-Persia and Greece, the second and third empires. It is only logical, in the historical scope that we as a civilization know to be fact, that the fourth Empire--the beast--is indeed the Roman Empire.

Daniel 11: **...Behold, there shall stand up yet three kings in *Persia*; and the fourth shall be far richer than them all: and by his strength through his riches he shall stir up all against the realm of *Greece*...**

The Book of Daniel is pivotal to end time prophesy because it is very specific about kingdoms and battles. It specifically names Babylon, Medo-Persia, and Greece, and alludes to the Roman Empire both in its original state and in its end-time state. The 10th, 11th, and 12th chapters of Daniel follow Medo-Persia's consumption by Greece, the intervention of Rome, and the end-time Roman Empire which will wage war with the saints. The 12th chapter opens up with a verse concerning the angel Michael, and also with an allusion to the resurrection of the dead during the end time:

Daniel 12: ...**And at that time shall Michael stand up, the great prince which standeth for the children of God's people: and there shall be a time of trouble, such as never has been since there was a nation even to that same time: and at that time the people shall be delivered, every one that shall be found written in the book. And many of them that sleep in the dust of the earth shall awaken...**

The twelfth chapter of the Book of Daniel alludes to the same end time prophecies as Jesus gave on the Mount of Olives. After the kingdoms of the earth are defeated, including the Roman Empire which will be present and active at that time, Jesus will return to earth and gather his elect from the four winds. *"..them that sleep in the dust of the earth shall awaken..."* It will immediately follow the tribulation which, as Daniel writes here and which Christ mentions on the Mount of Olives, will be *"...a time of trouble, such as never has been since there was a nation even to that same time...."*

Although many of Daniel's prophecies were fulfilled by the time Jesus had begun His ministry on earth, the "dual events" element of these prophesies made them all significant to the end time. We see this in Revelation 13, in Jesus' own prophesies on the Mount of Olives in Matthew 24, Mark 13, and Luke 21; and we see it in the concluding verses of the 12th chapter of the Book of Daniel:

Daniel: ...**But you, O Daniel, shut up the words, and seal the book, even to the time of the end: many shall run to and fro, and knowledge shall be increased....Go thy way, Daniel; for the words are shut up and sealed till the time of the end.**

The Books of Daniel and Revelation, especially Revelation 13, should not be read on their own, isolated from one another. They should be read together, referencing one another as a reader flip-flops between the two books to understand the symbolism in each. Daniel 2 should be read with Daniel 7; Daniel 7 with Revelation 13. Daniel 8 with Daniel 2, 7, 11, and 12. And the entire book of Revelation with the entire book of Daniel. In reading the Bible in this manner, one can gain a personal understanding of the prophetic symbols as they relate to the end time. And one can finally throw away man-contrived definitions and childhood myths surrounding the beast in Revelation 13. By reading these two books together, we know the beast is not a man, not an animal, not an antichrist, or not some mythical pegasus. It is the Roman Empire, which has changed times and laws and which will make war with the saints, causing widespread global havoc just prior to the second coming of Jesus Christ.

Canyon Adams

Chapter 7

The Beast in Not a Man

For some people who do not thoroughly read or study the Bible with any regularity, the beast of Revelation 13 may be their only exposure to an end-time presence that will cause chaos in the world. And as I have mentioned earlier, this presence is often thought of as being a man, an animal, a monster, an antichrist, or any number of created or invented demons borne out of the imagination of man. Most often, the beast is thought of as a sort of political or religious man who will be an antichrist and will put all true believers of God and Jesus to death. And since the numbers 666 are widely known to be associated with followers of the beast, it is often believed that the world will be forced to have these numbers tattooed on their foreheads and wrists as a sign of faithful obedience to the beast.

But let's stop and think about that for a moment. Here we are today, in the age of information. We have news programs on practically every channel on TV and radio: hundreds and hundreds of news programs with all kinds of different venues and agendas. We have newspapers available in virtually every city in the USA and in most places throughout the world. The internet has brought the entire planet and all of its information closer together, moreso than ever before in the history of the world. We have churches and religions throughout the seven continents, most of which know or have heard about the numbers 666. We have universities filled with scholars and professors; businesses and suburbs filled with thinking, logical, rational people. In the face of all this, how in the world, in all reality, could a law be passed which would ultimately lead to an entire world of people being tattooed with the numbers 666 on their foreheads and hands. Think about the absurdity of this scenario! Think of the insanity of the first news story that would hit the networks on the subject:

"Prince Badbeast of the worldwide government has declared that all citizens of the world must now be tattooed on their foreheads and their hands. Badbeast, in a statement released earlier today by his press secretary, has decreed that the numbers 666 must now be tattooed on the foreheads and the hands of every citizen on the planet Earth by April 15th of this year. Badbeast warns that after that date, any citizens not bearing the 666 tattoo on either their foreheads or their hands will not be allowed to buy or sell ...."

I mean, the thought is ludicrous when we stop to think about it. In a world of such vast amounts of information, such an event could never be possible. Collectively, we know enough about the numbers 666 to know that, if they were tattooed on our foreheads and hands, it would somehow be the "mark of Satan" mentioned in the Bible and that we should refuse. We may not understand it, but we would know that we should refuse it just because it's sitting there in plain and frightening view right in Revelation 13. Globally, there would be an uproar. Those who knew about the mark would broadcast or somehow disseminate the information to those who didn't. Church members would step forward by the millions to speak out and educate the rest of the world into resisting the mark. Political and religious advocates would be up in arms over such a violation of civil and religious rights has having a tattoo of religious consequence--or of any consequence for that matter--forced upon the flesh of human beings.

And sure, there are arguments (albeit weak ones) which can be made in belief of the possibility of such an event. "Well, people wouldn't be able to buy or sell without the mark. It says so right in the Bible." "The government-run military would enforce it, and people would be killed if they refused to have the mark." "The world will stop reading their Bibles and will forget about 666, and then the government will come in the back door and force the mark upon everybody before anybody catches on...." Etc. etc. etc. And we could go back and forth debating whether or not a worldwide decree of a 666 tattoo would ever be possible.

But the bottom line fact, however, is that the numbers 666 will not be a tattoo, or a visible mark, or anything that is placed on the flesh of human beings. It is something altogether different, something more spiritual and intangible in nature. And furthermore, as we have just discussed in the previous chapter, the beast mentioned in Revelation 13 is not a man. It is not an antichrist or a world leader. It is not a Prince Badbeast or any other human being or sub-human being that has come or will *ever* come to the earth. The beast mentioned in Revelation 13 is a *kingdom*: an empire or world government. The beast in Revelation 13 is the Roman Empire.

Let's take a look at Revelation 13 and walk through it piece by piece to analyze just what is being said here.

Revelation 13: **And I stood upon the sand of the sea, and saw a *beast* rise up out of the sea, having *seven heads* and *ten horns*, and upon his horns *ten crowns*, and upon his *heads* the name of blasphemy.**

Here, John is recording what is being revealed to him in vision. As we discussed previously, the beast he is seeing, with its seven heads and ten horns, is the Roman Empire from which 10 successive kings will arise. In order to understand the meaning of the seven heads and ten horns, we must briefly revisit Revelation 17 again:

Revelation 17: **The seven heads are seven hills, on which the woman sits. They are also** *seven kings.....***The** *ten horns you saw are ten kings who have not yet begun to rule....*

Again, we understand that the beast is not a man, but a kingdom. From this kingdom, 10 kings will arise. In addition, 7 of the kings will be "ridden" so to speak by the woman in Revelation 17, the church. In addition, we see that the beast has blasphemous names written on its head. The word blasphemous is translated from the Greek word *"blasphemia"* which means *"reproachful speech injurious to God."* The Roman Empire will speak things injurious to God. We continue with Revelation 13:

Revelation 13: **And the beast which I saw was like unto a leopard, and his feet were as the feet of a bear, and his mouth as the mouth of a lion: and the dragon gave him his power, and his seat, and great authority.**

Again, we see the beasts introduced in Daniel 7, the lion, bear, and leopard, but here they are all combined by the most powerful beast, the Roman Empire. And also in this stanza we see that the beast--the Roman Empire--is granted power and authority by Satan, the dragon.

Revelation 13: **And I saw one of his heads as it were wounded to death; and his deadly wound was healed: and all the world wondered after the beast. And they worshipped the dragon which gave power unto the beast:**

power unto the beast: and they worshipped the beast, saying, Who is like unto the beast? Who is able to make war with him?

Rome, although founded by Romulus in 753 BC, did not become a full-fledged Empire until after the military campaigns of Pompey, Crassus, and Julius Caesar. The actual beginning of the Roman "Empire" is associated with the crowning of Augustus Caesar (Julius' grandnephew) dated at approximately 31 B.C. From that date forward, the Roman Empire remained an omnipresent world empire until its fall in 476 B.C., a little over 500 years. That is twice as long as the United States has been a country. It was an all encompassing, all consuming world power that appeared as though it would never end. But when it did fall, however, in 476 A.D., it seemed as though it had been "*wounded to death.*" Other governments moved into Rome and set up their own kingdoms. The Roman Empire remained "dead" for approximately 78 years, until its restoration under Justinian in 554 A.D. In the above passage of Revelation, John is talking directly about this fall and restoration of Rome: "*one of* (the beasts) *heads* (appeared*) *wounded to death; and his deadly wound was healed.*" Once healed or restored, it then appeared that the Roman Empire would never again be conquered, that it would never be a lesser power. The world wondered after the beast and paid great tribute to its rulers, acknowledging that they stood for dominion and great strength over the world.

Incidentally, the word "*wondered*" in the above passage was translated from the Greek word "*thaumazo*" which means to "*have great admiration, admire, marveled.*" After the restoration of the Roman Empire, the world did indeed marvel and have great admiration for it. It seemed eternal and invincible.

Revelation 13: **And there was given unto him a mouth speaking great things and blasphemies; and power was**

given unto him to continue *forty and two months.*

Forty two months are equivalent to three and one half years.
Or as we have heard it expressed before, "*a time, times, and
half a time*" (1260 days). Remember that in God's prophecies pertaining to the punishments of Israel, one day is
equivalent to one year. So, in essence, we are talking not of
1260 days here, but of 1260 *years*. And the beast, once revi-
talized from the "deadly wound," was *allowed to continue*
for *1260 years*. We merely need to reflect on history and do
the math now: The Roman Empire fell in 476 A.D. and was
restored in 554 A.D. It continued to flourish through twelve
centuries and the leaderships of 5 different empire movements: Italian, Frankish, German, Austrian, and French. It
included such leaders as Charlamagne and Otto the Great,
who, upon his crowning in 962 A.D., established the Holy
Roman Empire. It continued through to Charles V and
Napoleon in 1805.

Napoleon was, of course, a French leader; however, his am-
bition and purpose were the same as the many leaders before
him; Napoleon set out to unite Europe and be the leader of
the entire Roman Empire. He failed to do so and ultimately,
through political treatise and resolutions signed among
heads of Europe, dissolved the Holy Roman Empire in 1814.
This marked the end of the Roman Empire. And here is the
math: The time that had passed from the Justinian restoration in 554 A.D. to the dissolution under Napoleon in 1814
was.......1260 years. These are the 42 months mentioned in
the Book of Revelation above. We are definitely talking
about the Roman Empire! There can be little doubt!

Throughout the 1260 years, 5 of the 7 heads which are mentioned in Revelation 13 and 17 controlled the Roman Empire. After it's demise in 1814, an attempt was made once
again to unite the continent of Europe. Garibaldi rose in
Italy to unite the Empire in 1870, and his efforts crash-
landed after 75 years with the defeat of Mussolini and Hitler

in 1945.

Many people do not understand this fact, but World War II was all about the attempted reunification of the Roman Empire. No, it may not have been referred to as the "*Roman Empire*," but Hitler stepped forward in 1939 and joined forces with Italy's Mussolini to conquer the countries of Europe, attempting to bring them all under one system of control within a Germany/Italy governing head. It was an attempt to reunify the territory that had traditionally been a part of the Roman Empire. In this manner, World War II saw the rise of the 9th horn mentioned in Daniel 7, as well as the 6th horn of Revelation 13, and the 6th head of Revelation 17.

Let's pause for a moment and take a brief, chronological look at the Roman Empire. Rome was founded by the twin brothers, Romulus and Remus prior to the time of the Babylonian Empire. It was named after Romulus. As a minor force in the scope of power and politics, Rome gradually rose to the ranks of a contending political presence under the leadership of Julius Caesar in 50 BC. At that time, there was civil unrest in Rome; and Julius Caesar extended his political might to bring the opposing forces of Pompey and Crassus together. The three of them formed what is known as a "triumvuri," a three headed governing body: Caesar, Pompey, and Crassus. While their forces conquered neighboring territories, and were defeated by others, The Roman "Empire" flourished and expanded for 80 years, gaining power and territory, until the first emperor of the Roman Empire was officially crowned.

The first Roman emperor, Augustus Caesar, was the emperor during the ministry of Jesus. By that time, Rome truly was an Empire, and Augustus Caesar was the head of the entire territory. The empire flourished for centuries and brought forth such infamous emperors as Julian, Diocletian, Valens, Theodosius, Nero, and Constantine. The military

attacks from barbaric nations, which were constant throughout the reigns of the other emperors, eventually served to
weaken the empire and, ultimately, caused it to collapse under the rule of Romulus Caesar in 476 A.D.

After the fall of the Roman Empire, three other barbaric entities, as mentioned previously, claimed control over the empire: the Vandals, the Heruli, and the Ostrogoths. Their
reign lasted 78 years. Eventually, the Roman Empire was
resurrected to power; and with a joint effort between church
and Empire, the Vandals, Heruli, and Ostrogoths were elim-
inated, wiped cleanly out of existence. If we return to
Daniel 7, we can see what the new Empire and the "*little
horn*," that is, the "*church/government horn*" did to these
three barbaric entities as the Roman Empire began to "***heal
it's deadly wound***" and be revived:

Daniel 7: "...**it tore out three of the horns that were already there**..."

After the tearing down of barbaric rule, Justinian established
his Empire in 527 A.D. and it lasted until 565. During that
period of time, approximated at 554 A.D., the Imperial
Restoration of the Roman Empire was indoctrinated. Thus
marked the beginning of the revived Roman Empire. Also
at that time, Justinian, incorporating church and state, declared the official religion of the Roman Empire: Christianity. The "woman" who rides the beast was born! The
'**Great Babylon, the mother of all prostitutes and the
abominations of the earth,**' as mentioned in the Book of
Revelation, had been instated.

After Justinian, the Roman Empire survived through five
additional and very specific movements: (1)the Frankish
Kingdom under Charlamagne, (2) the Germanic based Holy
Roman Empire under Otto the Great, (3) the Austrian based
Hapsburg Dynasty under Charles V. (4)the French based
kingdom under Napoleon, and (5) the Italian based "Italian

Renaissance" of the nineteenth and twentieth centuries, beginning with Giuseppe Girabaldi and ending with the fall of Hitler and Mussolini in 1945.

If we follow the phases of the Roman Empire from the fall in 476 A.D, to the failed attempt at its restoration in 1945, we can see the 10 horns, 7 horns, and 7 heads mentioned in Daniel 7, Revelation 13 and Revelation 17. They are as follows:

First, the Fall of the Roman Empire. Then, the Vandals (1st Horn in Daniel 7, 1st Horn in Revelation 13,)......the Heruli (2nd horn, 2nd horn) .....The Ostrogoths (3rd horn, 3rd horn).......Justinian (4th horn, 4th horn, and 1st head in Revelation 17).......Charlamagne (5th horn, 5th horn, and 2nd head)........Otto the Great and the Holy Roman Empire (6th horn, 6th horn, and 3rd head)........Charles V (7th horn, 7th head, and 4th head)....... Napoleon (8th horn, 8th horn, and 5th head)...........Giribaldi/Mussolini/Hitler (9th horn, 9th horn, and 6th head)......

Remember, the beast in Revelation 13, the beast who carries the number 666, had 10 horns and 7 heads. By the end of WWII in 1945, the world had experienced 9 out of the 10 horns discussed in Daniel 7 and Revelation 13; as well as 6 of the 7 heads mentioned in Revelation 17. 9 out of 10. 6 out of 7. In both cases, all but one of the horns and one of the heads have manifested in world history. Today, as a world, we await the final horn and the final head, both of which, of course, are the same thing: the final resurrection of the Roman Empire.

In the last chapter, we briefly discussed the passage from Revelation 17 which told of the beast during the end time *"...which once was, now is not, and will come up out of the Abyss and go on to destruction."* We are currently living during the time of this abyss. It is the time between the 9th horn (Giribaldi, Mussolini, and Hitler) and the 10th and final horn (a resurrection of the Roman Empire yet to come). The uprising and world presence of the 10th horn will mark the final stage of an Empire that actually dates back to before the time of Jesus' life on earth, and this Empire will be the world power which will be in control at the second coming of Jesus. As Jesus returns, however, the Empire (the beast) will finally, once and for all, *"go on to destruction."* The questions we must ask ourselves now, in attempting to identify the nature and the future location of this beast, are "what will be the identity of this beast?" "from where will it come?" and "are there any indications, past and present, that might lead us to understanding this beast?"

The answer to the latter question is "Yes!" There are indications, past and present, that might lead us to understanding the beast. We can look at Napoleon and Hitler for a moment. As previously mentioned, Napoleon was from France, but the thrusts of his political and military campaigns were to unite Europe under a single governing entity. His objective was to bring the entire territory of the old Roman Empire under one system of government. Hitler and Mussolini attempted the exact same thing during WWII. Operating out of headquarters located in both Germany and Italy, the objective of Hitler was to unite Europe, Northern Africa, and the Middle East--the general locations of the original Roman Empire--and bring them all under one system of totalitarian government. Both Napoleon and Hitler failed at their missions; but the 10th head of the beast, the resurrection of the Roman Empire which is yet to come, will succeed at its mission. The 10th head of the beast will, once and for all, unite the countries of Europe, Northern Africa, and the Middle East into one governmental, economical, and military system.

The military and political thrust of the Roman Empire has always been to expand its territories, increasing the magnitude of its power. Throughout history, the Empire has operated under a system of conquer and control, uniting its surrounding territories and governing them under a single ruling body of government. It stands to reason that a final resurrection of the Empire, the 10th and final head of the beast, will attempt to accomplish the very same objectives.

Let's look at Europe for a moment. It currently consists of gigantic powers in both economics and resources, yet each of these powers are divided and separated from one another. Germany operates as its own entity. France as its own entity. Italy as its own. Etc. Unlike the United States, in which individual states would be relatively ineffective on the global scene if it were not for the federal governing system--the system of the United States of America--under which they operate, Europe currently does not have such a united system. Yet world leaders throughout history have recognized the potential power of a united Europe and many, such as Giribaldi, Napoleon, Hitler, and Mussolini, have extended their mights to accomplish such a union. The tenth head of the beast will be successful in its attempts to unite Europe and bring it under one national system.

Economically speaking, the unification of Europe is currently in process. The European common market, which still operates under a nationally individualized monetary system (i.e. Germany has its own monetary system, France has its own, etc.). is currently in the process of phasing in a national monetary system, under which all European countries will utilize the "Euro" as their unified system of money. Beginning in January, 1999, the Euro has started to become phased in. This "phase-in" period is scheduled to run through July of 2002, three and a half years. (Does that 3 and a half years ring a bell? Maybe it's just coincidental.) During the "phase-in" period, the countries belonging to the European common market will phase out their current national money systems and phase in the Euro. After July, 2002, the Euro will be the only legal monetary system utilized in the European common market. Economically, Europe will be unified by a monetary system beginning in

2002. This is not a small step. Such unification allows for greater free trade and free importing and exporting between otherwise independent countries. A unification of such magnitude creates a single market in which social, economical, agricultural, governmental, and fiscal policies can be created. It is a single step, but not a small step, towards a united Europe and, ultimately, the resurrection and unification of the Roman Empire. To keep abreast of the beast's uprising from the current day abyss; that is, to watch the Roman Empire be resurrected and restored for one final time before the second coming of Jesus, we all need to keep our eyes and our ears and our minds focused towards Europe. It is the union of the European countries that will form the 10th head of the beast.

From Romulus to Augustus Caesar to Justinian to Adolf Hitler, the beast has been present in the world throughout the ages. Nine horns and six heads have come and gone, and now we merely await the final horn and the final head to arise--AND FALL--before the second coming of Jesus. And this final resurrection of the Roman Empire will be the force which brings about absolute devastation in the world as we know it. As Jesus said, *"...for then shall be great tribulation, such as was not since the beginning of the world to this time, no, nor ever shall be. And except those days should be shortened, there should no flesh be saved..."*

For those who remain doubtful that the beast is the Roman Empire, consider a few of the following points:

Romulus and Remus founded Rome on seven hills. They were ecstatic about coming upon this land with seven hills because they worshipped seven celestial bodies: the sun, the moon, Mercury, Venus, Mars, Jupiter and Saturn. This may have been their motivation for settling there and encompassing all seven hills, which they named Palatine, Aventine, Capitoline, Esquiline, Quarinal, Viminal, and Caelian. It is no secret today that Rome exists in the midst of seven hills; it is a well known characteristic of its geography. Now, consider what is revealed to John in Revelation 17: **"This calls for wisdom and understanding. *The seven heads are seven hills...*"** We learn that they have dual meaning and are also seven kings. But the seven hills, with all other things considered, is a hard fact to refute.

Consider the holocaust for a moment. Does it remain a mystery why 6 million Jews were exterminated during WWII? The Jewish people, as we have already discussed, are descendents from the tribe of Judah, one of the 12 tribes of Israel, God's chosen people. The holocaust, as well as other atrocities inflicted upon God's people throughout the ages by the beast, had been prophesized by both Daniel and John (through Jesus):

Revelation: *...and it was given unto him to make war with the saints and to overcome them...*

Daniel: *...while I was looking, that horn made war on God's people and conquered them.*

Daniel: *...he will speak against the Supreme God and oppress God's people*

It is common knowledge that the saints were sadistically persecuted and oppressed under the hands of the Roman Empire. History reflects the regular casting of the saints to the lions in the Coliseum, Christians being burned at the stake or forced to fight armored gladiators who killed them for public entertainment. The painful and public execution of the saints was commonplace under Roman rule.. It is believed that over 50 million of God's people were martyred throughout the centuries under the Roman Empire; not counting, of course, the 6 million that died under Hitler's regime. This is not coincidental nor is it an easy fact to dispute.

Consider also this fact: Rome was named after Romulus, a man. Again, in figuring out the identity of the beast, we are asked to have understanding: " **He that hath understanding, let him count the number of the beast; for it is the number of *a man...* "**

We also read that the beast will"....**causeth all, both small and great, rich and poor, free and bond, to receive a mark in their right hand, or in their foreheads: And that no man might buy or sell, save he that have the mark, or the *name of the beast*, or the *number of his _name_*.** We learn that the *"number of his name"* and the *"number of a man"* is the infamous 666.

We can now examine the numbers 666 and determine just what, exactly, they mean. The first place to examine the meaning of 666 would, of course, be within this Greek numerical system because it was the set of numbers from which 666, as John wrote them down, was derived. It was not the Roman system. It obviously was not the American numerical system. So, to understand 666, we need to look at the number system from which it came: the Greek numerical system.

We all have some basic knowledge of Roman numerals (IX, V, XII, etc.). We understand that in the Roman numerical system, letters are used to symbolize numbers. For example, I=1, V=5, X=10, etc. The New Testament, in which the Book of Revelation appears, was written in the Greek language. And just like the Roman numerical system, the Greek numerical system also uses letters to symbolize its numbers.

The following is a table of the Greek numerical / letter symbol system which was present at the time the Book of Revelation was written:

1 alpha	10 iota	100 rho
2 beta	20 kappa	200 sigma
3 gamma	30 lamda	300 tau
4 delta	40 mu	400 upsilon
5 epsilon	50 nu	500 phi
6 digamma	60 xi	600 chi
7 zeta	70 omicron	700 psi
8 eta	80 pi	800 omega
9 theta	90 koppa	900 sampi

Again, the founder of Rome was Romulus, a man. In New Testament Greek, his name was also referred to as the name "Latienos." It meant, in short, Latin Man or Roman Man; and it came to be attached to all men of Rome. Roman men were in essence considered Latienos, but the original use of the word was rooted and attached to Romulus himself.

Now, if you spell out the word Latienos and attach its Greek numerical symbols: L=30, A=1, T=300, I=10, E=5, N=50, O=70, S=200, you get (30+1+300+10+5+50+70+200), the sum of which is 666.

Remember the way in which the message is written in Revelation: **"Let him that hath understanding count the number of the beast:** *for it is the number of a man;* **and** *his number* **is six hundred threescore and six."** The number of a man. The word "Latienos' not only referred to the man who founded Rome, but to all men who were born out of Rome. The number 666 merely stands for the men of Rome, or Roman Man.

Over the years, as I have researched the number 666 and

have tried to prove and disprove its attachment to Romulus, I have run across some very crazy and misinformed interpretations of what the number might mean. I have found definitions ranging from "the number of black slaves brought over on the first Spanish ship" to "computer chips in the foreheads of every citizen in the world" to "the three secret numbers engraved on the Pope's crown," to a whole host of contrived, far reaching, and illogical possibilities. One interesting thing I did find, however, had to do with the Roman numeral system. Whereas the Greek alphabet incorporated numbers for *all* of its letters, the original Roman Numeral system incorporated only a few, six to be exact. The original six letter-symbols in the Roman numerical system were as follows: I for **1**, V for **5**, X for **10**, L for **50**, C for **100**, and D for **500**. IVXLCD. 1-5-10-50-100-500. (M was later added.) Add those numbers up and you also get **666**. This, of course, is strangely coincidental and interesting at best; because the original number 666 was derived from *"**the number of a man**,"* which was Latienos, or Latin Man, or Roman Man.....all leading back to Romulus, a man, all directly related to the men of the Roman Empire.

As we continue to put together *"...a little bit here, a little bit there...,"* we can begin to understand how the pieces so tightly fit. We are rapidly approaching the end of God's 6000 years of man's rule. We live in a time where people are *"going to and fro"* and *"knowledge is increased."* Almost a full 6000 years have passed since the creation of Adam; and we know we have a 1000 year millenium of peace in front of us, which can only come after the resurgence of the final head of the beast, followed by a great tribulation of the peoples of the earth, and brought to a climactical pinacle with the second coming of Jesus. These events are not that far off! The beast we have been discussing from the Books of Daniel and Revelation has already manifested 9 of its 10 horns and 6 of its 7 heads. WWII marked the end of the 9th horn and the 6th head.

This means that there is only 1 more head and 1 more horn to go. And these, of course, are the same thing. They are the final restoration of the Roman Empire, the unification of Europe with its surrounding territories, which, as we know from Daniel 2 and Daniel 7, will be present on the earth and be in supreme power when Jesus returns.

Let's look at the remainder of Revelation 13:

Revelation 13: **And he opened his mouth in blasphemy against God, to blaspheme His name, and His tabernacle, and them that dwell in heaven. And it was given unto him to make war with the saints, and to overcome them: and power was given him over all kindreds, and tongues, and nations.**

Remember, the word "him" is not referring to a man; it is referring to the Roman Empire. Only the number 666 was referring to a man, as in *"the number of a man"*; but the beast is not a man; it is a kingdom.

Revelation 13: **And all that dwell upon the earth shall *worship* him,**

A funny word, this word "worship." It is derived from the Greek root word *"kuon"* which means *"dog."* and the direct word *"proskuneo,"* which means *"to kiss a masters hand (like a dog licking his master's hand).* It also means *"to kiss the hand in show of homage and reverence."* When I first stumbled across this particular definition, well after the time I had already realized that the beast was the Roman Empire, I thought, "Hmmmmm, now where on earth do we see *that* happening? Where do we see people all over the earth kissing the hand which represents the Roman Empire?" Of course, I was thinking of the Pope, and how people all over the world bow and kiss his ring. To me, it seems like a very obvious sign, and a very symbolic parallel of the world "worshipping" the beast, like a dog licking the hand of its

master. People doing the physical act and the physical manifestation of what the world has done, and will do in the future, regarding the worshipping of the beast.

We continue with Revelation 13: **And all that dwell upon
the earth shall *worship* him, whose names are not written in the book of life of the Lamb slain from the foundation of the world. If any man have an ear, let him hear.
He that leadeth into captivity shall go into captivity: he
that killeth with the sword must be killed with the sword.
Here is the patience and the faith of the saints.**

**And I beheld another beast coming up out of the earth;
and he had two horns like a lamb, and he spoke as a
dragon.**

Remember, as mentioned earlier, the Roman Empire--the
beast--had fallen in 476 A.D. and was restored by Justinian
in the 6th century. This restoration was the rebirth of the
old Roman Empire, and it is referred to here in the Book of
Revelation as *"another beast,"* When this *"other beast,"*
this imperial restoration of the Roman Empire took place,
Justinian declared "Christianity" to be its official religion.
"Christianity" was, of course, what had by that time become
the Catholic religion. Through Justinian, then, the Roman
Empire was forming a hand-in-hand political relationship
with the Catholic religion. It was a virtual marriage between the government and the church; and it is this government / church relationship that is spoken about here as
"looking like a lamb" (Jesus) but *"speaking as a dragon"*
(Satan). The Roman Empire and it's accompanying church
would present the facade of *"the lamb"* but its underpin-
nings would be that of *"the dragon."* It would be, in
essence, a government and a false religion forming a single
entity of church and state. And this, of course, all ties in
with the Holy Roman Empire and the Roman Catholic
Church.

Speaking of which, the history of "Catholicism" and "Christianity" is interesting. The Bible shows us that both are a split away from the original teachings of Jesus.

After the death of Jesus, His apostles, ultimately spear-headed by Paul, founded the church and began to spread the "good news" throughout the territory. By 42 A.D., there were various sects of religions present in the area, all preaching different versions of what Jesus had taught. There were the Pharisees, the mystery religion of Simon (not the apostle Simon Peter), the converting Gentile religions, and the followers of Paul, to name a few. At some point between 42 A.D. to 53 A.D. (historians continue to debate about the exact date within this 10-year time frame), there was a summit--or a meeting of council--held in Jerusalem between the apostles and the Pharisees and other religious leaders of the time. The meeting is recorded in the Book of Acts 15. It was basically a debate between the church of Jesus and the other forms of "Christianity" which were springing up, concluding that it would be permissible for Gentile followers of Jesus to continue in some of their customs. This was done because the apostles decided, *"...we should not make it difficult for the Gentiles who are turning to God..."* The Gentiles, of course, were the people who were not descendents from the tribe of Israel, including citizens within the Roman Empire. This council meeting in Jerusalem marked the break between the "Israel-based, God-based church" and the "Gentile-based church," which had been founded in the religious base of paganism. A letter was then sent from the apostles up to Antioch, and it was addressed *"...to the Gentile believers in Antioch, Syria, and Cilicia..."*

Antioch, the center of Roman and Greek cultures at the time, was the capital of the Roman Province of the East. It was there that the term "Christian" was first given to the *Gentile* believers, and also where the many Gentiles, including Romans and Greeks, first heard and came to accept the teachings of Jesus. And it was also in Antioch that the Catholic church was born.

As the Israel-based and Gentile-based churches continued to increase the distance between their divisions, the Gentiles began to claim that their religion was not affiliated with Paul, but with Peter. Paul had, of course, preached in Rome and throughout the territories of the Roman Empire, and he had acquired a general following. The Gentiles did not disown Paul's teachings, but they cleverly resorted back to what Jesus had said to Peter in Matthew 16:

Matthew 16: *"...Blessed are you, Simon* (Peter)....*and I tell you that you are Peter, and on this rock I will build by church..."*

The Gentiles of the time looked to Simon Peter as the rock upon which their belief system--their church--was built. Even today, the Catholic church makes its claim that their lineage of Popes and leaders dates all the way back to Peter. They believe that Jesus was speaking of a "universal" church which would be founded on the rock of Peter. The word Catholic, incidentally, was derived from the Greek word *"katholikos"* which means *"universal."* Therefore, the Catholic church claims it is the one true "universal" church with Simon Peter as its first Pope. In making this claim, Catholic doctrine, which was actually founded in the practices and fundamentals of the Babylon Mystery Religion, often refers to a verse in 1 Peter which, they believe, makes reference to this Mystery Religion--the Babylonian religion--which had been founded in the Babylonian Empire and practiced throughout the Roman Empire:

1 Peter: **Your sister church in Babylon, also chosen by God, sends you greetings...**

This statement, of course, was not referring to the church *OF* Babylon. It was referring to the church *IN* Babylon, a small segment of Paul's followers who happened to be in the location of Babylon. It's important for us to know this because we must understand that the Babylon Mystery Religion was not "*also chosen by God*." Quite the contrary! The Babylonian Mystery Religion was an idol worshipping, emperor worshipping, sun worshipping abomination to God. To take pride in being rooted in it is foolish; it would be the equivalent of taking pride in claiming that the sun and the moon are your gods. In fact, it's a very similar thing. The religion did worship both the sun and the moon. And it is a detestable religion in the eyes of God.

Now, I have a theory that I would just like to throw out here as a little bit of food for thought. It is, in a sense, just another one of those "man made" theories that I detest, but it is not about the Bible or about any scriptural information contained therein. It is, instead, a theory about the Catholic church. And I have never been able to prove or disprove it, mainly because much of the information available on the subject is clouded and vague at best. Early Catholic literature makes certain references but nothing definite. My theory, basically, is that the Catholic religion was founded on the wrong person. Not on Simon Peter, the rock of Jesus' church, but on Simon Magus, also known as Simon the Sorcerer mentioned in Acts 8, an active practitioner and high priest of the Babylonian Mystery Religion.

The Babylonian Mystery Religion was, as I have mentioned, founded in Babylon and rooted deeply in paganistic rituals. It was practiced by Belshazzar and other kings of the Babylonian Empire. Based on the worship of idols and planets, it managed to thrive throughout the Medo-Persian, Greek, and Roman Empires. Julius Caesar was a practitioner of the Mystery Religion; it was one of the many ways in which he paid homage to the priests and pontifs of Babylon. Caesar's title of "Pontifix Maximus" was in essence claiming high priesthood of Babylonian paganism. The emperor Constantine, who professed Christianity for both the church and state of Rome, was also a Pontifix Maximus of the Mystery Religion.

When "universal Christianity" *(katholikos)* flourished in the Roman Empire, it incorporated elements of the Mystery Religion with elements of the Israel-based / Jesus-based church. And it claimed to be founded on the Apostle Simon Peter. But consider for a moment, Simon (Magus) the sorcerer:

Acts 8: **But there was a certain man, called Simon, which beforetime in the same city used sorcery, and bewitched the people of Samaria giving out that he was some great one: To whom they all gave heed, from the least to the greatest, saying, "This man is the great power of God." And to him they had regard, because of the *long time which he had bewitched them with sorceries.* Now when the apostles which were at Jerusalem heard that Samaria had received the word of God, they sent unto them *Peter* and John:**

Then they laid they their hands on them, and they received the Holy Ghost. And when Simon (the sorcerer) **saw that through laying on of the apostles' hands the Holy Ghost was given, he offered them money, Saying, "Give me also this power, that on whomsoever I lay hands, he may receive the Holy Ghost." But *Peter* said unto him, "Your money will perish with you because you thought that the gift of God may be purchased with money."**

Consider these points: Simon the sorcerer had practiced his sorcery for such a long time in the city of Samaria that the people began to refer to him as *"the great power of God."* He exalted himself and claimed to be a *"great one."* Simon Peter (the rock of the church) and John were both present and *"they"* baptized the people of Samaria, including Simon the sorcerer. Either John or Peter had to baptize Simon;

and my guess--according to my theory--is that Peter baptized Simon. (That is to say, Simon Peter baptized Simon the sorcerer). Peter refused to take money in exchange for God's gift of the Holy Ghost. But my theory is that, after Peter and John left Samaria, Simon the sorcerer continued to exalt himself and practice his sorcery, claiming that, since he was baptized by Peter, his religion was therefore founded in the true church. This word spread to neighboring Caesaria and up to Antioch and was eventually incorporated into what was becoming known as "Christianity," or "universal Christianity. (*katholikos*)"

Simon Magus is more widely known and accepted as the father of the Gnostic religion, which, like Catholicism, claims to be the one true and original church. Gnosticism was the first teaching to refer to the "*christos*" or "*inner Christ*," while basing its founding principles on the components of both the Babylonian Mystery Religion and the early form of Gentile-based "Christianity." While some may beg to differ, Gnosticism and Catholicism are not very dissimilar in many of their founding beliefs. In fact, the "Ecclesia Gnostica Catholica," or "*Gnostic-Catholic Church*," was eventually founded in France in the early century. And notice some of the lines from its Creed:

Creed of the Gnostic Catholic Church: **We believe in one secret and ineffable Lord; and in one Star in the Company of Stars of whose fire we are created, and to which we shall return; and in one Father of Life,** *Mystery of Mystery,* **in His name Chaos, the sole viceregent of the** *Sun* **upon the Earth.....and in one Womb wherein all men are begotten, and wherein they shall rest,** *Mystery of Mystery, in Her name BABALON...* **We believe in the Serpent...** *Mystery of Mystery....***and in one** *Gnostic* **and** *Catholic Church...*

To me, this Creed is so powerful and so revealing as to the

195

background of both the Gnostic and the Catholic religions that it is almost frightening. It is the perfect manifestation of what the Bible points out, in the Book of Revelation, regarding the false church and about *"Mystery Babylon the Great, Mother of All Whores and of the Abominations of the Earth."* And it is such a revelation of the ultimate agenda of the Catholic church.

Now, again, it is just my theory; but it seems very possible that the founder of the Gnostic faith, Simon Magus, high priest of the Babylonian Mystery Religion, could also have been the first Pope of the Catholic religion, instead of Simon Peter the rock, upon who the Catholic church so readily attaches its lineage. Both churches were founded in the paganistic rituals of the Mystery Religion. And I have yet to read, or see, or hear, or have pointed out to me, how in the world the Catholic religion *really* has justified attaching itself to Peter. The thought to me is, actually, extremely absurd, especially in light of the fact that every Pope in the history of the Catholic church has been forbidden to marry; yet, Peter himself WAS MARRIED:

Matthew: **And when Jesus went into Peter's house, he saw *his wife's* mother laid and sick of a fever.**

1 Corinthians: ...**don't I have the right to follow the example of the other apostles and the Lord's brothers and *Peter*, by taking a Christian *wife* with me on my trips?**

Catholicism religion is based in the Mystery Religion. It is purely paganistic in nature, filled with idol worship and holy days born right out of Babylon. It claims to be "Christianity." It claims to be the original and universal church. And, as John points out in Revelation 13, it rode the beast. It is the church that is referred to in Revelation as looking like a lamb and speaking like a dragon. And consider also this passage from Revelation 17:

Revelation 17: **The woman was dressed in purple and scarlet** (another strange resemblance to the Catholic religion)**, and covered with gold ornaments, precious stones, and pearls. In her hand she held a gold cup filled with abominable things and the filth of her adulteries. This title was written on her forehead: Mystery Babylon the Great, Mother of All Whores and of the Abominations of the Earth.**

"Mystery" is not just tossed in there as an expendable word. It refers directly to the Babylon Mystery religion. The word "abomination," again means something that is detestable to God, especially as it is used in reference to an idol. The Babylon Mystery Religion, like the Catholic religion, surrounded itself with idol worship. Its entire essence was that of worshipping man-made idols and planets and people. Like the Catholic church, the Babylonian Mystery Religion constructed wooden idols and sculptures to bow down to and worship. And in Revelation 17, the religion is referred to as *"the Mother of all Whores."* Definitely not a favorable church in the eyes of God.

In Revelation 18, we see the Mystery Religion again: **"Fallen! Fallen is Babylon the Great. She has become a home for demons. ....for all nations have drunk the maddening wine of her adulteries."**

After the split between the Israeli-based and Gentile-based church, the term "Christianity" was coined to refer to the *non*-Jewish, or *non*-Israeli religion. It primarily referred to religion that was not based in Jerusalem, referencing a non-Jewish-based set of beliefs and practices. Throughout the ages, and even today, we have a universally acknowledged a distinction between the Jewish religion and Christianity. "Christianity" became the religion of the Gentiles during the Roman Empire, and it was incorporated with the religion which had already been practiced in the Empire from its inception: the pagan based Babylon Mystery Religion.

When the Book of Revelation speaks of *"Babylon the Great, mother of all whores,"* it is referring to the Mystery Religion, the Gentile conceived form of "Christianity" from which all other religions were born. This "Christianity" ultimately split once again into Catholic and Protestant orientations. The Catholics, of course, denounce the Protestant orientation because, as they quickly point out, the Catholic religion (*(katholikos)* is the one and only true church. This theocentric attitude of the Catholic Church can be seen in, for example, the following passage of a sermon spoken by Saint Augustine to the people of Caesarea around 390AD:

"No one can find salvation except in the Catholic Church. Outside the Church you can find everything except salvation. You can have dignities, you can have sacraments, you can sing 'alleluia', answer 'Amen', have faith in the name of the Father, the Son, and the Holy Ghost, and preach it too; But never can you find salvation except in the Catholic Church."

I have to scratch my head over this one. This is a very clear indictment of how the Catholic church has historically placed belief in the church over faith in Jesus. It is just a snap shot of the blasphemous way in which the Catholic church conducts itself. If salvation could only be attained throughout the Catholic Church, why didn't Jesus at least mention it once during His time on earth? Why didn't any of the apostles or any of their predecessors, the prophets, mention this all important church? If salvation could only be found in the Catholic Church, why did Jesus even need to come to this world? The type of teaching and church theocentricism revealed by Saint Augustine is truly not an isolated incident. The Roman Catholic Church has been preaching very much the same thing for nearly 2000 years.

By the time of that sermon, the terms "Catholic" and "Christian" meant the same thing in the Roman Empire. All other forms of "Christianity" were thought of to be abominations in sight of the church; however, as Jesus points out in the Book of Revelation, both "Christianity" and "Catholicism," from which all idol-worshipping religions were derived, were abominations in the sight of God. *"Mystery Babylon the Great, Mother of All Whores and of the Abominations of the Earth."* After the Roman Empire fell and was resurrected under Justinian, the reborn beast increased in its power and affiliation with the Catholic "Christian" church. The government / church entity served as a foreshadowing to the beast that will come out of the abyss in the end time.

And he exerciseth all the power of the first beast before him, and causeth the earth and them which dwell therein to worship the first beast, whose deadly wound was healed. And he doeth great wonders, so that he maketh fire come down from heaven on the earth in the sight of men, .

And he deceiveth them that dwell on the earth by the means of those miracles which he had power to do in the sight of the beast; saying to them that dwell on the earth, that they should make an image to the beast, which had the wound by a sword, and did live. And he had power to give life unto the image of the beast, that the image of the beast should both speak, and cause that as many as would not worship the image of the beast should be killed.

And he causeth all, both small and great, rich and poor, free and bond, to receive a mark in their right hand, or in their foreheads: And that no man might buy or sell, save he that had the mark, or the name of the beast, or the number of his name.

Here is wisdom. Let him that hath understanding count the number of the beast: for it is the number of a man; and his number is six hundred threescore and six.

Shortly, we will discuss the mark of this Roman man, which, as the Book of Revelation explains, the beast will "....**causeth all, both small and great, rich and poor, free and bond, to receive a mark in their right hand, or in their foreheads: And that no man might buy or sell, save he that had the mark, or the name of the beast, or the** *number of his name.*"

Chapter 8

The Mark of the Beast is Upon Us Now
(And Has Been For Centuries!)

---

666 is not the mark of the beast. It is the *number* of the beast: the number of a man. Note again the following 2 passage from Revelation 13:

Revelation: **Here is wisdom. Let him that hath understanding count *the number of the beast*: for it is the *number of a man*; and his number is six hundred threescore and six.**

Revelation: **And he causeth all, both small and great, rich and poor, free and bond, to receive a *mark* in their right hand, or in their foreheads: And that no man might buy or sell, save he that had *the mark*, *or the name of the beast*, or *the number of his name*.**

These passages must be read carefully. The number 666 is *"the number of the beast"* and *"the number of a man."* The *mark* of the beast, however, is a mark placed in the right hands and the foreheads of *"all."* And the statement reads that no man might buy or sell unless he has *"the mark"* or *"the name"* or *"the number"* of the beast. The *"mark"* isn't 666. The *"number"* is. The number 666 is exactly that: *"the number."* It is not the *"mark."* This is significant because, as we search for understanding of the beast's "mark," which is placed in the hand and forehead, we have to be very clear that it is not necessarily the number 666. And we have to be very clear about how *"all, both small and great, rich and poor, free and bond,"* receive the mark; and how no man can buy or sell unless he has the mark, or the name, *or* the number 666.

Notice in Revelation 15 how the two are separated:

Revelation 15: **And I saw as it were a sea of glass mingled with fire: and them that had gotten the victory over the beast, and over his image, and over *his mark*, and over *the number of his name*, stand on the sea of glass, having the harps of God.**

In the last two chapters, it was determined that the Roman Empire is the beast. Romulus, a man, was its founder; and the number 666, *"the number of a man,"* is the number of Romulus according to the Greek word "Latienos" calculated within the Greek numerical system. It is also a number that applies to each man of Rome by virtue of the label Latin Man or Roman Man.

John wrote the Book of Revelation around 90-95 A.D. It was a time shortly after the reign of terror by the emperor Nero, and a time in which the Roman Empire was enforcing both emperor worship and the religious gravitation toward the Babylonian Mystery Religion, which, at the same time, was rapidly incorporating more and more characteristics of the Mystery Religion, combining Christian symbolism with Babylonian practices. It was a time of the first beast: the Roman Empire between 31 B.C and 476 A.D. John was in the present tense of the first beast and writing about how this beast would eventually fall, *"receive a mortal wound,"* but how it would be resurrected and, in essence, be brought back to life. He was, of course, writing about the fall of the Empire in 476 and the resurrection in 554. He saw *"another beast,"* which was the resurrected Empire under Justinian, rise up and cause all the earth to worship (pay homage) to the first beast whose *"deadly wound"* had been healed. John was writing about a time in *his* future: the fall of the Empire 300 years in his future and the healing of the Empire's deadly wound approximately 400 years in his future.

In terms of the number 666, it was the second beast, the resurrected Roman Empire, which *caused* the earth to pay homage to the first beast and to receive the mark.

Revelation: *...he exercises all the power of the first beast before him, and causes the earth...to worship the first beast whose deadly wound was healed....and he had power to give life unto the image of the beast....and he causes all, both small and great, rich and poor, free and bond, to receive a mark in their right hand, or in their foreheads...*

This beast was in John's future, but it is in *our* past. The second beast (the reborn Roman Empire), which caused all the inhabitants of the earth to "receive the mark" and pay homage to the first beast (the old and fallen Roman Empire) was on earth in 550 A.D. And while it perpetuated its existence for almost 1400 years through 9 of its 10 horns, leading up to 1945, the beast of which John speaks, and the mark, were both present on the earth at the time of the Justinian Empire in 554 A.D.

In 95 A.D., John wrote Revelation 13 about events that would take place less than 500 years in his future. So, while the Book of Revelation is written in future tense, all readers today can refer to much of it in PAST tense; although, some of it should still be viewed in future tense. Some, but not all. And this may cause confusion because we know the Roman Empire will once again be present on earth. And that is true. The 10th and final horn of the Roman Empire will rise and establish the Empire in grand scale prior to the second coming of Jesus. Whereas the 9th horn--Hitler and Mussolini--failed to reestablish the Empire, the 10th horn, the unified continent of Europe coupled with the antichrist and a global military might, will succeed in resurrecting the 10th and final horn of the beast. It will be present on earth at the time of Jesus' return. The Book of Daniel and the Book of Revelation make this fact very clear.

But we need to understand that, while this 10th horn is yet to come and will come in our near future, the beast and the *mark of the beast* have been present on earth since 550 A.D. The mark of the beast has been upon the entire world for over 14 centuries. It's not a tattoo or brand or computer chip or anything else; the mark of the beast is something completely different than any of these things.

Which brings us back to determining just what this mark is all about. The best place to start is by looking at where the mark will be placed: *"...in their right hand, or in their foreheads..."* The mark of the Roman Empire will somehow be placed in the right hands and/or the foreheads of all the inhabitants of the earth who follow the beast; that is, who will pay homage to the original Roman Empire. Some believe that a sort of tattoo or brand will be placed in the flesh at one of these locations of the body; the rationale being that the forehead is visible for all merchants of the world to see (for the buying and selling component), or that a mark in the right hand could be run across a sort of barcode scanner, which are in most stores today, in order to make engaging in commerce simple and efficient; and, of course, to make the entire world blindly dependent upon the mark for "buying or selling..." But casting this man-invented, baseless malarkey aside, we can use the Bible to see that there is a far greater and more significant reason for the placement of the Roman Empire's mark in the hands and foreheads of the entire world.

God also has a mark. And many people do not realize that God's mark, which has nothing to do with tattoos in the flesh or the convenience of mercantilism, is also placed in the hands and foreheads of His followers. Consider the following passages:

Exodus (concerning Passover, the Feast of Unleavened Bread, and God's Law): "**...and it shall be for a sign unto you *upon your hand*, and for a memorial *between your eyes*, that the Lord's law may be in thy mouth: for with a strong hand has the Lord brought you out of Egypt...**

Deuteronomy (concerning the 10 Commandments): "**...now these are the commandments....And thou shalt bind them for a *sign upon your hand*, and they shall be as frontlets *between your eyes*...**"

Deuteronomy (concerning the Commandments, Laws, and restraint from idol worship): "**...therefore shall ye lay up these my words in your heart and in your soul, and bind them for a *sign upon your hand*, that they may be as frontlets *between your eyes*.**

In the above passages, the word "*frontlets*" was translated from the Hebrew word "*towphaphah*" which means "*mark*." So God, in essence, was saying that His commandments and His laws and festivals would be a "***sign upon your hand***" and a "***mark* between your eyes**," which is basically the forehead. We know that God did not tattoo or brand the children of Israel with these marks. And we also know that man *thinks* and *worships* with his head and *works* with his hands. When God was telling the children of Israel to walk in His statutes and to bind those statutes as a sign upon their heads and a mark between their eyes (foreheads), He was

Canyon Adams

instructing them to act and conduct their lives in accordance
to His laws, which they would manifest by *thinking*, *worshipping*, and *working* according to His words.

Proverbs: **Keep my commandments and live; and my law
as the apple of your eye. Bind them** (the commandments
and laws) **upon your fingers, write them upon the table of
your heart.**

No, God is not instructing Israel to literally tattoo or brand
His laws and commandments upon their physical hearts; a
21st century team of cardiac surgeons couldn't even pull
that particular feat off. He is instructing them to *feel* His
laws and commandments. As He did in the Books of Exodus and Deuteronomy, God instructed Israel to *think* and
feel and *work* according to His ways. And so, in the Book of
Revelation when Jesus is giving John an account of the
things that were to come, He is showing him a world which
will *think* and *feel* and *work* according to the ways not of
God, but of the beast: the Roman Empire. And as we read
the Book of Revelation, we find out exactly what will happen to those who have the mark of the beast and are thinking, acting, worshipping, and working according to that
mark; and what will happen to those who have the mark of
God and are thinking, acting, worshipping, and working
according to *that* mark:

Revelation: **Hurt not the earth, neither the sea, nor the
trees, till we have *sealed* the servants of our God *in their
foreheads*.**

Revelation: **And the third angel followed them, saying
with a loud voice, 'If any man worship the beast and his
image, and receive his mark in his forehead, or in his
hand, he too will drink the wine of God's fury....'**

Revelation: **And the smoke of their torment ascendeth
up for ever and ever: and they have no rest day nor**

206

night, who worship the beast and his image, and whosoever receiveth the mark of his name..... Here is the patience of the saints: here are they that *keep the commandments of God*, and the faith of Jesus.

Revelation: **The first angel went and poured out his bowl
on the land, and ugly and painful sores broke out *on the
people who had the mark of the beast* and *worshipped* his
image.**

Revelation: **And I looked, and, lo, a Lamb stood on the
mount Zion, and with him a hundred forty and four
thousand, having his Father's name *written in their foreheads.***

Clearly, the mark of the beast and the mark of God are located in the same place: in the forehead and in the thoughts
of mankind. Some men will follow the beast and, thus, have
the *mark* of the beast. Others will follow God and, thus,
have the mark of God. But in neither case is the mark a tattoo or a brand or a computer chip. The mark is merely the
thinking, feeling, worshipping, and working in accordance
to either God or the Roman Empire. And not the Roman
Empire of the future but the one of old; the Roman Empire
dating back to Romulus, crowning its first emperor with Augustus Caesar, falling with its mortal wound in 476 A.D.,
and being resurrected in 554 A.D. The mark is the way in
which individuals of the world think, feel, worship, and
work in accordance to *that* Roman Empire that determines
whether or not the individual has the mark of the beast or
the mark of God.

And notice this: God's mark related to the keeping of His
commandments and festivals and laws. It was the feeling
and the thinking and the worshipping and the working in
relation to *those* laws that were considered to be manifestations of their observance. God talked about the Passover,
the feasts, the commandments, and the Sabbath, indicating

that they would be a sign between Israel and Him forever:

Exodus: **Speak also unto the children of Israel, saying, 'Verily my Sabbaths you shall keep: for it is a *sign* between me and you throughout your generations...You shall keep the Sabbath therefore; for it is holy unto you: every one that defileth it shall surely be put to death..for whosoever does any work therein, that soul shall be cut off from among his people. Six days may work be done; but in the seventh is the Sabbath of rest, holy to the Lord... Therefore, the children of Israel shall keep the Sabbath and observe the Sabbath throughout their generations...it is a *sign* between me and the children of Israel forever'**

This sign was forever, and it was to be bound in the hands (work) of the children of Israel as well as in their foreheads (thinking and worshipping). Throughout their generations, God's people were to adhere to the laws and the festivals and the Sabbaths and the commandments of God. They were to have God's sign. On the contrary, however, those who adhered to the laws and festivals and commandments of the Roman Empire would also have a sign in their hands (work) and in their foreheads (thinking and worshipping). It would be a sign contrary to God's; and in the end, those people with the Roman sign would receive the horrific last plagues, whereas God's people would be spared from them all.

So, one might sigh a breath of relief here, concluding that he or she is safe from the mark of the beast. We, as a society, may believe this as well, acknowledging that we go to church and pray to God and have very little to do with the Roman Empire. Many may believe that the Roman Empire is something ancient and remote and irrelevant to our present day lives. Some may believe that, since they are not Catholic but "Christian," belonging to possibly the Baptist or the Methodist or the Lutheran church, they are not involved in any way with the Roman Empire or the Catholics. But let's reexamine two passages from Revelation regarding the beast:

Revelation: (the beast) "....**causeth** *all***, both small and great, rich and poor, free and bond, to receive a mark...**

The beast would cause "all" to receive the mark: the meager, the great, the famous, the rich, the poor, the free, the enslaved, the imprisoned. All! The Roman Empire would be so powerful and so all-encompassing that it would cause "*all*" to receive the mark.

And notice this statement:

Revelation: (The woman riding the beast, symbolic of the church): **This title was written on her forehead: Mystery Babylon the Great,** *Mother of All Whores and of the Abominations of the Earth.*

All worldly religions--Catholic and Protestant: Baptist, Lutheran, Methodist, Presbyterian, Pentecostal, etc. etc. etc. were born out of the one great whore, the one great religion and church: the Babylon Mystery Religion / Gentile-based "Christianity." This religion is the woman who rode the beast, and the religion that ultimately became integrated with the beast. And it is through the fundamentals of this Gentile-based religion that "*all*" are forced to bear the mark of the beast.

Remember, God's mark in the forehead and hand were placed there in relation to His followers' adherence to His commandments, festivals, and laws. The mark of the beast, in the forehead and hand, are placed there in relation to its followers' adherence to commandments, festivals, and laws of the Roman Empire.

Now, let's revisit what was said about the beast--The Roman

Empire--in Daniel 7: *"...he will try to change the set times and the festivals."*

We have already discussed God's 7 appointed Holy days: Passover, the Feast of Unleavened Bread, the Day of Pentecost, the Feast of Trumpets, the Day of Atonement, the Feast of Tabernacles, and the Final Day. In addition, God appointed weekly and annual Sabbaths which were to be observed. How many people today follow these feasts and Sabbaths? How many churches observe these Sabbaths and holy days?

On the contrary, how many people and churches observe *these* holidays ("holy days"): Christmas, Easter, and Good Friday? How many churches hold services on God's appointed weekly Sabbath (Saturday, the 7th day of the week), and how many hold services on the *changed* Sabbath (Sunday, the 1st day of the week)?

By answering these questions, we draw closer to understanding the mark of the beast. We can begin to see the distinct contrast between God's appointed holy days and the other holidays which were born out of somewhere else. Out of "Christianity? Out of the *"Katholikos /* universal" Catholic church? Out of the Babylonian Mystery Religion? Before we even begin to answer those questions listed above, compare for a moment God's 7 Holy days with just some of the Catholic church's annual feasts and days of observation. The following is a slightly abridged list of the holy feasts and days of observation of the Roman Catholic Church:

Octave of Christmas - Solemnity of Mary, Mother of God; Epiphany, Conversion of Apostle Paul Feast, Baptism of Our Lord Feast, Presentation of Our Lord Feast, Chair of Apostle Peter Feast; Joseph, Husband of Mary Solemnity, Annunciation Solemnity. Mark Evangelist Feast, Apostles Philip and James Feast, Apostle Matthias Feast, Visitation Feast, Holy Trinity Solemnity, Corpus Christi Solemnity,

Solemnity, Birth of John the Baptist Solemnity, Apostles Peter and Paul Solemnity, First Martyrs of the Church of Rome. Thomas Apostle Feast, Mary Magdalene Memorial, Apostle James Feast, Martha Memorial, Transfiguration Feast, Deacon Lawrence and Martyr Feast, Assumption Solemnity. Apostle Batholomew Feast, Birth of Mary Feast, Triumph of the Cross Feast, Apostle Matthew Feast; Michael, Gabriel, Raphael Archangels Feast. Luke Feast. All Saints Solemnity, All Souls Day, Feast to Saint John Lateran, Andrew Feast, Christ the King Solemnity, Immaculate Conception Solemnity, CHRISTMAS, Holy Innocents Feast, oly Family...

The list goes on and on. The Catholic religion virtually changed time and festivals and incorporated such things as days of observance dedicated to saints and apostles, much like the emperor-worshipping practices of the Mystery Religion. The Roman Catholic religion is abundant with man-made holidays; however, unlike God's holy days and festivals, all of which He explains in great detail in the Bible, _none_ --I repeat, _**NONE**_--of the above "holy days" of the Catholic church are mentioned *anywhere* in the Bible, Christmas included! And note also that the reverse is also true: not one of God's holy days or festivals are included in this list of Catholic holidays. Which brings us back to the statement in Daniel 7:

"(the beast) *will try to change the set times and the festivals.*"

To understand the mark of the beast; the mark of thinking, working, and worshipping, we can simply look at these contrasting holy days and festivals; but for full comprehension, one must also examine the contrasting Roman and Julian calendar systems as well. As previously mentioned, God's calendar begins in the month of March/April. The days and months in God's calendar are not named after rulers and gods and planets, and there are 360 days to the year. The

Roman calendar, however, is something completely different. Beginning in January, all days and months are named for either gods, Roman leaders, or planets; and there are 365 days to each Roman/Julian year.

The original Roman calendar was formulated by Romulus (Latienos / 666) and contained only 10 months and 304 days. King Numa, who succeeded Romulus, made several significant adjustments to the calendar, beginning the year in Martius (March) and ending it in December. The 10 months at that time were Martis, Aprilis, Maius, Junius, Quntilis, Sextilis, September, October, November, and December. February-Termi (in honor of Terminus, god of boundaries, was added as the first month, and then Janus was added in honor of Janus, the sky god, who was quoted as saying, *"The ancients called me Chaos..."* (Refer back to the Gnostic-Catholic creed). Janus was thought of as the supreme god, and his month was, of course, changed to January. Early Romans considered the beginning of each day, month, and year sacred to Janus. Eventually, his month was placed before February and used to begin the new year.

The Roman calendar, which in no way resembled God's calendar, remained the same from the time of Numa through the reign of Julius Caesar. In 46 B.C., Caesar created what is now known as the Roman/Julian calendar. Caesar's Julian calendar contained 365 days, including 2 new months which were eventually named July (after Julius Caesar) and August (after Augustus Caesar). The days of the week included Sunday (after the sun), Monday (after the moon), Tuesday (after the pagan god Theus), Wednesday (after Woden, another pagan god), Thursday (after Thor, another pagan god), Friday (after Freia, a pagan goddess), and Saturday (after Saturn). Upon the incorporation of calendars created by both Romulus and Caesar, the Roman calendar was officially a full-blown tribute to the pagan practice of worshipping planets, gods, and emperors.

As the calendar evolved, eventually, with the reign of Constantine, the weekly Sabbath was *changed* from Saturday to Sunday. In a fully disclosed tribute to the "god of the sun,' the Roman empire *changed* God's very important day of rest, symbolic of the final 1000 years of God's plan, from the 7th day to the day-of-the-sun: Sunday. The following passage was a recorded declaration of Emperor Constantine regarding the Empire's mandated move to Sunday worship:

"On the venerable *day of the Sun*, let the magistrates and people residing in cities rest, and let all workshops be closed. In the country however persons engaged in agriculture may freely and lawfully continue their pursuits because it often happens that another day is not suitable for sowing or planting; lest by neglecting the proper moment for such operations the bounty of heaven should be lost."

The Catholic (*"universal* Christian") church at the time of Constantine, ordered their religious observances to be conducted on Sunday as well, stating *"Christians shall not Judaize and be idle on Saturday, but shall work on that day."* they consciously and overtly changed God's law, separating their Gentile-based /Babylonian Christianity from the religious practices of Judah / Israel. The practice continued throughout the ages and, ultimately, became incorporated into the practices of "Christian" societies throughout the world. Today, we of course see evidence of Sunday worship all around us. The following statement from the Pope in the 1990's reveals how the Catholic church continues to reinforce the importance of worshipping on *"the day of the sun"*: *"In obedience to the third Commandment, Sunday must be sanctified, above all by participation in holy Mass."* Here is the Pope, a man who is quick to support the importance of Sunday worship but slow to acknowledge the importance of remembering the commandments. *"Remember the Sabbath"* is the 4th commandment, not the third!

213

Aside from a change to Sunday worship, the Roman Empire and the Catholic Church implemented two universally accepted "holy days": Christmas and Easter. Like the change of the Sabbath day to Sunday, these two holy days have been embraced and observed by almost all other churches and religions in the world that dare to call themselves "Christian." Yet, both "holy days" are firmly rooted in the Babylonian Mystery Religion's worship of planetary gods.

Easter was adapted into "Christianity" from the pagan festivals for Ishtar and Tammuz. Ishtar was the great mother goddess of fertility and the heavens. Tammuz was her youthful lover. In Babylon, it was believed that Tammuz died and rose again. The spring festival of Ishtar, from which the word Easter is derived, celebrated fertility and rebirth, incorporating such symbols as rabbits (symbolic of abundant fertility) and eggs (symbolic of pure fertility). In Babylon as well as in the Roman Empire, the tribute to Ishtar and Tammuz was done by weeping for the death of Tammuz until the sun rose at dawn, which was thought to bring rebirth to Tammuz as well as to the world. The worshipping was actually directed at the god of the sun, which brought life and abundant fertility in honor of Ishtar.

It was very similar to the way in which "Christians" celebrate Easter today, facing the east during a sunrise service and feeling enlightened as the sun rises to symbolize the resurrection of Jesus. This practice was born out of the Roman Empire, incorporating the original pagan rituals of Ishtar/Tammuz as Easter became a "Christian" holiday. But let's look at the Book of Ezekiel in the Bible where this celebration is recorded and where we can witness, first hand, God's reaction to such a festival:

Ezekiel: **Then God said to me.... 'lift up your eyes.... do you see what they do? The *great abominations* that the house of Israel is committing here? Turn again, and you**

will see *greater abominations.*' And He brought me to
the door....then He said to me, 'Go in and behold the
wicked abominations they do here.' So I went in and
saw...all the idols of the house of Israel portrayed upon
the wall.....Then he said to me, 'turn again and you shall
see even greater abominations that they do'....behold,
there sat women *weeping for Tammuz.* Then He said to
me, 'Have you seen this, O son of man? Turn again and
you shall see *greater abominations* than these'.....there
were about twenty five men with their backs toward the
temple of the Lord, and their faces toward the east; and
they *worshipped the sun toward the east.* Then God said
to me, 'Have you seen this, O son of man? Is it a light
thing to the house of Judah that they commit these *abominations?*'

The Isthar celebration, weeping for Tamuz and facing the
east at sunrise, which ultimately became the "Christian"
holiday of Easter, was a detestable, abominable practice in
the eyes of God. The above passage from Ezekiel 8 cannot
make that point any clearer. Yet Isthar, or Easter, is practiced by "Catholic" and "Christian" churches throughout the
world today.

Even greater in "Christian" practice than the holiday of
Easter is the celebration of Christmas. Originally celebrated
in Babylon as the Sacaea festival, it was a time in which
slaves and masters traded places as a showing of goodwill
between men. The Sacaea was a celebration to the god of
the sun, showing the peace and good intentions of mankind
in an attempt to please the sun and ensure its return to earth
day after day. The celebration lasted for several days during
the winter solstice and eventually evolved to include feast-
ing, drinking, and continual celebration. The decoration of
trees and giving of gifts was originally attributed back to
Nimrod's practices of leaving gifts for the gods upon an ev-
ergreen tree. As the practice became incorporated into Roman custom, it included the giving of presents between

friends and family, the decoration of trees, large feasts; and very often, participation in drunken revels and sexual orgies beginning with encounters under the mistletoe. The celebration evolved to be called "Saturnalia" in honor of the planet and god of Saturn. Christmas is clearly a Roman-based, pagan-based holiday.

And so, as we look at the big picture, we see that God implemented a calendar, a weekly system of 6 days of work and a 7th day of rest, and an annual system of significant holy days and festivals. He declared that the observance of these things would be a sign between Him and His people forever, and that it would be bound as a sign in the hands and as a mark on the forehead. Then we see the beast, the Roman Empire, whose mark is also in the hand and the forehead, *changing the times and the laws* by implementing a new calendar, a new set of festivals and holy days, a new system of days and months which pay homage to pagan gods and planets and emperors. And we see the entire "Christian" world adhering not to God's system, but to that initiated by the Roman Empire. We see "Christians," in essence, wondering after the beast.

The mark of the beast is the adherence to the Roman Empire's system of days and weeks and festivals and first-day-Sabbaths and holy days. It is the observance of the Sun-day Sabbath, the celebration of Christmas and Easter; the day-in day-out unconscious homage we all pay to pagan gods through the observance of the Roman/Julian calendar, complete with its days and months for the planets, gods, and emperors. The entire world adheres to this system, echoing the words of Revelation 13: *"...he causeth all, both small and great, rich and poor, free and bond, to receive a mark in their right hand* (symbolic of work*), or in their foreheads* (symbolic of thinking and worshipping)" The mark of the beast is the working and thinking and worshipping according to the ways of the Roman Empire. And as we examine the remainder of that verse in Revelation, we see that the beast caused *all* to work and think according to the Roman Empire, *"... And that no man might buy or sell, save he that had the mark, or the name of the beast, or the number of his name."*

The word "*sell*" in Greek is "*poleo,*" and its meaning is identical to what the word means in English, which is "*to barter*" or "*to sell.*" The word "*buy,*" however, is translated from the Greek word "*agorazo,*" which means "*to be in the market place, to attend it, to do business there.*" These two definitions are significant because they add a broader dimension to the meaning of *"..no man might buy or sell, save he had the mark...*" The activities and actions of a man who has or does not have the mark of the beast are not merely limited to buying and selling, which the advocates of the computer chip theory would like to believe. Instead, the man who does not have the mark of the beast cannot "*be in the market place,*" or "*attend the market place,*" which is to say that he cannot "*attend*" his business. In other words, the man who does not adhere to the Roman calendar of days and weeks and months and holidays cannot be in the market place or attend his business. He simply cannot *do* business. And as a society, we know this to be true. If a store owner closed his store on Saturday, according to God's calendar and plan, his business would suffer. The Roman calendar and religious customs allow full commerce on Saturdays but have, in the past, restricted business on Sun-day, the day of worship for the beast. Saturday is, in fact, one of the busiest shopping days of the week.

(Incidentally, I at one time owned a novelty/specialty clothing store on the main street of a small resort town in northern Michigan. I conducted full 9 am - 9 pm store hours from Sunday through Friday, but I kept the store closed on Saturdays. Tourists couldn't understand it. The townspeople couldn't understand it. One of the city father's called me up and said, "You know, you really need to keep your store opened on Saturday. Last weekend, there was a crowd of people looking through the windows and wondering why you were closed. You're going to lose a lot of business that way." And he was right. Being in a resort town that was filled with weekend tourists every Saturday, I probably sacrificed 2/3 of my potential business by closing on Saturday. But I had a conviction in my heart that said I was going to adhere to God's Sabbath and not contribute to the flagrancy of the beast. And consequently, the business of my little store suffered immensely.)

Businesses of the world are run and scheduled according to the Roman calendar. Public, parochial, college, and university school systems are also structured around the calendar and the Roman holidays of Christmas and Easter. The public conscience is conditioned to think in terms of the Roman Empire's days and weeks and holidays. We expect to take Easter breaks and Christmas vacations. Virtually no business or commerce is conducted on Christmas Day and New Years Day; yet, business is transacted as usual on Passover, the Day of Atonement, and all of God's other feasts and Sabbaths. The entire industrialized world adheres to the mark of the beast. Imagine a potential employee, telling the interviewer of a large corporation, "Well, I'm a hard worker, but I do take off for Passover, seven days for the Feast of Unleavened Bread, another seven for the Feast of Tabernacles....." The rejection buzzer would immediately go off in the employer's head: "Bzzzzt! Next!" Unless a person has the mark of the beast, he or she simply cannot "*attend the market place.*" Consider for a moment, the general population of the United States--the children of Israel from Manasseh-- who adhere entirely to the Roman calendar. Who among this group, *great or small, rich or poor, free or bond,* follows God's calendar or all seven holy days of God? Yet, how many from that same population freely call themselves "Christian" or "Catholic," and follow the religious traditions of the Roman Empire? Now consider the numbers of people doing the exact same thing in Europe, in Canada, in South America, in Mexico, in Australia, in the United Kingdom. The entire world wonders after the beast.

This is what the mark of the beast is all about! And it is not, by any means, a small or insignificant thing in the eyes of God. The church may condone it. The Pope may grant it his highest blessing. On the surface, it may seem as though everything has been structured to worship and appease God. It is, after all, supported by "Christianity." But God is appalled by it:

Ezekiel: **The *priests* break my law and have no respect for what is holy. They make no distinction between what is holy and what is not....they ignore the Sabbath. As a result the people of Israel do not respect me. They have no respect for the holy places...**

Deuteronomy (in relation to nations practicing idol worship and rituals similar to Babylon): **Take heed to yourself that you do not get snared by following these nations . . . and that you don't inquire about their gods, saying, "How did these nations serve their gods?" and saying "I will do likewise." You shall not do likewise unto the Lord your God, for every abomination to the Lord, *which the Lord hates*, have these nations done to their gods . . .**

Matthew: **"But in vain they do worship Me, teaching for doctrines the commandments of men,"**

The mark of the beast has been upon the entire world, including the entire "Christian" world, for centuries. Those who have it will suffer each of God's last plagues. But those who have God's mark instead will escape the plagues. *"This calls for wisdom."* It is up to each individual to decide upon the beast and upon the mark. It takes study and investigation, a heart open for understanding; and above all things, it takes prayer. Just as God conditioned the children of Israel for 40 years in the desert to understand and follow

His 7 day week and Sabbaths, the beast has conditioned the world for nearly two milleniums to follow its week and its own set of traditions and Sabbaths. And such conditioning is not an easy thing to break; it is rooted generations and generations deep, right in the center of our civilization.

But with God, all things are possible. And with grace and understanding, a heart can throw off the burdensome mark of the beast and replace it with God's own mark of perfection and beauty, of meaning and significance. The mark of the beast is, indeed, upon us all. But it can be rebelled against, rebuffed and resisted. We, as a culture and as individuals, can either receive the mark of God or the mark of the beast. And the choice is completely ours.

Chapter 9

Tribulation
(Some Die, Some Survive)

In the general realm of religious study, there often exists a
bit of confusion in regard to "the tribulation," which is mentioned several times in the New Testament in reference to
the end time woes cast upon mankind. I have used it myself
to mean several things. Jesus spoke of "tribulation" on the
Mount of Olives, and the book of Revelation mentions it frequently in its description of end time events. However,
there seems to remain a bit of ambiguity as to just what the
word "tribulation" means, what it is referring to, and what
specific events will occur in the end time during the great
"tribulation."

The word "*tribulation*" was translated from the Greek word
"*thlipsis,*" which means "*pressure, affliction, a pressing together.*" It is generally used in reference to the end time
catastrophes which will be bestowed upon the world just
prior to Jesus' coming. As a general definition, it is often
used to encompass *all* of the end time catastrophes, such as

wars, famines, diseases, earthquakes, death, destruction, chaos, and world horror in general. The Bible, however, uses it in a more specific sense to refer to the end time persecution of the saints. Some Bible translations use the words *"tribulation"* and *"great persecution"* synonymously. If we reexamine Jesus' words on the subject, we find that the tribulation is clearly something separate than the other end time catastophes:

Matthew: **And you shall hear of wars and rumours of wars... and there shall be famines, and pestilences, and earthquakes... All these are the *beginning* of sorrows. *Then shall they deliver you up to be "afflicted," and they shall kill you....*And then shall people betray one another and hate one another. And this gospel of the kingdom shall be preached in all the world for a witness unto all nations; and then shall the end come.**

Therefore, when you see the abomination of desolation, spoken of by Daniel the prophet...(head for the hills!)...For then shall be great tribulation, such as was not since the beginning of the world to this time, no, nor ever shall be...

Immediately after the tribulation of those days shall the sun be darkened, and the moon shall not give her light, and the stars shall fall from heaven, and the powers of the heavens shall be shaken...and then shall all the tribes...see the Son of man coming in the clouds of heaven with power and great glory.

It is important to distinguish the tribulation from the other end time events because, if we can understand what it means and where it fits into the sequence of events which will occur prior to the coming of Jesus, we will know when it is upon us and how close we actually are, at that time, to the end of man's 6000-year rule and the beginning of the 1000 years of global peace and prosperity on the planet. To that end, I have dedicated this particular chapter to looking specifically at the great tribulation as it preludes other atrocities that will befall mankind in the 11th hour of civilization as we know it.

There are actually three catastrophic movements that will occur during the end time. They are (1) the beginning of sorrows, (2) the tribulation, and (3) the Day of the Lord.

The "beginning of sorrows" are the signs which we have already discussed: wars, famine, diseases, false christs, and earthquakes, It will be a time of general upheaval in the world which ultimately will culminate in the *abomination of desolation* being set up in Jerusalem and great military fallout in the land of Judaea. It will be a time that will mark the "*birth pains*" of tribulation, a time of trouble and chaos leading up to a boiling climax of wars and persecutions and killings and large scale death and destruction in all areas of the world. Like *birth pains*, this tumult will gradually increase and intensify . After this time, the tribulation--or persecution of God's people--will encompass the entire earth.

Traditionally, many religious practitioners have labeled "tribulation" as the last great day of God's wrath upon the sinful people of the world. Those who believe in the secret rapture theory generally proclaim that Jesus will secretly come to earth to carry His believers off to heaven just prior to the tribulation, leaving only the sinners behind to face all the horrors of tribulation and God's wrath upon the world. They have often attached the term "tribulation" to the events which occur during the "seven trumpets" in Revelation 8-11 and the "seven bowls of God's anger" mentioned in Revelation 16, which we will talk about in the following chapter. The fact is, however, that the tribulation is something that will happens *to* God's people. It will include a grand scale martyrdom of the followers of God and Jesus that will happen just prior to the release of God's undiluted anger and

223

wrath upon the world. The tribulation will not be a time of God's wrath on sinners. It will be a time of *Satan's* wrath on *the saints*, a final attempt by Satan to persecute and slaughter the people of the earth who worship and belong to God. And ironically, this slaughter of believers will be accomplished through the "Christian" church working hand in hand with the beast and the false prophet (The Roman Empire and the antichrist posing as Christ) to isolate and annihilate all true believers in God and Jesus. Real followers of Jesus will be put to death by a government run, Gentile-based "Christian" church which believes itself to be the one true universal church. Perplexity and confusion will blanket the entire earth.

The tribulation, however, should not be confused with "The Day of the Lord," which occurs immediately *after* the tribulation, as can be understood here by comparing an excerpt from the Gospel of Matthew with one from the Book of Joel:

Matthew: **Immediately *after the tribulation* of those days shall the sun be darkened, and the moon shall not give her light, and the stars shall fall from heaven, *and the powers of the heavens shall be shaken...***

Joel: **The sun shall be turned into darkness, and the moon into blood, before the great and terrible *day of the Lord* come.**

"The Day of the Lord" is written about extensively in both the New and the Old Testaments. *After* the time period of tribulation caused by Satan, God's wrath will be poured out with great fury into all the world. It will be a time of God's unleashed, undiluted anger towards the sinful, corrupted conditions of the world. It will be a day filled with a wrath that will rip fiercely through the earth and through all of those who joined in the ways of Satan and in Satan's persecution of the saints. The Day of the Lord will burn with great rage through a world which, for 6000 years, has moved further and further away from God's wishes and closer and closer into the grips of Satan and the beast. It will be a time like none other in history. The Day of the Lord will *follow* the great tribulation and will mark the final episode in the 6000 years of mankind's corruption of the world.

The following are a few of the several Bible passages which discuss The Day of the Lord:

Isaiah: **Behold, the *Day of the Lord* cometh, cruel both with wrath and fierce anger, to lay the land desolate: and He shall destroy the sinners thereof out of it.**

Jeremiah: **And the slain of the Lord shall be at that day from one end of the earth even unto the other end of the earth: they shall not be lamented, neither gathered, nor buried; they shall be dung upon the ground.**

Joel: **The sun shall be turned into darkness, and the moon into blood, before the great and terrible *day of the Lord* come.**

Isaiah: **Behold, the *Day of the Lord* cometh, cruel both with wrath and fierce anger, to lay the land desolate: and he shall destroy the sinners thereof out of it.**

Isaiah: **Howl ye; for the *day of the Lord* is at hand; it shall come as a destruction from the Almighty.**

Jeremiah: **For this is the *day of the Lord*...a day of vengeance**

Isaiah: **And it shall come to pass in that day, that the Lord shall punish the host of the high ones that are on high, and the kings of the earth upon the earth.**

Joel: **Alas for the day! For *the day of the Lord* is at hand,**

225

and as a destruction from the Almighty...

Amos: Shall not the *Day of the Lord* be darkness, and not light? Even very dark without brightness in it?

Obadiah: For the *day of the Lord* is near upon all the heathen: as you have done, it shall be done to you. Your reward shall return upon your own head.

Zephanaih: The great *day of the Lord* is near...the mighty man shall cry there bitterly.

The Day of the Lord will be filled with God's wrath. And it will *follow* tribulation, which will be a time period of Satan's wrath. Compare the verses above, which basically talk about God's anger and vengeance upon sinful mankind, with the verse below from Revelation 7, which speaks of the reward to all those followers of God's way who come out of tribulation:

Revelation: After this I looked, and behold, a great multitude which no man could number, from every nation, from all tribes and peoples and tongues, standing before the throne and before the Lamb clothed in white robes, with palm branches in their hands, and crying out with a loud voice, "Salvation belongs to *our* God who sits upon the throne, and to the Lamb!"

Revelation: Then one of the elders addressed me, saying, "Who are these, clothed in white robes, and from where have they come?" I said to him, "Sir, you know." And he said to me, "These are those who have come *out of the great tribulation*; they have washed their robes and made them white in the blood of the Lamb. Therefore are they before the throne of God, and serve Him day and night....They shall hunger no more, neither shall they thirst any more....For the Lamb in the midst of the throne will be their shepherd, and He will guide them to

springs of living water; and God will wipe away every tear from their eyes."

The followers of Jesus who come out of the great tribulation, or the *great persecution,* will be fully rewarded with everlasting peace and happiness. They will not suffer the final plagues of God cast down upon mankind in the Day of the Lord. They will either be spared and will change *"in a twinkling of an eye"* when Jesus returns. Or they will be murdered by their persecutors and resurrected at Jesus' return. In either case, those who were martyred throughout the ages, or persecuted and martyred during the great tribulation, will live and reign with Jesus forever.

Revelation: **They shouted in a loud voice, "Almighty Lord, holy and true! How long will it be until you judge the people on earth and punish them for killing us?" And each of them was given a white robe, and they were told to rest a little while longer, until the complete number of other servants and believers were killed, as they had been.**

Here is where we can put several of the passages previously discussed together to understand how they pertain to the victory of the saints during the tribulation. In the Book of Daniel, we saw how the saints would be handed over to the beast but how they would ultimately prevail. In the Gospels of Matthew, Mark, and Luke, we read of persecution and tribulation and how the days will be shortened for the elect's sake. In Revelation, we read about how the beast will make war with the saints, how God's people will be marked in their foreheads *prior* to the 7 last plagues, and how the faith and the patience of the saints will be victorious. And we read in several places where the believers and followers of Jesus will be resurrected or *changed* at His coming and will live and reign with Him for 1000 years. This is all good news for those of us--now, in the past, and in the future--who believe in Jesus and who are willing to follow Him and be persecuted and martyred on His behalf. For the martyr, the end is a beautiful and peaceful victory!

But, a couple pieces of information should be discussed at this point. First, lets discuss the difference between believing *in* Jesus and believing *on* Jesus. Believing *in* Jesus is not necessarily believing *on* Him or following in His ways. There are many practicing and self-proclaimed "Christians" who feel it is enough to merely believe in Jesus, to believe that Jesus exists. These "Christians" believe that the mere belief that Jesus lived and was crucified, buried, and resurrected is enough to avoid such end time persecutions and enter into His kingdom at the second coming. But faith and believing *on* Jesus is more than just believing He existed. Satan and his demons not only believed *in* Jesus and believed that Jesus existed, they actually talked to Him face to face; but they are not considered believers. Nor faithful. Consider the example of the two demon-possessed men written about in Matthew 8:

Matthew: **...And when Jesus came to the other side, to the country, two demon possessed men met Him coming out of the tombs. They were so fierce that no one could pass that way. And behold, the demons cried out, "What have you to do with us, Son of God? Have you come here to torment us *before the appointed time*?" Now a herd of many swine was feeding at some distance from them....And the demons begged of Jesus, "If you cast us out, send us away into the herd of swine....And He said to them, "Go!" And the demons came out and went into the swine; and behold, the whole herd rushed down the steep bank into the sea and perished in the waters.**

This passage from Matthew shows the story of Satan's own demons not only believing *in* Jesus, but immediately identifying Him and asking Him for a favor. Which He granted! These demons knew Jesus, believed *in* Him, and believed in His power. But they did not follow Him or believe *on* Him..

They did not belong to Jesus. And they consequently perished in the waters.

Believing *in* Jesus and believing *on* Him are two completely different things. Believing in Him is merely an act of believing that He existed. The demons believed *in* Him. Believing *on* Jesus, however, is believing and *acting* on His word. Following Him. Adhering to His commandments and lessons. Placing one's faith and one's life *on* His foundation. During tribulation, many will believe *in* Jesus, but many of those who believe *on* Him and follow His ways in opposition to the beast will be persecuted and put to death, consequently avoiding the fierce anger of God's wrath.

Another point in relation to following Jesus is that the "Christian" (and the Catholic) churches teach that membership in their church bodies somehow equate to the following of Jesus. We saw this in an earlier chapter, where Saint Augustine was quoted as overtly stating how salvation could only be found through the Catholic church. We see this in most of the practicing churches today, who believe to some degree that those on the inside of the church are followers of Jesus and belong to Him, while those on the outside do not follow Jesus and consequently do not belong to Him. But as we follow the Books of Daniel and Revelation and begin to understand the foundation of the "Christian" and "Catholic" churches, we find that maybe just the opposite is true. That true followers of Jesus have come out of the church to follow Him. And that those who remain inside the church may be simply believing *in* Jesus and not *on* Him.

In Revelation 18, a passage in which the Babylonian Mystery Religion is discussed, God is addressing those who merely believe *in* Jesus and are wrongly following in the ways and teachings of the "Christian" or Catholic church:

Revelation: ...**He cried out in a loud voice: "She has fallen! Great Babylon has fallen!... For all the nations** have drunk her wine—the strong wine of her immoral lust...Then I heard another voice from heaven, saying, *"Come out, my people! Come out from her!* You must not take part in her sins; you must not share in her punishment! For her sins are piled up as high as heaven, and God remembers her wicked ways...For she keeps telling herself: 'Here I sit, a queen! I am no widow, I will never know grief!' Because of this, in one day she will be struck with plagues— disease, grief, and famine. And she will be burned with fire, because the Lord God, who judges her, is mighty.

This is a portrait of a church which believes it will never know grief, but upon which will pour all the plagues of God's wrath. It is a portrait of those who stay in the church and believe in Jesus, as opposed to believing on Him, while wondering after the beast and participating in pagan-based religious practices. It is the portrait of "Christian" and *Katholikos* religion; and the voice from heaven is telling its members, "Come out of her, *my people*....You must not share in her punishment!" We have already read about how God's people will be marked in their foreheads (thinking and worshipping) before the 7 last plagues are poured out. And we know that true saints will be persecuted during tribulation. In Luke 21, it is also pointed out that the church will be a participant in the persecution of the saints:

Luke: "...for they shall deliver you up to councils; and in the *synagogues* you shall be beaten: and you shall be brought before rulers and kings for my sake, for a testimony against them..."

This church-led persecution of the saints has taken place in history in the Roman Empire, and it will take place once again, during the resurrection of the Empire through the reunification of Europe, in the time just prior to Jesus' return, during the tribulation. So, when we discuss the tribulation and the way in which the followers of Jesus will be martyred, we need to understand just what being "on the inside" and "on the outside" of the "Christian"/ *katholikos* church is all about. Because the end result for the persecuted and martyred saints is clearly filled with reward and peace. But one must first *"come out of her"* and come out of the beast as well to be counted worthy of escaping the final plagues of God's wrath.

Luke: **Watch therefore, and pray always, that you may be accounted worthy to escape all these things that shall come to pass, and to stand before the Son of man.**

2 Peter: **...the Lord knows how to rescue godly people from their trials and how to keep the wicked under punishment for the Day of Judgment...**

Not all will die during tribulation. Many of the saints will be persecuted and put to death. Others will remain until the coming of Jesus. Some of the saints will remain alive during the 7 plagues of God but will escape the wrath and torment therein. But shortly after those days of tribulation, the Day of the Lord will come, and the wrath of God will burn with heated fury against all of those who refused to hear His word and follow in His ways.

Canyon Adams

Chapter 10

7 Seals, 7 Trumpets, and 7 Bowls

In general, The Book of Revelation is about the history and completion of all things according to God's plan. As Jesus reveals the end time to John, He does so by showing some events in groups of 7. For example, in the first three chapters, He shows and addresses the 7 churches. In chapters six through nine, He shows 7 seals and 7 trumpets. In Chapter sixteen, the 7 bowls of God's wrath are revealed. There is a reason for the use of this number. The number 7 is God's whole and complete number, as in the 7 days of creation, the 7 holy days, and the 7000 year plan. Seven days make a complete week; seven holy days make a complete annual example of God' plan. 7000 years make a complete plan. And the number 7 applied in the Book of Revelation signifies the completion of all things according to the workings of God. For example, when Jesus is addressing the seven churches in Revelation 1-3, He is not merely talking to the seven churches which existed during the time of the Book's writing, but to the seven *ages* of the church that existed or will exist since the first time Jesus was on earth until His second coming.

In the same manner, the seven seals in Chapters 6-9 show seven movements that will occur during the end time, beginning with the birth pains, carrying through to the tribulation, and ending with the 7 final plagues upon the earth. In short, the 7 seals show a progression through time, culminating with the 7 final plagues

After that time period of tribulation caused by Satan, God's wrath will be poured out undiluted into all the world. As mentioned earlier, there will first be "*the beginning of sorrows*," then "*great tribulation*," then this third time period known as "*The Day of the Lord*," which will occur directly between the time of great tribulation and the second coming of Jesus. The Day of the Lord will be a time of God's unleashed, undiluted anger towards the sinful, corrupted conditions of the world. It will be filled with a wrath that will rip fiercely through all of those who joined in the ways of Satan and in Satan's persecution of the saints. It will burn with great rage through a world which, for 6000 years, moved further and further away from God's wishes and closer and closer into the grips of Satan and the beast. It will be a time like none other in history. Here is how it is described in various passages in the Bible:

Isaiah: **Behold, the day of the Lord cometh, cruel both with wrath and fierce anger, to lay the land desolate: and he shall destroy the sinners thereof out of it.**

Joel: **The sun shall be turned into darkness, and the moon into blood, before the great and terrible day of the Lord come.**

The Day of the Lord will immediately follow the great tribulation and will mark the final episode in the 6000 years of mankind's corruption of the world. But it is very important to understand, especially for those holding fast to the rapture theory, that the tribulation will happen prior to the Day of the Lord; and it will include the worldwide persecution of all people belonging to God and Jesus.

Jesus was the "co-author" of the Book of Revelation. John wrote it, but it was about the revelations given to him by Jesus. John served more or less as a reporter or scribe to the material that Jesus was revealing to him. And the 7 seals that Jesus showed him in Chapters 6-9 are the exact same things Jesus showed His disciples on the Mount of Olives in Matthew 24, Mark 13, and Luke 21, which we have thoroughly discussed in Chapter 4 of this book. The Book of Revelation and the Gospel of Matthew discuss the same end time prophesies. Therefore, in the following paragraphs, to illustrate the identical nature of these prophesies, I have alligned the 7 Seals discussed in Revelation 6-9 with the Mount of Olives prophesy recorded in the Gospel of Matthew:

Seal One: A rider on a white horse sent out to conquer.
Matthew: **And Jesus answered and said unto them, Take heed that no man deceive you. For many shall come in my name, saying, I am Christ; and shall deceive many.**

Seal Two: A rider on a red horse with power to take peace from the earth and make men slay each other.
Matthew: **And ye shall hear of wars and rumours of wars:**

Seal Three: A rider on a black horse carrying a scale and measuring wheat and barley for a days wages.
Matthew: **famines**

Seal Four: A rider on a pale horse with the power to kill with famine and plagues and the wild beasts of the earth.
Matthew: **pestilences, diseases**

Seal Five: Slain saints asking for vengeance, but being told to wait until their fellow servants and brothers are also killed for their beliefs. Martyrdom.

Matthew: **Then shall they deliver you up to be afflicted, and shall kill you: and ye shall be hated of all nations for my name's sake.**

Seal Six: An earthquake. The sun turning black, the moon turning blood red, and the stars falling from the sky.
Matthew: **Immediately *after the tribulation* of those days shall the sun be darkened, and the moon shall not give her light, and the stars shall fall from heaven, and the powers of the heavens shall be shaken...**

Seal Seven: Seven angels with seven trumpets representing the 7 last plagues.
Matthew: The Gospel of Matthew does not talk about these last plagues specifically, and there is a reason for that. Jesus on the Mount of Olives was talking to His disciples. They were His followers. They didn't need to know about the last plagues because Jesus' followers--at that time, throughout the ages, at present, and in the time of the end-- will not be affected by the last plagues. The plagues were only meant to hurt those who will not have the seal of God in their forehead. And many saints will already have been killed in the tribulation. With the opening of the seventh seal, the 6000 years of man's rule will face its ultimate climax. The seventh seal reveals seven trumpets, which are the 7 plagues of God's wrath. These plagues are (1) hail and fire mixed with blood and the destruction of one third of the earth. (2) the destruction of one third of the sea, (3) the destruction of one third of the rivers and many resulting deaths, (4) one third of the sun, one third of the moon, and one third of the stars are affected, (5) the opening of an abyss and the release of locusts which torment people on earth with a scorpion-like sting for five months, (6) the killing of one third of mankind, (7) loud voices sounding from heaven that say, *"The kingdom of the world has become the kingdom of our Lord and he will reign forever and ever..."*

So up to this point, in Revelation 11, the end-time signs have been revealed by Jesus and reported by John. We are shown the seven seals, which are opened one by one over a course of time and which parallel the signs that Jesus gave to his disciples on the Mount of Olives. The seven seals end with the opening of the seventh seal, which reveals the seven trumpets of the final plagues of God's wrath. The seven seals lead directly up to the seven trumpets.

And the seven trumpets in Revelation 8-11 parallel the seven bowls of God's wrath described in Revelation 16. Notice the similarities between the seven trumpets, which were outlined above, and the seven bowls, which appear in their entirety below:

Revelation: **Then I heard a loud voice speaking from the temple to the seven angels: "Go and pour out the seven bowls of God's anger on the earth!" The first angel went and poured out his bowl on the earth. Terrible and painful sores appeared on those who had the mark of the beast and on those who had worshiped its image.**

Then the second angel poured out his bowl on the sea. The water became like the blood of a dead person, and every living creature in the sea died.

Then the third angel poured out his bowl on the rivers and the springs of water, and they turned into blood. I heard the angel in charge of the waters say, "The judgments you have made are just, O Holy One, you who are and who were! They poured out the blood of God's people and of the prophets, and so you have given them blood to drink. They are getting what they deserve!" "Lord God Almighty! True and just indeed are your judgments!"

Then the fourth angel poured out his bowl on the sun, and it was allowed to burn people with its fiery heat.

They were burned by the fierce heat, and they cursed the name of God, who has authority over these plagues. But they would not turn from their sins and praise his greatness.

Then the fifth angel poured out his bowl on the throne of the beast. Darkness fell over the beast's kingdom, and people bit their tongues because of their pain, and they cursed the God of heaven for their pains and sores. But they did not turn from their evil ways.

Then the sixth angel poured out his bowl on the great Euphrates River. The river dried up, to provide a way for the kings who come from the east. Then I saw three unclean spirits that looked like frogs. They were coming out of the mouth of the dragon, the mouth of the beast, and the mouth of the false prophet. They are the spirits of demons that perform miracles. These three spirits go out to all the kings of the world, to bring them together for the battle on the great Day of Almighty God. Then the spirits brought the kings together in the place that in Hebrew is called Armageddon.

The significance of this location, Armageddon, has inspired a great deal of question and speculation throughout the ages. It is generally--and rightfully--believed that the "Battle of Armageddon" will be the final confrontation between the nations, a belief which is reinforced by the above passage, which states it will be a battle *"on the great Day of Almighty God,"* and the way the verse is juxtaposed with the one below, in which a loud voice from the throne says, *"It is done!"* in reference to the first 6000 years of God's plan. But just how and where this battle will take place has often been confusing to many. Advocates of the rapture theory believe that God's people will be secretly gathered and swept off to a safe and secret place while the rest of the world will be left to fight it out until the planet's utter destruction. Others believe that countries will merely sit back and launch nuclear missiles at one another until the entire planet explodes into molten nothingness. In whatever manner such a battle will take place, it is important to know *where* it will take place.

The key indication of where this battle will take place is as follows: *"in the place that in Hebrew is called Armageddon."* The New Testament was written in Greek whereas the Old Testament was written in Hebrew. The word *"Armageddon"* can be broken down into two Hebrew words, *"har"* and *"Megiddo."* The word *"har"* is Hebrew for "mountain, or hilly area," and the word *"Megiddo"* was actually a location north of Judaea, in the territory of Manasseh. The battle of Armageddon, then, could actually be named "the battle of the hill (or mountain) of Megiddo." This gives us a location of the final battle. It will not be in the United States, nor Europe, nor Russia, nor Canada, nor Asia. It will be in the Middle East, in the land of Judaea, near the mountain of Megiddo.

This location reinforces what Jesus said on the Mount of Olives, as recorded in the Gospel of Luke:

And when ye shall see Jerusalem compassed with armies, then know that the desolation thereof is near. Then let them which are in Judaea flee to the mountains; and let them which are in the midst of it depart out; and let not them that are in the countries enter thereinto. For these be the days of vengeance, that all things which are written may be fulfilled.

Here we see that those in Judaea should flee, and that those *in the midst of it* should depart out, because the desolation of the area is about to occur. This final area of battle, the Battle of Armageddon, will be in the land of Judaea; this is also the area in which Jesus will come

239

down to earth with His saints. After descending with a
great spectacle, gathering his elect from throughout the
world as every eye watches, Jesus will come down on the
Mount of Olives, in the midst of this battle area. And He
will overthrow the kings and the beast and establish His own
kingdom headquartered in Jerusalem. But this will be after
the seventh and final plague upon mankind, which, after the
nations are gathered for the Battle of Armageddon, will be
poured out into the air:

**Then the seventh angel poured out his bowl in the air. A
loud voice came from the throne in the temple, saying,
"It is done!" There were flashes of lightning, rumblings
and peals of thunder, and a terrible earthquake. There
has never been such an earthquake since the creation of
human beings; this was the worst earthquake of all! The
great city was split into three parts, and the cities of all
countries were destroyed. God remembered great Babylon** (the mystery religion: "christianity") **and made her
drink the wine from his cup—the wine of his furious
anger. All the islands disappeared, all the mountains
vanished. Huge hailstones, each weighing as much as a
hundred pounds, fell from the sky on people, who cursed
God on account of the plague of hail, because it was such
a terrible plague.**

One interesting point is that while mankind is stricken with
these terrible plagues, he will remain stiff-necked and rebellious and, instead of repenting and turning to God for rescue
and salvation, he will curse God with the same contemptu-
ous attitude that brought about the plagues in the first place.
Another interesting thing about The Day of the Lord is what
is written about it in the Book of Jeremiah:

Jeremiah: **"...Alas! for that day is great, so that none is
like it: it is even the time of _Jacob's_ trouble, but he shall
be saved out of it."**

As we discussed in Chapter 2, the original blessing of a promised land was given by God to Abraham, who then passed it along to his son, Isaac. Isaac passed the birthright along to his son, Jacob, whose name was changed to Israel. Jacob/Israel passed the blessing on to the sons of Joseph, Ephraim and Manasseh, who migrated north and west out of the original promised land and, ultimately, became Great Britain and the United States. When Jacob/Israel passed along the blessing to Ephraim and Manasseh, he said, *"...may they be called by my name..."* Ephraim and Manasseh, then, became known as "Jacob" or "Israel" or "the children of Israel," although the latter refers generally to all the tribes whereas the first two--Jacob and Israel--refer specifically to the United States and Great Britain. So, when Jeremiah speaks of the Day of the Lord as being *"even a time of Jacob's trouble,"* he is saying, within the context of dual events, that the day will even be a time of trouble for the United States and Great Britain, collectively the wealthiest and most powerful nations on earth. But even prior to that time, the power and wealth of both countries--the United States/Manasseh and Great Britain/Ephraim--will be dwarfed by the resurrected Roman Empire beast of Europe and the Middle East.

But note what else Jeremiah writes: "...**it is even the time of Jacob's trouble, but *he shall be saved out of it.*"** The United States and Great Britain will not be utterly destroyed by the end time wars. They will be present and salvaged, if only in part, during the Day of the Lord. We see an allusion to this again in Revelation 7:

Revelation: ...**"Do not harm the earth or the sea or the trees, until we have sealed the servants of our God upon their foreheads."** And I heard the number of the sealed, a hundred and forty-four thousand sealed, out of every tribe of the sons of Israel:

12,000 sealed out of the tribe of Judah, 12,000 of the

tribe of Reuben, 12,000 of the tribe of Gad, 12,000 of the tribe of Asher, 12,000 of the tribe of Naphtali, *12,000 of the tribe of Manasseh*, 12,000 of the tribe of Simeon, 12,000 thousand of the tribe of Levi, 12,000 of the tribe of Issachar, 12,000 of the tribe of Zebulun, *12,000 of the tribe of Joseph*, 12,000 of the tribe of Benjamin.

Note that the children of Israel are mentioned here, but with a few subtle differences. First, the tribe of Dan is *not* mentioned. Secondly, the tribe of Manasseh *is* mentioned, yet, Manasseh was the son of Joseph, the *grandson* of Israel. It is unusual for him to be mentioned here under the sons of Israel. Third, the tribe of Joseph is also mentioned, which would encompass both Joseph and his son, Ephraim, in light of the fact that Manasseh was mentioned.

There has been a great deal of speculation written about the significance of the numbers 144,000 and the 12,000 from each tribe. I profess to know very little about the truth behind the 144,000. I have read reams and reams of man-conceived ideas about what the numbers could mean, but nothing concrete or proven by the Bible itself. It is one of those things in scripture that I have resigned to accept as a continued mystery. But I have always read this particular chapter of Revelation with more fascination concerning the absence of Dan from the listing of Israel's children and the inclusion of Manasseh instead. What does that mean? Some Bible scholars believe that Dan was excluded because the antichrist will arise from that tribe. Others believe that Manasseh was mentioned instead because, by revealing the United States, the youngest and newest of the countries, a more concise idea of time regarding the Day of the Lord could be measured. All of that, too, is speculation. The important point is that, consistent to Jacob being saved out of the wrath of God, it is mentioned in Jeremiah and reinforced here in Revelation with the listing of both Joseph and Manasseh.

(And just a repeated warning: you may read many things about the 144,000, some of which may come directly from respected church personnel or world renowned religious speakers. Some of it may sound very plausible and logical. But do not believe any of it! There is nothing in the Bible which explains or reinforces any definition of the 144,000 or the 12,000 from each tribe of Israel. And any time we search outside the Bible to find answers for concepts and questions which arise inside the Bible, we fall prey to confusion and misunderstanding. And as mentioned in 1 Corinthians: *"...God is not the author of confusion..."* Satan is the author of confusion and of all lies. We need to be careful when we look outside the Bible for answers of any sort.)

As God's people are sealed and His wrath intensifies upon the world, great heavenly signs will appear and men will recognize that the Day of the Lord has arrived. With great fear, they will run for cover and try to hide from the wrath upon the land.

Revelation: **"...and I saw the Lamb break open the sixth seal. There was a violent earthquake, and the sun became black like coarse black cloth, and the moon turned completely red like blood. The stars fell down to the earth, like unripe figs falling from the tree...The sky disappeared like a scroll being rolled up, and every mountain and island was moved from its place. Then the kings of the earth, the rulers and the military chiefs, the rich and the powerful, and all other people, slave and free, hid themselves in caves and under rocks on the mountains. They called out to the mountains and to the rocks, "Fall on us and hide us from the eyes of the one who sits on the throne and from the anger of the Lamb! The terrible day of *their* anger is here..."**

For 6000 years, God has been patient with mankind and has, for the most part, subdued his anger. In the Day of the

Lord, all of that anger will be unleashed with great fury and vengeance. And it will not only be the anger of God, but the anger of Jesus as well. It will be the terrible day of *their* anger. But it can be avoided. And from it, we can all escape.

244

Chapter 11

The Earth Will Not Be Destroyed By Man

By now, it should be pretty evident that, although it has become a very hot political topic of the liberal left, the earth cannot and will not be destroyed by man. God made the earth and all that is in it. He handed it over for man to use and control for 6000 years. When He takes it back, He will place Jesus on its throne for another 1000 years. And *then* God Himself will destroy the earth. And the heavens. And He will create a new heaven and a new earth will be much better than the first:

Revelation: **Then I saw a new heaven and a new earth, for the first heaven and the first earth had passed away...**

The earth will not be destroyed during the birth pains of the end. It will not be destroyed during the tribulation, nor the Day of the Lord, nor the Battle of Armageddon. It will not be destroyed during the second coming of Jesus. It *will* be harmed. It will be burned and ravished. Some of its areas will be laid desolate. But it will not be destroyed, a fact which is a testimony to the power and the perfect logic of God. Remember in the beginning, in Genesis 1, God, through Jesus, created and recreated the earth from the void and desolate state it had been rendered prior to the creation of Adam and Eve. It may have been darkened and desolate because of the corruption of the angels led by Lucifer. But with its recreation, it was made beautiful and plentiful; and it was handed to mankind as a gift upon which to flourish and prosper. As mankind has grown more and more corrupt, the anger of God has grown greater in its intensity. Finally, in the end, in the Day of the Lord, God will unleash His pent up anger and frustration; and He alone will bring darkness and desolation upon the earth, just like He may have done when the angels grew corrupted and rebellious.

But think of the seasons for a moment. According to God's calendar, the new year begins in the spring. Everything begins fresh and new and beautiful. The seasons pass. Eventually, the winter comes and, especially in places like here in Michigan, the land is pretty much rendered desolate by the cold and ice. Plant life dies. Wildlife hibernates. A certain seasonal "death" occurs. But in the spring, the desolation and dead-like state of the land is brought to life once again. Plant life flourishes. Animals come back out and go about their business. The birds begin chirping. The skies and the air become clear and clean again. New life begins. And the seasons continue to evolve like that year after year for all generations to experience.

Such is the case with God's plan. The lives of men and women begin anew at birth and continue until death, but they will not remain permanently dead. They will be resurrected to life once again, either during the first resurrection or the second. Like the events of the seasons, the deaths of men will once again be turned into life. In the same manner, the lives and generations of mankind, from Adam and Eve until the coming of Jesus, have worked in very much the same way. The new world dawned with Adam and Eve. It will end as we know it with the Day of the Lord and the coming of Jesus. And the dead state which occurs at that time will once again be brought to life. The natural order of God is birth and death and rebirth. And God's way is everlasting, and it cannot be altered or destroyed or prevented or derailed by man. Mankind is pompous and self-grandiose to believe otherwise.

And this brings up another point: false prophets. The one who comes to mind most immediately is Nostradamus. Some of his predictions have been interpreted to come true. But the events of July, 1999 have proven him a false prophet. What happened in July, 1999? Nothing! Certainly not the end of the world which Nostradamus predicted. And many false prophets like Nostradamus have come and gone, all completing the work not of God but of Satan. They are sometimes called prophets, and sometimes fortune tellers and psychics. We see them on the TV talk shows. We read about them in the tabloids. They have given many people false hope and have predicted world events that simply have never come true. Here are some passages from the Bible which discuss false prophets:

Deuteronomy: **When a prophet speaks in the name of the Lord, if the thing does not come about or come true, that is the thing which the Lord *has not* spoken.**

Matthew: **Be on your guard against false prophets; they come to you looking like sheep on the outside, but on the inside they are really like wild wolves.**

2 Peter: **False prophets appeared in the past among the people, and in the same way false teachers will appear among you. They will bring in destructive, untrue doctrines...,**

1 John: **Beloved, believe not every spirit, but try the spir-**

its whether they are of God: because many false prophets are gone out into the world.

I mentioned very early in this book, in the first chapter, that one should never believe another man's interpretation of the Bible. I meant this to encompass all men and all writings, including my own writings in this book. One should always--ALWAYS--turn to the Bible and rely on it as the sole source of interpretation for all scripture and all major world events past and present. I intended this to also apply very strongly to the teachings and predictions of false prophets and psychics. They are especially dangerous because, very often, their workings are deceitfully believable; and they serve to lead people away from the true prophesies of the Bible. We read how Simon the Sorcerer deceived many in Samaria and, ultimately, proved himself ungodly when he offered to pay money and buy the power of the Holy Ghost from Peter. His sorcery was believable, but his doctrine was not from God.

In the same manner, the doomsday prophets of the modern day who stir up fear and anxiety, and very often anger, with their predictions and diatribe regarding things like the depletion of the ozone, the earth's upcoming lack of oxygen due to the destruction of the rainforest, etc. etc. etc. must be viewed with a strongly critical and skeptical eye. They are not from God. Their predictions and calculations will not come true. Man will not destroy the planet! The Bible clearly states in many many places that the earth will be fully functioning during the Day of the Lord, and that Jesus will come to earth to live and reign for 1000 years. And in the end, God Himself will destroy the heavens and the earth. Not man. Not the polluters. Not the war-mongers. Not the tree cutters and the users of spray deodorants and other fluorocarbons. Man will not destroy the earth. He may pollute it, but the Bible shows in no uncertain terms that he will not destroy it.

Chapter 12

The News Is Good. Really!

And so, as we come to the end of this book, my hope is that it is merely a new beginning; a bridge between the burning desire of question and the warm security of knowledge. An open door into the intense world of the Bible and its prophesies. My prayer is that each reader, touched in his or her own way with even the slightest twinge of uncertainty or curiosity, opens the Bible and delves into its beauty and simplicity to find the answers he or she so seeks. The answers truly are all there in relatively straight-forward language; the trick becomes moving past the definitions and limitations imposed by mankind and the church, and venturing off onto new avenues and into new dimensions of understanding and inquiry. With the Bible, every question should beget an answer, and every answer should beget another question. In that manner, the breadth of knowledge which can be extracted from the Bible is never ending; and there becomes an entire lifetime of learning and understanding that can be discovered from its pages.

The end of the world will never happen until God makes it

happen according to His plan, after the 1000 years of peace and rest under Jesus have blanketed the entire earth. But the end of civilization, as we know it, could very well happen in our lifetime. We are very near the end of the 6000 years stemming from Adam and Eve, possibly within 33 to 50 years to the day. The sun is slowly sinking on the age of man, and the 1000 year sabbath of God and Jesus is just over the horizon. To compare our present day and age to the symbolic seven day week, we are living during a time period comparable to late Friday afternoon. The sun is on its way down and the Sabbath is drawing very near. To compare our time with the seven holy days of God's calendar, three of the holy days have passed and we are in the last days of the sixth month, waiting for the Feast of Trumpets to blast in a new era of peace and happiness. All of this is very good news!

We are approaching a time of complete abundance and prosperity, the end of all tears and pain and of every last hurtful, dangerous, and disasterous thing known to mankind. A golden era like no other golden era in the history of life. The government of Jesus. On earth! For 1000 years. A time of complete fairness and equality and happiness and harmony throughout the entire earth and in every far reaching corner of the planet. Joy and happiness and safety and life throughout the whole orchestra of humanity! The news is, indeed, very VERY good!

But when we turn on the TV and listen to all the doomsday prophets--the charismatic orators and preachers of our manmade religions--we hear of things like heaven and hell and eternal fire and damnation. We are painted a picture of a relentlessly punishing God and a humble, indifferent Jesus. We hear daily threats of global meltdown, nuclear annihilation, and the supposed approach of mankind's extinction through mankind's own disasterous means, none of which the Bible teaches, enforces or confirms. Instead of hearing the beautiful news of a planet at peace, we hear of the inevitable doom of both man and earth.

And okay, I will concede that mankind will grow worse as time progresses; this fact is plainly discussed in the Second Book of Timothy:

2 Timothy: ...**in the last days perilous times shall come. For men shall be lovers of their own selves, covetous, boasters, proud, blasphemous, disobedient to parents, unthankful, unholy....traitors, heady, highminded, lovers of pleasures more than lovers of God.....ever learning, and never able to come to the knowledge of the truth...... evil men shall wax worse and worse, deceiving, and being deceived...**

But I am also mindful of what is written in Second Peter 3:9:

2 Peter: **The Lord is.....patient with us, not willing that any should perish, but that all should come to repentance.**

It is consistent with God's plan that none of us perish but that we all come to salvation and be saved. God's desire is that we all turn toward Him and be counted worthy to live and reign with Jesus for 1000 years. In doing so, we will escape the fierce wrath of the Day of the Lord. We will rest in the comfort of Jesus. We will be appointed power and authority in all parts of the world, reigning with Jesus in an earthly government of undiluted peace and righteousness for an entire millenium.

The road between then and now will, indeed, be rocky. Darkness will fall upon the earth. Death, disease, disaster, and evil will run rampant in every culture and in every corner of the world. Wars, famines, earthquakes, and deadly plagues will literally wipe out billions of people. Believers in God and Jesus will be put to death by the government of a united Europe and it's faithful sidekick, the church. Afterwards, the sun will be darkened and the moon will turn blood red. And the fierce wrath of God will rage unbridled upon the planet. Death will be everywhere! People will lose faith and continue to turn away from God.

And then, at the last trump, in the twinkling of an eye, Jesus will descend from the heavens to gather his elect and take back control of the entire world. The dead in Jesus will be resurrected. Living men will be changed to immortal beings. And together, the dead and the changed will rise up into the air to meet Jesus, and they will descend with Him in glory onto the Mount of Olives. Governments will topple. And the 1000 years of peace and beauty shall immediately begin!

The news is good! The news is VERY VERY good!

We have reached the end of this book, but we can now embrace a new beginning of biblical study and understanding. I hope that the information I have offered up within these pages has inspired a desire for such an adventure. I have merely been a messenger delivering a very brief and partial message. The whole message awaits between the covers of the Bible. Not in the church. Not on TV. But in the vast universe between Genesis 1:1 and Revelation 22:21. Within the world of those pages, true understanding exists and true spiritual knowledge can be obtained. By everyone!

A journey into the Bible is never ending; it can last a lifetime, and the results can make us happy and whole and filled with the spirit of Jesus and of God forever. It is a journey that will conquer all fears and inhibitions and will lead us past the empty end-time rhetoric and into the crystal clear conclusion that the news of God's plan for mankind is very good.

The news is VERY VERY VERY good!

OTHER BOOKS
BY
CANYON ADAMS

♦ **Addiction in the White House: Disgrace of the U.S. Presidency**

♦ **666: The Beast Revealed**

♦ **Reviving Your Embryo-Self**

**AVAILABLE THROUGH
BOOKWORLD SERVICES, INC.
1933 Whitfield Park Loop
Sarasota, Florida 34243
1-800-444-2524**

Or At Your Local Bookstore

ABOUT THE AUTHOR

Canyon Adams is currently a doctoral candidate at the University of Southern California earning a Ph.D in Psychology. His education includes a Master of Arts in Counseling from Central Michigan University, a Master of Fine Arts (MFA) in Writing from Antioch University in Los Angeles, and a B.S. in Education from Central Michigan University. As an educator, counselor, entrepeneur, consultant, and writer, he has spent over two decades researching biblical references and end-time prophesy. His other books include **The Signs: Prophesy for 2000 A.D. and Beyond**; **Addiction in the White House: Disgrace of the U.S. Presidency**; and **Reviving Your Embryo-Self**.

Canyon Adams currently resides in Saginaw, Michigan. He can be contacted at **canyonadams@netscape.net**